D1218749

TO ANNA

The story of an African famine

ယ

The story of an African famine

Gender and famine in twentieth-century Malawi

MEGAN VAUGHAN

CAMBRIDGE UNIVERSITY PRESS
CAMBRIDGE
LONDON NEW YORK NEW ROCHELLE
MELBOURNE SYDNEY

Published by the Press Syndicate of the University of Cambridge
The Pitt Building, Trumpington Street, Cambridge CB2 1RP
32 East 57th Street, New York, NY 10022, USA
10 Stamford Road, Oakleigh, Melbourne 3166, Australia

First published 1987

Printed in Great Britain at the University Press, Cambridge

British Library cataloguing in publication data

Vaughan, Megan
The story of an African famine: gender
and famine in twentieth-century Malawi.
1. Famines – Malawi – History
I. Title
363.8 HC935.Z9F3

Library of Congress cataloguing in publication data

Vaughan, Megan.
The story of an African famine.
Bibliography.
Includes index.
1. Famines – Malawi – History – 20th century.
2. Food supply – Malawi – History – 20th century.
I. Title.
HC935.Z9F38 1987 363.8'096897 86–20727

ISBN 0 521 32917 5

VN

Contents

Maps

Illustrations

Preface

This book aims to reconstruct the history of a famine which took place in Malawi (then Nyasaland) in 1949–50. When I began the research I thought that I had set myself a well-defined and limited task, and believed that by carefully piecing together the jigsaw of historical evidence I would end up with a picture which would not only be complete in itself, but might also make some contribution towards the more general analysis of the problem of famine in Africa. As with many such tasks, however, this one turned out to be more complex than I had initially thought. Having assembled what archival evidence I could find, I then conducted interviews with people who had lived through the famine. Their representations of the event were sometimes difficult to accommodate. What weight, for instance, should one give to the information that the goats sold by famine victims changed into snakes when taken home by their new owners? I decided, however, that such representations were an integral part of the history of the famine, and so deserved to be centrally incorporated alongside the crop statistics. This made the task of writing the book a challenging one. To reconstruct the event I have had to move constantly between levels of analysis – from the household hearth to the global grain markets, and back. If famine were simply the result of the failure of a maize crop, then this would not be necessary, but famines are never as simple as that.

The bulk of the research for this book was carried out in 1982–3, when I was lecturer in the Department of History, Chancellor College, University of Malawi. The research was completed while I held the Chapman Fellowship at the Institute of Commonwealth Studies, University of London, and the book has been written from the African Studies Centre, University of Cambridge, where I hold the Smuts Research Fellowship. I owe a debt to all these institutions, but especially to the University of Malawi, which provided me with a research grant for the fieldwork, as well as vital institutional support. I would also like to thank the Government of Malawi for granting me access to the National Archives, and the Ministry of Agriculture in particular, for permission to consult documents falling within the forty-year rule. I am also very grateful to the staff of the National Archives of Malawi for their patient assistance.

The students of Chancellor College stimulated my interest in the famine and helped me energetically in the fieldwork. Special thanks for help in the field are due to Humphrey Chindenga and John Yesaya.

Many people have read and commented on earlier drafts of this book, but I owe particular thanks to William Beinart, Andrew Butcher, David Hirschmann, John Iliffe, John McCracken, Henrietta Moore, Terence Ranger, Amartya Sen, and Landeg White.

Glossary

chilangano *chitekere*	varieties of fast-maturing cassava
chinkhoswe	marriage surety or guardian of a partner to a marriage
dambo	grass-covered plain which becomes flooded in the rains and retains moisture in the dry season
dimba garden	a dry season garden made on *dambo*-type land
ganyu	casual labour performed in the peasant agricultural sector
kachasu	a strong, locally made liquor, resembling gin
lobola	brideprice
matuto	mounds of earth, built by the farmer, into which seeds are planted
mbumba	the matrilineal sorority group of the Yao and Nyanja
mopane	indigenous woodland of lower altitudes
nkhokwe	grain-bin used for storage of maize
thangata	labour rent exacted from African tenants on European-owned estates
ubombo	a concept describing the breakdown of family and community solidarity; greed
ulendo	a journey, usually referring (in this text) to the colonial officers' tours of their districts

Introduction

Famines gather history around them. In the Blantyre District of Southern Malawi many people remember the famine which occurred in 1949–50, and many more have been told about it. There are stories and songs and recollections of the famine: accounts of foraging and migration; of 'famine disease' and death; of both the cohesion and the disintegration of communities and families; of selflessness and the extremes of individualism. Survivors of the famine can give close accounts of the events of that year. They begin with the abnormal weather conditions – what the clouds looked like and what this meant; how high the crops grew before they died, and which crops survived; the names of the children who starved and the husbands who left; the wild foods eaten and their methods of preparation; the minute details of the famine relief system – the coarseness and the colour of the grain distributed, the size of the tins which acted as measures, the behaviour of the queuing people who waited to receive it. Older people can tell stories of famines that went before – the 1922 famine and the famine of 1903 which drove people into the area from Mozambique. They say that nothing comparable to 1949 has happened since. People calculate their ages by reference to it, and women consciously keep the communal memory of the event alive when they sing the pounding songs they composed then.

This book tells the story of that famine and draws on the memories of those who lived through it. But in analysing the events it moves beyond them both geographically and temporally, to look at long-term historical change and remote policy making, tracing these back to the stories, songs and personal memories.

Writing at a time when a major famine dominates large parts of Africa, one is struck at a certain level by the similarities between the stories and images of 1949 and those emerging from the current famine, despite the fact that the latter is on a vastly greater scale.

Television cameras now witness the distress of the starving, but the brutal fact is that starving people look much the same everywhere and at all times. Writers on famine have always been struck by these similarities. Sorokin's book (Sorokin, 1975), written of Russia in the 1920s, ranges widely both geographically and over time in a survey of starvation; Aykroyd's work (Aykroyd, 1974) surveys famine throughout the world and through history, as do more recent collections of papers on the subject (Cahill, 1982; Aziz, 1975; Hopkins and Puchala, 1978); and Amartya Sen's work elaborates a general theory of famine analysis from a wide range of contemporary and historical examples (Sen, 1981). In the International Disaster Institute's journal, *Disasters*, famine is just one category of crisis knowing no geographical or social bounds, and articles on famine sit side by side with accounts of hurricanes in Australia and earth tremors in Wales.

Sometimes the comparative analysis can sink into the banal. Although there is increasing evidence for variation in human calorific needs, and hence in the ability to withstand regular shortages, at the very *extremes* of deprivation the human body everywhere responds in much the same way. Hence it has been possible for the physiologists of starvation to draw on the closely observed experience of concentration camp dwellers of World War Two to help them understand the physical process of starvation in very different circumstances.[1] For the social scientist, however, there are limitations to the usefulness of exploring the fact that starvation manifests itself in similar ways everywhere. A more useful form of comparative analysis is that undertaken by Sen (Sen, 1981), which attempts to identify a general theory of causation with a view to influencing policy in helpful ways.

My own analysis of the 1949 famine tends in two directions. In the last resort, a wide-ranging book such as Sen's still lays stress on the importance of understanding the specificities of the social, economic and political structures in which famine is situated. Whilst a general framework can be elaborated, there is still a great need to understand these structures in detail. At one level, then, this story of the 1949 famine is firmly located in time and space. Without a clear picture of the existent social and economic frameworks, and the historical processes which gave rise to them, it is impossible to understand the structure and texture of the famine as it emerged. Put in Sen's terms, we need to understand *who*, *when* and *why* people starve. The superficial physical similarities in the process of starvation, from Imperial China to modern Africa, obscure vast differences. The same degree of food shortage may have widely different results in different communities. At the extreme, social and political structures can determine whether a famine occurs at all. There are cases, as Sen has shown, where famine has not been the result of any obvious 'food availability decline', and so must be seen in large part as a social phenomenon (Sen, 1981).

One dimension of this study incorporates the 1949 famine as both a product of and a window on the social and economic history of Malawi. The economic history of which it forms a central part is the history of agricultural production and change.[2] The famine occurred at the end of a decade of unprecedented colonial interest and intervention in food production systems in Malawi. In analysing the famine we need to understand how changes in food production related to other changes in the economy over a long period. In particular, to relate them to the development of local wage labour systems and labour emigration, to the production of export crops and the extension of the market, and crucially (but with more methodological difficulty), to population dynamics.

All of these are issues which relate to more general debates on the economic history of Africa, as well as to the 'current crisis' in African food production. The post-war period was one in which policies were formulated and world economic patterns emerged, which have exerted a lasting influence on Africa. The institution of food aid, for instance, has its genesis in this period, and government intervention in marketing (over which many of the current debates on African agriculture revolve) reached new levels. The history of this one famine reveals some of these wider trends and indicates how they can be played out over a specific event.

The social history of which the famine forms a part is less accessible, but closely linked to these economic developments. It is in the realm of social change, and particularly in the area of family and kinship structures, that a crisis such as a famine can be of most use to the historian of Africa. Whilst there are always dangers in viewing any society through a crisis, the evidence which emerges from the famine, when treated with care, is indispensable to an understanding of social change in Malawi. Changes in agricultural production and employment generated new patterns of social and economic differentiation. Some levels of these are more visible than others in the historical record. Using data on wages, and estimates of subsistence earnings, we can attempt to define income groups in Malawi by the 1940s. But how these were located in relation to kin and family structures is more difficult to discern. It is precisely this latter relationship, however, which is central to any analysis of longer-term change and the process of class formation.[3]

The famine generates data normally unobtainable, and provides a window on social structure at a particular point in time. I try in Chapter 5 to explore how this juncture relates to longer-term changes in marriage and kinship structures. Whilst few studies of famine place much emphasis on these, an examination of the 1949 famine leads one to see them as crucially important. If we are to understand why some people starve and not others, then we need to know the individual's economic entitlements both in normal and crisis times, but also to see how these are meshed with social relations.

In part, then, this book is intended as a contribution towards a more complete social and economic history of Malawi, and thus in small part towards the history of modern Africa. The second dimension of the study, however, is seen as a contribution towards the general analysis of famine. Throughout the book I use comparative material when this appears illuminating, and in examining the comparative literature on famine there seems to me to be a case for re-assessing the forms of analysis used to explain famine in Africa both today and in the past. Much discussion of African food supply and famine appears to be conducted in isolation from that of other geographical areas and historical periods.[4] There may, of course, be very good reasons for this isolation, and they may be related to the elements of specificity and detail which I have already mentioned as being central to the understanding of the 1949 famine. At the same time, however, the intellectual traditions of African studies may also have contributed to the domination of certain types of analysis. This is not purely an exercise in intellectual history. As the story of the 1949 famine makes plain, the way in which administrators perceived the causes and nature of the problem to a large extent determined how they acted to remedy it, and this could have 'life-and-death' implications for individuals and communities. The same argument can be applied to the current famine in Africa. Perceptions of the longer-term viability of food production systems in semi-arid Africa, of the role of climatic change and population growth, of the functioning of the market and the effects and side-effects of food aid, all ultimately determine the institutional response of politicians and donors to the immediate spectacle of the starving.

In the next section of this Introduction, I examine some of the most influential of the approaches used to analyse African food supply problems and attempt to contextualise them.

Famine and food supply – Africa in comparative perspective

In Chapters 2 and 3 I outline in some detail the theories employed by contemporary observers to account for the occurrence of famine in 1949. All of these theories recur in some form in the present-day literature on 'food crisis' in Africa.

The first of these theories was a neo-Malthusian one. It held that the 1949 famine had been caused by a long-term (but recently accelerated) environmental deterioration which rendered food production precarious. The environmental deterioration was brought about by population pressure and the 'improvident' use of the soil made by African agriculturalists. The second theory also explained the famine in terms of a decline in food production, apparently caused by competition for land and labour presented by cash crops, and in particular by tobacco. The third, and related, theory was that state intervention in the marketing of food crops and interference in free trade mechanisms resulted in a marketing inefficiency which discouraged the production of food surpluses and ultimately placed national food supply in jeopardy. With few stocks in hand, one year's shortfall could easily be translated into a famine.

Malthusian and neo-Malthusian theories have had wide application. They dominated in the nineteenth-century British approach to famine in India, in analyses of famine in pre-revolutionary China and pre-industrial Europe. Such theories are widely used to explain present-day food supply problems in Africa. Their application to African circumstances is nothing new, but there has since the 1960s in particular been a broadening of their scope and application. Global equations of food supply and population began to be made in the post Second World War period, and in recent years this statistical approach has been married with a widespread 'ecology' movement in the industrialised countries of the West. This has given rise to a particular variety of neo-Malthusian theory to which I will return later. I begin, however, with a brief look at the application of Malthusian theories in the history of India.

A number of writers, including Klein (1984), McAlpin (1983) and Ambirajan (1979), have documented the influence of Malthusian and Social Darwinian ideas on the famine policies of the British. Much of the discussion on India aims ultimately to explain the *decline* of major famine which took place at the end of the nineteenth century, and the 'demographic revolution' which began around the same time. Ira Klein has argued that the administrative and economic weapons needed to conquer famine in India were available long before they were put into practice. The factor inhibiting their application was the prevailing theory that 'India would have been pauperised, its work ethos shattered, and an importunate populace of government dependants would have been created by the early distribution of famine relief' (Klein, 1984, p. 189). This fear of the consequences of famine relief was tied closely to ideas about long-term food supply and population dynamics. To rescue the semi-starved in any single famine 'only would have postponed a calamitous reckoning when a swollen population multiplied beyond its subsistence' (Klein, 1984, p. 189). When married to Social Darwinian theories, the belief in Malthusian checks and balances operating through famine generated some sobering statements from administrators of British India. Ambirajan quotes Sir George Couper's confidential memorandum on famine expenses submitted to the Viceroy in 1881. Couper argued that by keeping the starving section of the population alive, the problem would only be exacerbated – famine would occur even if there was a slight shortfall in agricultural production. Furthermore, such action would interfere with the process of natural selection and this would be disastrous for society as a whole:

> If we are to secure that a class of men – so low in intellect, morality and possessions, the retention of which makes life valuable, as to be absolutely independent of natural population checks – shall be protected from every cause, such as famine and sickness, which tends to restrain their numbers by an abnormal mortality, they must end up by eating every other class in the community. (Ambirajan, 1979, p. 9)

The shift away from such attitudes and the possibilities for intervention which this shift allowed, go some way towards explaining the decline of major famine in India.

Malthusian theories have also been popular in explaining the occurrence of famine in pre-revolutionary China. Mallory's remarkable book on famine in China, written in 1926 (Mallory, 1928), in fact gives considerable weight to political and wider economic factors, but much of his argument nevertheless rests on equations of population, aggregate production and consumption needs. Famine becomes inevitable as population increasingly outstrips food supply, and food production fails to keep pace in part because of the absence of 'scientific agriculture', but also on account of deforestation and the general deterioration of the environment (Mallory, 1928, pp. 85–6, 109–10).

All of these arguments are echoed closely in the historical sources on famine in Africa, and in Chapter 2 I outline in detail how they were applied to the specific case of Southern Malawi in the 1940s. Variations on these theories continue to recur in the literature on modern Africa. The current 'agrarian crisis' in Africa provides a focus for a wider concern, which has existed particularly since the Second World War, over global viability in the face of high rates of population increase in the Third World. In a report typical of the genre, the Washington-based Worldwatch Institute reported in February 1985 that Africa was on 'the verge of human crisis on an unprecedented scale as a result of the fastest population growth of any continent in history, widespread soil erosion and the neglect of farming' (*The Guardian*, 16/2/85). In such analyses the famine in Africa is seen as one particularly visible part of a crisis facing the continent as a whole, and ultimately the entire world.

Thomas Poleman has traced this school of thought back to the immediate post-war period when global analyses of food supply first began to be attempted (Poleman, 1977), and in Chapter 3 I describe the impact of some of these ideas on official thought as applied to Malawi in this period. Beginning with the Food and Agriculture Organisation's World Food Survey of 1946, Poleman outlines the development of what he sees as the 'myth of imminent global starvation' (p. 383) through to the dramatically pessimistic conclusions of the 1974 World Food Conference which concluded that one quarter of the population of the Third World (excluding China) was inadequately fed – five hundred million people on the brink of starvation. It is not so much this conclusion that Poleman challenges, as the analysis used to reach it, and its potentially misleading consequences. As Poleman points out, the 'lifeboat' analogy so often used in these global analyses is hardly a useful framework in which to study a world in which food supplies are so unevenly distributed. Furthermore, the severe limitations of the data at this massively aggregate level are such as to disallow many of the conclusions. To begin with, there is as yet no scientifically satisfactory definition of individual food needs, and viewed historically the tendency has been for these to be overstated. Since the 1940s nutritionists have generally revised their estimates downwards. An imminent global food crisis can simply vanish overnight when a slightly different figure is fed into the calculator. The analogy of the world as a lifeboat also assumes a dietary homogeneity, and this assumption has come under increasing scrutiny since the mid 1960s. Poleman argues that such analyses under-estimate the real agricultural growth which has in fact taken place in the Third World in the last forty years, and are based on models liable to over-react to any faltering in this growth in so far as it affects the industrialised countries. Two earlier major 'crises' in global food supply – in the mid 1960s and the early 1970s – provide good examples of the sensitivity to panic and the opportunities for political leverage which such models contain, as well as demonstrating the vulnerability of global aggregates to distortion.

The mid 1960s panic, Poleman argues, resulted almost exclusively from two successive droughts in India. Because the Indian production figures bulk so large in the total aggregate for the Third World, any fluctuation in Indian output has a marked influence on the total index. An apparent 'world food crisis' thus appeared. The reverse could just as easily take place, however, as was to be demonstrated shortly afterwards. By the late 1960s the impact of the introduction of high-yielding wheat varieties in the Punjab was being felt. The result was that the food production index for all low-income countries rose steeply. By 1969 the FAO was suggesting that the major food problem of the future might be excessive production and storage limitations rather than scarcity (Poleman, 1977, p. 388). But the second 'crisis' occurred soon after this prediction, in the early 1970s. Its causation was complex. Unfavourable weather and poor crops in India and the Sahel contributed, but probably more important were the running down of food stocks and holding down of production in the United States, coupled with a crisis in the Soviet agricultural sector which resulted in heavy buying on the world grain market. The 'world food crisis' of the 1970s, then, had at least as much to do with the industrialised countries as with the Third World.

Despite the clear evidence for the inadequacies and distorting effects of such global analyses, the image of the world as 'lifeboat' lingers on in much of the literature on food supply. Increasingly the focus is on Africa where a number of factors combined in the 1970s and again in the 1980s to produce widespread and severe famine. If neo-Malthusian models are misleading when applied to the world as a whole, are they nevertheless applicable to Africa?

Sara Berry (Berry, 1984) has argued that aggregate production data for the continent of Africa is subject to the same distortions and difficulties as those outlined for the global data. The World Bank, FAO and other agencies argue that since 1960 population growth, urbanisation and rising urban incomes have caused demand for marketed foodstuffs to outstrip productive capacity. Food imports have increased and at the same time the costs of other essential imports, especially petroleum based ones, have risen sharply. Aggregate agricultural production data for Africa is used to support the case for greater foreign intervention. The perceived 'crisis', and especially the drama of the Sahel in the 1970s, has produced an unprecedented amount of aid-donor activity. Berry argues that in the wake of the Sahelian drought donor activity in some Sahelian countries grew so intense that local officials were fully occupied in administering foreign aid, and competition among donors became an impediment to their own as well as their hosts' efforts to reach agricultural producers.

Sara Berry demonstrates convincingly that not only is the African production data extremely unreliable, but also that it obscures the fact that agricultural performance in Africa has varied a great deal from one crop to another and one area to another, and for a variety of reasons. There is no one causal factor, and certainly one cannot explain what is happening to African agriculture today by using aggregate production data to postulate a simple relationship between food and population.

Moving back to 'global analyses', one result of the 'crises' of the 1960s and 1970s has been the generation of much interest in the issue of food supply amongst the public of the industrialised Western countries. This interest partly reflects the extension of media coverage of Third World famine. But it also relates to a trend amongst some sections of Western populations towards a revision of their own dietary habits, and is closely linked with a general interest in ecological and conservationist matters. Widely read books such as Colin Tudge's *The Famine Business* (Harmondsworth, 1979), recognise that the 'world food problem' is not so much one of overall shortage at a global level as of maldistribution of available food supplies. The remedy is seen to lie, at least in part, in a revolution in Western eating habits towards cheaper, more energy-efficient foods. Though Tudge recognises 'distribution' to be the crucial problem, he does not make it clear how redistribution can be effected. Also lingering at the back of this analysis is the conservationists' image of the population time-bomb. In this case, however, the answer is seen to lie with 'us' rather than with 'them'.

Though very pervasive and influential, neo-Malthusian theories do not provide the only framework used to analyse current food supply problems in Africa, and neither did they in the past. In Chapter 3 I describe the 'food versus cash crop' theory as it was applied by contemporaries to the 1949 famine. The political context within which this theory was employed in the 1940s was quite specific, but nevertheless there are parallels with some current analyses of Africa. The latter are usually very much more sophisticated and they rarely limit themselves to one causal factor, but they do rest on similar assumptions about the nature of African agrarian society.

In its simplest form this theory states that in the course of the colonial period

African farmers were encouraged or coerced either to grow export crops themselves to the detriment of their food production, or to work on European-owned plantations with the same results. This economic pattern is seen to have been continued into the post-colonial period, and is held ultimately responsible for the occurrence of famine in modern Africa.

Depending on the region studied, some analyses place emphasis on the creation of 'labour reserves' within African economies as being responsible for a decline in food production (Arrighi, 1970; Arrighi and Saul, 1973). Some, more than others, see the creation of class divisions within African societies as being important.[5] All see capitalist expansion, under the aegis of state intervention, as creating a new type of vulnerability to food shortage. According to this general theory, in the course of the commercialisation of agricultural production and exchange, or through the development of a labour market, Africans have been rendered dependent on market exchange to meet their basic consumption needs, and are thus very vulnerable to price changes. Commercialisation has distorted 'subsistence' economies and destroyed the insurance mechanisms in-built in these, without replacing them with any new forms of security.

This argument has been highly influential in African historiography, and also influences many perceptions of present-day famine in Africa. Much of the work written within this framework has been highly sophisticated, and is especially convincing when applied to local case studies which are closely documented. Mike Watts' work on the history of famine in Northern Nigeria is one such example (Watts, 1983; Shenton and Watts, 1979). Watts sees the undermining of the pre-colonial 'moral economy', combined with the contradictions in the development of capitalist relations as they developed in Northern Nigeria, as having created an unprecedented vulnerability to famine:

> the effect of the particular form of capitalist development in Northern Nigeria was to rupture the cycle of peasant production, to expand commodity production, and to individuate peasant society . . . the tissues of the moral economy were stripped away, making peasants vulnerable to both market crises and capricious climate. The mode of capital accumulation in Northern Nigeria expanded the role of the market yet blocked social development along other lines. The colonial state was incapable of regularising conditions of production in Northern Nigeria and often contributed directly to the vulnerability of the peasants upon whom it ultimately depended. (Watts, 1983, p. xxiii)

An important element of Watts' analysis and that of other writers is the portrayal of pre-colonial African subsistence economies as basically self-sufficient, adaptive and cooperative. Watts holds that the use of the 'moral economy' concept need not imply an idealised Rousseauian past, and that in the case of Northern Nigeria the 'moral economy' arose out of the class structure of the society itself, and in the historically specific form of relations between nature and society in the Sokoto Caliphate (p. 89). Watts describes the mechanisms of insurance against possible food shortage which existed in pre-colonial Hausaland. He argues that both the systems of production themselves, and the social systems in which they operated, provided some insurance against wholesale disaster. As elsewhere in Africa, the pre-colonial agricultural system of the Hausa had evolved crop combinations, patterns of inter-cropping and the use of drought-resistant strains in adaptation to the precarious environment. Social factors were just as important – patterns of redistributive and reciprocal gifts, revolving credit schemes, and a strongly paternalistic ideology all reinforced the ability of the Hausa to withstand a shortfall in food supply. The inter-generational household, the *gandu*, permitted an averaging-out of consumer/producer ratios of component nuclear families, and thus reduced their level of vulnerability (p. 140).

Similar structures have been described for the nomadic pastoralists of the savanna–Sahelian zones. Work on these areas from a human-ecological perspective has uncovered a highly sophisticated and complex survival strategy employing a variety of adaptive mechanisms including the use of micro-environments to grow staple grains, systematic migrations, and cooperation and exchange between farmers and nomads (Scott, 1984).

Raynault's analysis of the 1970s in the Sahel in 'Lessons of a Crisis', concludes that monetization of the Sahelian economies has been a disaster (Raynault, 1977). Raynault argues that there has been a progressive breakdown of old structures with their collective control, and that these structures have been replaced by an immature form of market economy. The inherent risks of agricultural production in the Sudano-Sahelian belt have meant that no very profitable exploitation by colonists has ever taken place there. External forces dominate, but the money they introduce passes through the community without taking root. The solution is for agrarian societies to 're-establish their control over the total functioning of the system of agricultural production', and they will only gain this control 'in so far as they are able to discard the spirit of competition and the individualisation of productive activities to which they have been brought by the development of the market'.

Raynault's conclusion is radical. The future of Sahelian agriculture cannot be assured through heavy investment and increased appeals for 'aid', but is predicated on rural populations having a greater degree of independence from the vagaries of a market whose rules can only operate to their disadvantage (p. 27). Raynault does not pay any close attention to the consequences of differentiation within the peasantry, and his analysis (and others like it) assumes a unity of the 'rural community' which goes far beyond the 'moral economy' as described by Watts.

There are real dangers in misrepresenting the pre-capitalist past and over-estimating the capacity of subsistence economies to withstand natural disaster.

Diulde Laya's interviews with farmers and livestock owners in Niger in the 1970s are interesting from this point of view (Laya, 1975). Comparing the crisis of the 1970s to experiences in the past, interviewees showed a clear perception of how the nature of famine had changed, but the changes did not necessarily reflect favourably on earlier periods. In the early part of the century there had been less mobility in food supplies and less likelihood of a famine-stricken region being relieved by supplies from elsewhere:

The last three years could not be like those we have talked of [in the past]. Why? Because at the present time, provided one has the means, one finds something to eat; there was no food in the previous years, and when those who had gone to look for some returned, there were already some deaths in their family. Today people die of hunger only if they do not have the means. (p. 64)

Another interviewee put it even more succinctly:

People no longer die from famines, since there are motor cars now. (p. 60)

The argument that capitalism has failed to 'develop' Africa is a common one, but used in very different ways by different writers. At the extreme are populists like Raynault who suggest complete withdrawal from the market, though even in his work it is sometimes difficult to discern whether he sees 'too much' or 'too little' capitalism as the causal factor. Analyses of the Ethiopian famine of the mid 1970s strike out at both 'feudalism' and 'capitalism'. The policies of a 'semi-feudal' regime, and the fetters imposed by 'pre-capitalist modes of production' are cited as contributory factors, but are seen to act in combination with the 'commercialisation of subsistence agriculture and pastoral economies, and the orientation of these towards export, leading to the impoverishment, eviction, and in the end the total ruin of the poor peasant and nomad' (Hussein, 1976, p. 10).

As Berry has pointed out, the 'too much' or 'too little' capitalism debate is a largely sterile one. More profitable is the approach of French Marxist writers who pose the problem in terms of the 'articulation of modes of production', and examine the inter-relationships between an externally dominated capitalism and an indigenous pre-capitalist base.[6] When employed by writers such as Watts, in a carefully documented study, this model seems helpful. But quite often such analyses are highly theoretical and seem far removed from the diverse histories they attempt to encapsulate.

We have moved some distance from the simple 'food versus cash crops' theory. The analyses I have outlined here vary greatly in their sophistication and emphasis, but some still do equate 'cash crops' with the market economy, and 'food crops' with subsistence, and then go on to describe how one undermines the other. As I show in Chapter 3, such equations do not hold up for the case of the 1949 famine, and I suspect will not hold up for many other African cases.

Ultimately all these analyses are concerned to understand the nature of the development of capitalism in Africa, and the effects it has had on peasant communities and their food supply. This connects with the third theory of the 1949 famine held by contemporary observers which I have labelled the 'marketing-board' theory. This theory relates to a wider historical debate, very evident in the literature in nineteenth-century India and Europe, around the issue of free trade versus intervention (McAlpin, 1983; Post, 1977). It also relates to a body of literature on contemporary Africa which sees African government marketing and pricing policies as the main causal factors behind the perceived crisis in food production, and the occurrence of famine.

Robert Bates' work is the best known of this school of thought and it has been highly influential (Bates, 1981). Bates and others argue that agricultural pricing policies are biased against peasant food producers in order to satisfy the need for cheap foodstuffs on the part of the more articulately political urban population. In some instances this involves the importation of foodstuffs for urban consumers – imports ultimately paid for through the taxation of the peasantry.

There are variations in this broad line of argument. Michael Lofchie argues that food production has suffered from the bias in favour of export crops, and that there has been *inadequate* government intervention and support for food production (Lofchie, 1975). The under-capitalisation of the food-producing sector, and the 'absence of marketing agencies to assist in the transportation and sale of food produce' are seen as culpable. Most writers, however, take the view that there has been too much inappropriate and damaging intervention in African food production and marketing on the part of overweight bureaucracies. These bureaucracies may arise from either capitalist or socialist-oriented regimes. The literature on Tanzania, for instance, in explaining the occurrence of food shortages there in the 1970s, and the increasing volume of food imported, points a finger at the *ujamaa* villagisation programme and its chaotic effects (Coulson, 1977). Discriminatory pricing policies, inappropriate intervention, and inefficient and corrupt marketing agencies are generally held to blame for declines in food production over much of Africa.

Sara Berry has labelled this school of thought 'rational peasants and imperfect structures' (Berry, 1984, pp. 70–1). The assumption inherent in it is that higher crop prices and a free trade policy would relieve food deficits. Berry points out that this case rests on several propositions about farmers' behaviour which are derived from rational choice analysis – that farmers usually increase production of a crop when its price rises; that domestic markets are reasonably competitive so that an increase in the official price will result in higher prices for most producers, and that what is true for one crop will be true for agricultural output as a whole.

Henry Bernstein has recently examined the convergence of right and left-wing criticism around the pathology of the post-colonial state (Bernstein, 1985). Like Berry, he advocates a closer examination of the nature of capitalism in Africa today, and in particular a re-examination of the class place of the peasantry.

In Chapter 3 my examination of the 'marketing-board theory' as applied to the 1949 famine indicates that we need to look carefully at the effects of state agricultural policies on *different sections* of the African agrarian population, and that we especially need to consider in any analysis the existence of a group of rural food purchasers.

These then seem to be the broad categories of analysis currently employed to explain African food supply problems. Whilst current analyses are generally more sophisticated than those employed by colonial observers in the 1940s, the continuities and connections are notable. It is beyond the scope of this book to test these theories in a wider context, but in the following section I indicate some of the directions in analysis which appear most helpful.

John Post's book, *The Last Great Subsistence Crisis in the Western World* (1977), describes the famine crisis in Europe of 1815–16. The title of the book is in fact misleading as the crisis it analyses is in no way adequately described as a 'subsistence crisis'. Unusually adverse weather conditions precipitated a crisis in food production, but this was imposed on an already stagnating Western economy, suffering post-war dislocation and major readjustments in trade and industry, including a high rate of unemployment (p. 36). Although the majority of Europe's working population was still made up of subsistence peasants and agricultural labourers, the 'crisis' can only be explained with reference to the linkages between the agricultural and non-agricultural sectors of the economy.

This analysis fits broadly with Amartya Sen's entitlement view of famines, set out in his influential book, *Poverty and Famines* (1981). Sen argues that starvation need not be related directly to food supply or a Food Availability Decline (FAD). Food is heavily commoditised and an individual's command over food may depend on the assets he or she possesses, or labour power which can be converted into food. There are a number of different ways in which an individual may have command over food, and these Sen calls 'entitlements'. Famines occur when exchange entitlements collapse, leaving some individuals or groups without any command over food.[7]

Post's analysis, like Sen's, points to the necessity of imposing some separation between explanations of shortfalls of food production and explanations of famine. This distinction is nothing new, but in analyses of African food supply problems it is frequently ignored. The major theories I have outlined in the previous section are for the most part concerned with the analysis of long-term problems of food production, seen variously as the product of ecological crisis, dependency, or local manipulation of markets. Whilst long-term problems of food production must inevitably play a large part in placing agricultural populations at risk of famine, they are not in themselves sufficient to explain the occurrence of famine.

Much recent literature on the history of famine in India makes this point very clearly. Early analyses of Indian famine matched quite closely many of the trends in current literature on Africa. Famines in nineteenth-century India were seen to result from the economic drain from India to Britain, and the heavy burden of taxation imposed on Indian peasants. Agriculturalists sold food grains in order to raise cash to pay their land revenue. Meanwhile, there was an increasing economic differentiation amongst the peasantry themselves, resulting in the breakdown of communal responsibility (Bhatia, 1967).

Criticisms of this analysis have taken two directions. The first is to subject to scrutiny the 'dependency theory' embodied here; and the second is to question the assumed pivotal relationship between subsistence production and famine. Michelle McAlpin (1983) argues that India became more able to withstand harvest shortfalls in the late nineteenth century, through improved transportation networks and the greater penetration of the market into rural areas. She likens this development to the experience of European states in the early part of the nineteenth century. She also argues that the forms of self-insurance practised traditionally by subsistence farmers were very expensive ones, requiring storage each year of twenty per cent of the year's consumption needs in order to be effective (p. 212). As transportation improved and the market penetrated, so higher prices ruled for agricultural produce and large flows of grain became common:

> The combination of the removal of need to self-insure, rising prices for agricultural goods (both absolutely and relative to non-agricultural goods) and better markets encouraged agriculture to expand production in general and the production of higher-value, more labour-intensive crops in particular. Both these changes tended to increase demand for agricultural labour and to exchange seasonal rural-migration. (p. 212)

Malthusian ideologies dominated. Early nineteenth-century *laissez-faire* philosophy ruled out direct interference by the state, and an effective famine policy could only come about when *laissez-faire* was seen to have failed. Most crucially, famine was only conquered with the growth of a *financial* commitment on the part of the government. Famine relief and administration involved the expenditure of considerable sums of money and a willingness to intervene in local markets to create employment and direct food supplies (p. 189).

A similar pattern has been traced for the history of famine in Europe (Post, 1977). From the sixteenth century onwards, improved transportation and market networks had made it increasingly possible for a shortfall in one area to be made up by imports from another, but the conversion of possibility into practice had to await the further development of the state in the nineteenth century. Following a pattern which has been described for a number of areas, growing markets could mean that a shortfall in grain in one region could raise prices in other areas where harvests were normal. In extreme cases, such as the 1848 famine in Ireland, food was exported from the same area in which famine was occurring (Woodham-Smith, 1962). In such circumstances malnutrition and death were less the result of absolute shortage than they were of high prices and low incomes (or unemployment). Food riots and blockages often resulted as people dependent on the market for food sometimes took direct action to prevent exports. Post describes how, in the 1816 crisis, European governments threw aside their reservations about intervention and secured imports of grain from other areas and, when necessary, distributed these at below the market price. Differential mortality rates in different parts of Europe are to be explained, according to Post, by the degree of responsiveness of governments to grain import opportunities:

> the importance of the willingness and ability of European governments to take advantage of large grain supplies now available from the Russian empire and American market is difficult to overestimate in any assessment of differential mortality rates. (p. 60)

The importation of food, combined with public works for the unemployed and the increasingly important role of private charity, explains the avoidance of a major mortality peak in this crisis, when compared to similar ones in the eighteenth century (p. 66).

The lesson of the European and Indian examples seems to be that famine can be solved when it is politically expedient to do so, and when the resources are available to make the importation and movement of food possible. Sen has made this point in an article comparing India and China (Sen, 1983), in which he argues that the political process in India is responsible for the end of outright famine. In India, 'the country's political system and press make information about potential famines hard to miss and hard for the government to ignore' (p. 55). However, the government intervenes to prevent the occurrence of famine, but at the same time non-acute, regular starvation goes on in India year by year, with between a third and a quarter of the population suffering. This kind of starvation is not as newsworthy or politically volatile as full-scale famine, but it helps explain the continued low life-expectancy of the majority of Indians. By contrast, China has a greater level of state provision and intervention, and has raised life-expectancy to around sixty-nine years. Chinese commitment to guaranteeing some food for all has been largely successful in ending the widespread chronic malnourishment suffered by so many Indians. On the other hand, evidence emerges of a massive famine having taken place in China in 1959–61 which had been 'covered-up' in a way which would have been impossible in India. The explanation of this contrast, according to Sen, lies in the nature of the political system:

> if there is an economic and political crisis in China which confuses the regime, it goes on diligently pursuing disastrous policies with confident dogmatism. There are no crusading newspapers and hard-hitting opposition parties to force a change . . . (p. 55)

Solving famine, then, depends on the existence of a political system in which the voice of the starving has leverage, but solving famine is not the same as solving chronic malnourishment and poverty.

Where does this leave our analysis of Africa? Some would argue that, despite the present evidence of massive suffering in a large part of the continent, the 'conquest of famine' has to some degree been achieved. Deborah Bryceson argues that both the colonial and post-colonial state in Tanzania has functioned to guarantee peasant reproduction through providing famine relief (Bryceson, 1980 and 1982). John Caldwell has analysed the evidence of the 1970–4 drought in the Sahel and Ethiopia and has concluded that the demographic impact – in terms of its effect on mortality – was much less than in previous droughts (Caldwell, 1977). The reasons he gives for this lessened effect on mortality are similar to those described for the history of Western Europe and India, with the added dimension of the provision of international relief. He places these explanations in three major categories. Firstly, the growth of national governments, international relief efforts and better communications; secondly, the increasing commercialisation of the agricultural economy; thirdly the expansion of the non-agricultural economy such that an increasing proportion of the rural community has relatives working in non-farm employment (p. 97). Following this argument through, Caldwell says that famines no longer act as 'Malthusian checks', and he projects large population increases in Africa in the short term as a result.

It is hard to accept the evidence for the 'conquest of famine' when millions are starving in Africa. The history of famine relief procedures in both the colonial and post-colonial periods is one of unpredictability and unreliability, and it seems highly unlikely that whole agricultural populations will have put their faith in such systems. Recent history confirms this. In the Sahel in the 1970s there was a bungling of food relief brought about by bureaucratic inefficiency, while in Ethiopia in the same period the Imperial government indulged in a massive cover-up of the famine, with international aid agencies apparently turning a diplomatic blind eye (Shepherd, 1975). In post-revolutionary Ethiopia, famine relief is subject to immense political manipulation at both the national and international level (Smith, 1983). Nowhere in Africa, it seems, if you are starving can you be sure that relief will come your way, and this is as true for the wealthiest country on the continent (South Africa) as it is for the poorest. Most countries in Africa fit neither the Chinese nor the Indian models outlined by Sen, as long-term poverty and malnutrition for some groups co-exist with full-scale famine.

During the 1949 famine in Malawi officials expressed the same kinds of reservations about intervention and food relief as have been described as dominating in India in the earlier part of the nineteenth century. In much of the current literature on Africa, food aid and famine relief continue to be regarded with some distaste. Yet a comparative analysis indicates that famine in other parts of the world has only been solved by direct intervention. It is of course essential to distinguish between food aid as an emergency measure and food aid as a longer-term strategy. Emergency food aid is essential to the alleviation of famine in Africa, and to criticise the way it has been administered and manipulated on occasions is not to say that anything could be achieved by doing away with it. More controversial is the subject of longer-term food aid and food importation, around which there is a large body of literature. The current orthodoxy amongst aid and relief agencies in Africa is that populations should be 'weaned off' food handouts as soon as possible after a crisis, and encouraged to resume their own food production. At one level this makes clear sense. Long-term recipients of food relief can become a privileged community within a country, cheap imported food can destroy the market for locally-produced foodstuffs and thus discourage production, and the distribution of 'alien' foods can permanently alter tastes in favour of foodstuffs which cannot be produced locally. Much of the criticism of food aid has, however, taken a wider political perspective (Thomi, 1978). Most commonly, food aid is seen as a particularly heinous form of dependence. As Africa as a whole slips into greater dependence on food imports and food aid, so, it is argued, its dependence on the exporters (the USA being the major one) increases. Food aid can be used as a foreign policy tool. Central America provides good examples of this, and in the 1974 Bangladesh famine American food aid was withheld because of Bangladesh's trade links with Cuba (Crow, 1984). Christopher Stevens has argued that although food aid may have many problems, dependence is not the most serious argument against it (Stevens, 1980). What is important is not whether a donor sees in food aid a way of creating dependence, but whether he actually succeeds. All aid can produce dependence, the real question is whether these risks are worth accepting:

> Countries that are not self-sufficient in food are dependent on those that have a surplus. However, this dependency need not be onerous for a rich country such as Britain; what is onerous is when a food shortage is combined with poverty. Such dependence could be alleviated by an increase in domestic food production or an increase in income. Food aid *per se* does not affect the position either way, unless it has an impact on one of these two variables. (p. 17)

It can also be argued that, if administered carefully to minimise its effects on producer price incentives and if channelled to 'target populations such as mothers and children, food aid can be seen as a precondition for the lowering of infant mortality and a decline in fertility. If 'market mechanisms' fail to alleviate hunger, then the case for intervention is stronger. One writer makes the point that the emphasis on increasing food production in the poorer countries contains the assumption that increased production will benefit the hungry. This is not necessarily the case, especially in areas of land shortage or marginal agricultural production (Christensen, 1978). Unless radical solutions are found to the problems of agriculture in such areas, then the poor are always likely to be dependent on means other than their own production in order to obtain foodstuffs. As a greater proportion of the income of the poor is spent on food, so the poor are more vulnerable to price fluctuations. If food aid or cheap imports of food can ensure a greater overall supply of food, then this is likely to be to their benefit.

One country which has built an entire economic and political system around food aid is Egypt (Thomson, 1983). Egypt's crucial political role makes it an example which cannot be easily generalised from – in the early 1980s, for instance, there was rivalry between the US and France over subsidised wheat sales to Egypt – but it is still a case worth considering. Egypt has achieved a high degree of food security with a decreasing domestic component. Domestic producer prices have fallen in the last twenty years and lack of incentives has resulted in relative stagnation in wheat production. But the Egyptian government has pursued a cheap food policy through imports, around 50 per cent of which are obtained through food aid (p. 181). Cheap imports help keep wage rates down, but at the same time by keeping the food costs of household budgets down they create the possibility for the expansion of a market for locally manufactured goods (p. 182). This is not to say that the Egyptian model could or should be followed (Egypt pays for its imports with oil and labour remittances, and its debts are piling up), but it is a caution against the assumption that food imports in themselves must be a bad thing.

It has been argued that the long-term problems of Indian famine and food supply were solved by an increasing diversification of the economy. This entailed a large proportion of the population ceasing to produce its own food and becoming dependent on the efficient and humane functioning of a government which could intervene to ensure food supply if 'market forces' undermined purchasing power. This dependence is also being created in Africa, but often without any accompanying expansion of agricultural and industrial production, which characterised Indian economic development. Thus African urban and, increasingly, rural, dwellers are dependent on their government's willingness to intervene to ensure food supply, but often in a situation where the government does not have internally generated supplies available to it, nor foreign exchange with which to buy imports. African governments, and

African populations, are left dependent on the international community and the will to solve famine at this level.

All of these questions appear to be some distance from the specificities of the 1949 famine in Malawi, but I hope to show how this one study can illuminate matters of wider relevance. Africa-wide analyses and prescriptions, such as I have just outlined, do little justice to the immense variations in economic, social and political configurations on the continent, just as aggregate production figures obscure the existence of variations in yield and productivity. The detailed study of one famine can demonstrate the relative importance and interaction of many of the factors discussed in this Introduction, from price-incentives and marketing policies, to ecological factors and the politics of food relief allocation. As an historical study it has other dimensions. The famine occurred during a crucial period of reorientation in the world economic system, which also saw the genesis of international relief and food aid (Aykroyd, 1974). It also occurred at a period when nationalist movements were making political headway in Africa. In Malawi the nationalist movement rested very firmly on the support of the peasantry, and thus the political implications of famine policy, and of agricultural policy, are of some significance. Finally, the course of the famine itself, its structure and form, provide insights into the processes of economic and social change taking place within one African community in this period.

The geographical focus of this account is the Blantyre District of the Southern Province. This was the area which was affected most severely, and it is from this area that much of the written documentation, and all of the oral accounts, are drawn. Other parts of the country were affected, however, and material is also drawn from these areas. They included the lakeshore area of Dedza District in the Central Province, as well as parts of the Southern Province outside Blantyre District – Zomba District, Port Herald District, Chiradzulu District and Mulanje District. In attempting to uncover the causes of the famine, the analysis moves into a wider arena, focusing on the territorial and international levels to discuss policies and wider economic structures bearing on the famine. Chapters 2 and 3 operate at this wider level, while Chapters 4, 5 and 6, focus on the Southern Province, and on Blantyre District in particular.

The book opens with a description of the famine in Chapter 1. The substance of this description then forms the basis for the discussion in the rest of the book. Chapters 2 and 3 examine contemporary theories of the famine, and in so doing they examine long-term trends in the agrarian economy of colonial Malawi. Chapter 2 concentrates on the theory that the famine was a 'Malthusian crisis' and critically examines this. Chapter 3 discusses the theories of 'cash versus food crops' and the 'Marketing Board' theory. In Chapter 4 I return to the structure of the famine itself in an attempt to understand who starved and why. This chapter concentrates on the crucial factor of employment, and classifies the population of the famine area by economic entitlement to food. Chapter 5 explores the dimension of gender and famine, and attempts to locate the events of the famine within a longer-term perspective on changes in marriage and kinship structures. In both Chapters 4 and 5 the famine policy of the government emerges as an important independent variable. Chapter 6 provides a description of post-famine adjustments, and concludes by relating the events of the 1949 famine to the wider issues discussed in this Introduction.

1

The 1949 famine

This chapter begins with a brief description of Blantyre District and surrounding areas of the Southern Province of colonial Malawi in the late 1940s. It then goes on to detail the events of the famine of 1949–50. This description focuses on Blantyre District where the famine was most severe, but it also draws on material covering a wider geographical area, in an attempt to relate government policy to local experience. As the famine progressed, so the linkages between local communities and wider economic structures became more crucial. The narrative traces these linkages, moving backwards and forwards between the local setting and a larger world.

Its history is written in its lay-out. There are none of the wide streets, running at right-angles, typical of Bulawayo, Johannesburg, Nairobi, or other African towns. Like Topsy, it has just 'growed'. (Norman, 1934, p. 33)

The town of Blantyre was prosperous in the late 1940s. Blantyre had never been the administrative capital of colonial Malawi,[1] but along with its 'twin' town, Limbe, it formed the commercial centre of the country. It was a town dominated by Europeans and tied closely to the settler economy.[2] With high tobacco prices, an expansion of construction, and an influx of demobbed African soldiers flush with money, the immediate post-war period was a good time for commerce. Blantyre had grown, somewhat raggedly, from its foundation as a 'township' in 1895, when it had been literally built around the twin pillars of Commerce and Christianity, in the form of the Church of Scotland mission on one ridge and a handful of trading companies on another. Its growth gave the appearance of being unstructured, but was never disorderly. The Blantyre Town Council, consisting of representatives of all European interests, had exerted enough control to ensure that racial segregation was enforced from the earliest date. Indian traders were confined to a small but central location, out of which they constantly agitated to expand. Europeans lived in the scattered suburbs of landscaped gardens. Africans were required to carry passes and letters from employers if they wished to stay in the township after dark. In the interests of 'health and sanitation' all but domestic servants were obliged to live in settlements beyond the township boundaries.

Since the township had been founded, one sanitation crisis after another had resulted in a recurrent theme of discussion in the Council – the need for the creation of 'native locations'. Native locations would enable the town authorities to enforce more easily legislation such as the ordinances against beer-brewing and prostitution, and they would simplify if not solve the water and sanitation issues. Some schemes were quite grandiose. All involved an element of segregation *within* the African urban community, as well as an imposed distance from European zones. Native locations would be subdivided into 'class zones', so that educated government clerks, would not have to rub shoulders with the 'raw Ngoni' labourers who in the early part of the century flooded in to work seasonally (Nyasaland Protectorate, Land Report, 1921). Despite half a century of schemes, little had been done by the 1940s. There were a few areas of employees' housing – the railway housing at Limbe and Mpingwe, the Imperial Tobacco Group's housing at Maone, the Church of Scotland compound, and housing for junior civil servants (Malawi Government, Blantyre Planning Team, Report 1975). The vast majority of African urban residents, however, lived in settlements approximating to 'villages' in the surrounding areas – in Ndirande, Mpingwe, Michiru, Chilimoni. Blantyre itself was a collection of scattered buildings, the spaces between them being gradually filled up, and at a quicker pace in the 1940s than ever before. The Church of Scotland mission dominated one side of the settlement, the Catholic cathedral the other. The railway station was connected to the centre of the town, which consisted of one main street of business buildings, and a 'native market' surrounded by Indian-owned stores. There was a High Court, the Queen Victoria Memorial Hall, a Lands Office and the Headquarters of the Provincial Commissioner for the Southern Province. European social life revolved around a sports club, a cinema, and a collection of hotels, some seedier than others.

Blantyre was built on the fortunes of European agricultural enterprise and fluctuated with that sector. By the 1940s tobacco was the dominant industry. Blantyre lay in the centre of the earliest area of European settlement – the Shire Highlands – and was surrounded by European-owned estates. The district of Blantyre was half-owned by Europeans, and the town served as both a manufacturing and service centre for this community's activities. Although the tobacco industry by this time had a second important focus in the Central Province, Blantyre and Limbe still constituted the main centre for tobacco processing – the large tobacco companies had their headquarters here, and their tobacco processing factories. The auction floors at Limbe were where the product was sold, packed and finally despatched on the train for export. Some fifty miles away lay Thyolo, and further towards Mozambique was Mulanje. These were the tea-growing areas of the country, and although Blantyre was

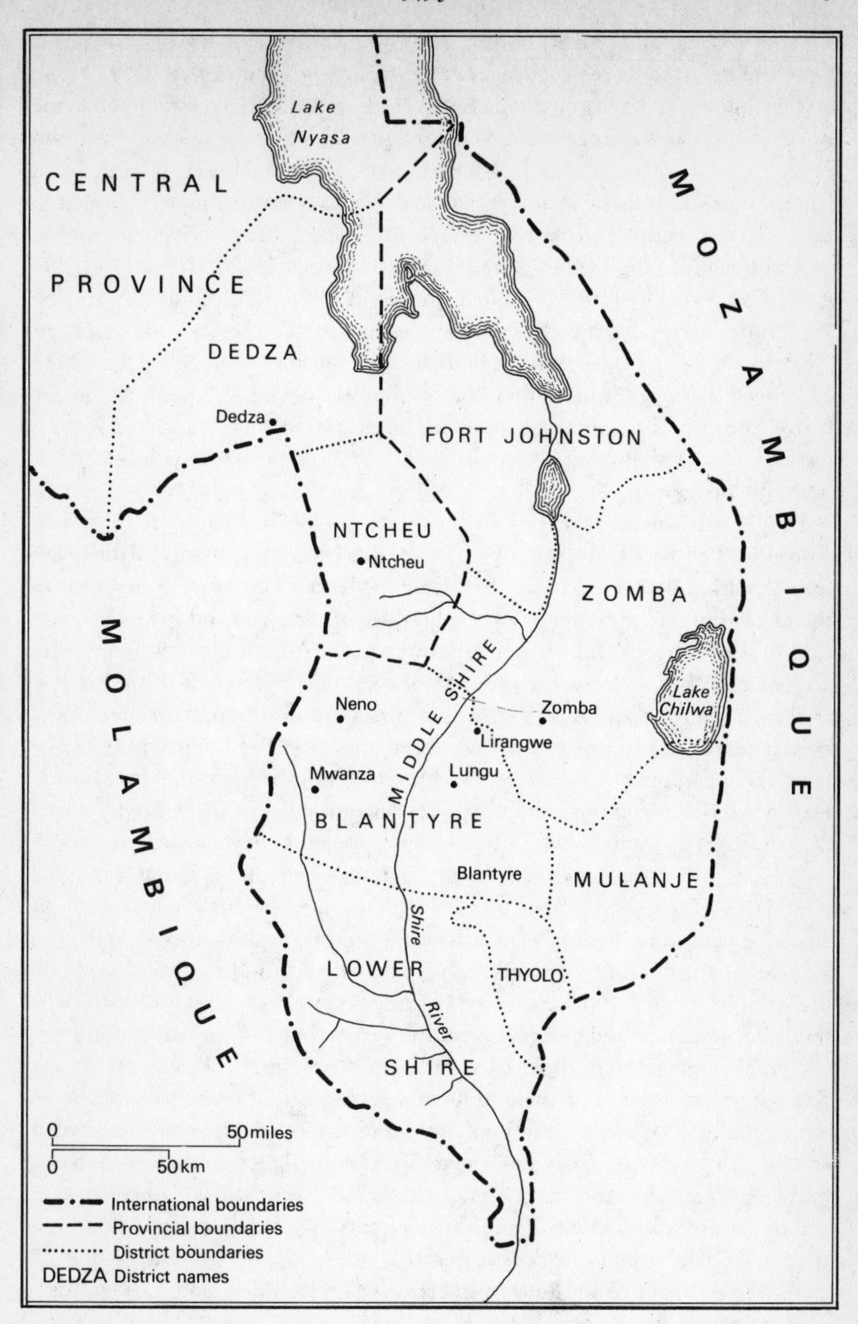

Map 1. Southern Province, Nyasaland, showing district boundaries.

not the centre for tea manufacture (this was carried out on the estates), it nevertheless acted as the main service centre for this industry as well.

The 'boom' in urban construction and commerce which was going on in the post-war period was largely due to the rise in tobacco prices and the expansion of that industry. More and more land was being put under the crop, more barns had to be built, more factories erected, and there was more money to invest in building and manufacturing industry. The European urban population began to enjoy a more highly developed service industry, as dairying and market gardening expanded to meet their needs, and various kinds of 'import substitution' were attempted with varying success. The 'New Look' crept its way slowly to the Indian stores of Blantyre, and, the women's page of the *Nyasaland Times* passed comment on it. Things materially became better for many European residents and life more comfortable, and must have seemed especially so as they read about the stringencies of post-war rationing back home in Britain.

Despite attempts to segregate and delineate the role of Africans in this urban complex, their participation took on a life of its own from an early date. From the 1880s local Blantyre Africans had developed service industries in response to the market provided by temporary migrant workers. Yao and Nyanja traders sold rolls of tobacco and various foodstuffs to the Ngoni estate workers who arrived in Blantyre for a few months of the year. A municipal market was established in 1901, and was an immediate success, and although the brewing of beer (and the beating of drums) was banned within the township, beer and *kachasu*[3] were readily available for purchase just beyond the boundaries. Hampered by restrictions on their areas of operation, by the licensing laws, and discriminatory credit laws, African entrepreneurs nevertheless made an increasing impact on the life of the town both within and without its formal boundaries. The 1931 Census Report listed amongst the 'native industries' of Blantyre the following: market gardeners, butchers, dealers in fowls and eggs, bicycle repairers, laundry owners, canteen owners, cobblers, dealers in lime, blacksmiths, charcoal makers, cutters of grass, sieve makers, sawyers, carpenters, photographers and tailors (Nyasaland Protectorate, Census Report, 1931, p. 27). Though some of these activities were carried on in the central market area, the main centres of these industries were in the peri-urban villages in which the bulk of the African population lived. Here the huts were crowded round with patches of maize and vegetables, and small plots of millet grown for brewing beer. Men either went off to work in the town each day, or engaged in a trade. Some were away altogether as migrants in South Africa and Southern Rhodesia. The women tended their patches of crops, bought and sold small quantities of produce and, most importantly, brewed beer and *kachasu*, for a predominantly male clientele.

The channels of economic activity emanating from Blantyre went far beyond the immediate peri-urban villages, however. This could be seen in the dry season as men and women from more rural areas brought long grass in to sell to the urban 'village' dwellers who needed to repair their roofs; or at almost any time of year (except the February to April 'hungry season') as women urbanites obtained the maize for their beer brewing, or vegetables for sale, from relatives in more distant villages of the district. But it was also the case that many of the men working in the town for periods, or those who came to buy and sell goods, actually had their homes further away from the 'peri-urban' village zone.

In 1945 Blantyre District had a population of 102,208 Africans (Nyasaland Protectorate, Census Report, 1945), and outside the town boundaries it was divided into a number of Traditional Authority areas – Machinjili to the south-east of the town; Somba to the south; Ntaja to the west; Kapeni, Matindi, Chigaru, Lundu, Mataka and Chitera to the north.[4]

The most densely populated parts of Blantyre District were the highland areas (with the town at their centre) where rainfall was most reliable and where opportunities for employment were close at hand. Moving north from the town one moved into Chiradzulu District, the most densely populated part of the larger Administrative Unit. Here there was a variety of communities living by different means – there were urban wage workers who walked or cycled into the town every day; workers on European-owned tobacco estates; African Trust Land tobacco growers and food producers (White, 1987). Despite the density of population, Chiradzulu District usually boasted a large marketed maize surplus, and had been known as the 'grain-bin' of the area. But the problems of crowding and erosion had been intensified with the expansion of tobacco cultivation in the 1940s, so that the people in this area were generally becoming more dependent on non-agricultural income. Moving south-east from Blantyre took one into another crowded district – Thyolo. Here again, maize surplus producers had long been feeding the urban dwellers, and erosion was being tackled here with an ambitious, but rather unpopular, conservation scheme organised by the Department of Agriculture, involving the construction of large bunds, and contoured banana plantations (Department of Agriculture Reports, 1945–9). The high rainfall in this area and the terracing made it sometimes look reminiscent of Chinese landscapes, as many an agricultural officer remarked. Side by side with the peasant producers, however, were large tea estates and communities of workers living in company 'lines' (workers' housing) or longer-term residents (known as tenants) living in villages on estate land. Further east still was Mulanje district, also a major tea-growing area, on the borders of Mozambique.[5] Going south from Blantyre took you into Chikwawa District, and down a dramatic escarpment into another world – the Lower Shire Valley. Looking down from the top of the escarpment one could see the river winding south and looking like a bright green snake, the intense cultivation of the floodplain imparting the colour. But farther away from the river the land was dusty and dry for much of the year, scattered with cotton fields, grazed where possible with cattle. The Shire Valley economy was a complex one, and subject to alteration imposed by ecological change, as well as more general influences – the cotton price, the rains, the labour market (Mandala, 1983). The fluctuations of the river had meant that large-scale population movements had long taken place in this part of the valley, and a new dimension had been added to this by the intervention of the colonial administration. This was an area seen to be most 'at risk' of famine, and colonial intervention in valley agriculture had a long history here. A long-standing pattern of labour emigration was one way in which the communities of Chikwawa (and those of the district further south, Port Herald) survived their risky environment.

North-west from Blantyre also took one into the Shire Valley – here it was known as the 'Middle Shire' – but less dramatically or abruptly. The rift valley was shallower here, the descent more gentle, and this is why the major routes from the river steamers to the town had taken this direction. There was still a marked contrast with the highlands, however. The wide-bottomed valley floor lay in a rain shadow – rainfall was less reliable, soils poorer and population sparser. Many of the people here had moved down from the crowded highlands from the 1930s onwards, though there had always been people here, living in scattered villages, and generally making the most of the wet soils of the river banks to grow their crops. In the 1940s river bank cultivation was under attack by agricultural officers, but on the drier land people grew maize, and some grew cotton as a cash crop. By the 1940s increasing numbers of men from this area were going to work as migrants outside the Protectorate, but communities here also maintained strong links with Blantyre, which was only 10–20 miles away. Many men who worked in Blantyre had their family homes in these areas, and returned at week-ends to help their wives farm. Depending on how far from the town they were, some of these women were able to go there to trade small amounts of foodstuffs, or the pots they made. Some found a nearer market for their beer amongst estate wage-earners. There were tobacco estates scattered around the Middle Shire Valley – mostly owned by one company, the British Central Africa Company (BCA), and some villages were 'tenant' villages built on BCA land. There was a lime-making and brick-making industry in the Lirangwe–Lunzu area of the middle valley which expanded with expansion of construction in Blantyre in the post-war period.

Before the advent of the railway system this middle part of the Shire Valley had lain on the most important transport route in the country. Coming from the Zambezi, up the Lower Shire, steamers were halted at Katunga's, from where head carriers took the goods up the escarpment to Blantyre. Goods destined to go north were taken down by carrier to Matope in the middle of the valley and loaded onto more steamers here. These boats plied up and down to the mouth of Lake Nyasa at Fort Johnston, and were owned by a variety of trading companies – the African Lakes Company (ALC), Sharrer's (later BCA Co.), Kahn's – all of which had stations dotted along the river which also acted as retail stores selling salt, cloth and imported hoes to local Africans.

The Shire River here was no longer a transport route by the 1940s, but the Matope Road was still an important route, and the railway from Blantyre now also lay along the valley floor, going north to the lake. Agricultural production was risky enough in the 1940s to make centrally important the economic ties with the markets and jobs of Blantyre, and the mines and farms of South Africa and Rhodesia, and this emerged clearly when this area fell victim to a drought and famine in 1949.

The rains failed in Blantyre District just after Christmas 1948. In fact the rainy season had begun well over the whole of Malawi, and even in mid December there were hopes for a good harvest of both food and cash crops. But after Christmas the rain ceased entirely in some parts of the country, and for January, usually the wettest month, there was practically no rain at all. The drought was particularly severe in the Southern Province, of which Blantyre District formed a part (Report on 1949 drought, MNA, MP 4/72).[6] Some rain fell on the highland areas in February, but the plains stayed dry until March. As the figures from the rainfall stations came in, they showed that it was an exceptional year for the Southern Province (see Table 1). By January there was considerable alarm being expressed over the prospects for food crops especially for the Southern Province and the lakeshore areas of the Central Province in Dedza District. Fortunately the higher areas of this Province (especially the high areas of Dedza and Lilongwe districts) were barely affected by the drought, and food crops looked good there.

Table 1 *Rainfall in inches*

	November–April 30		May–October 31	
Rainfall Station	1948/9	Average year	1948/9	Average year
Port Herald	19.81	33.22	4.74	2.22
Thyolo Boma	31.07	n.a.	9.22	n.a.
Mulanje	45.38	63.37	14.27	10.30
Chileka	13.82	n.a.	1.49	n.a.
Blantyre	17.66	n.a.	1.90	n.a.
Zomba	25.43	51.03	3.46	1.76
Nyambi	16.31	36.36	2.14	0.71
Fort Johnston	16.26	27.80	0.37	0.87

Source: Nyasaland Protectorate, Department of Agriculture, *Annual Report for 1949* (Zomba, 1950).

The pages of the *Nyasaland Times* were dominated by drought talk. By January 13th the government was issuing emergency communiqués and these were published and commented on in the paper. All Provinces were put on an emergency footing, one hundred European officers were sent into the field to arrange for the opening of root-crop gardens, and an order was passed for the emergency control of foodstuffs (*Nyasaland Times*, vol. 52, no. 5, 20/1/49). Meanwhile, the Department of Agriculture in Zomba was collating reports from the districts. The initial crop forecasts were very alarming. However, it soon became clear that within a very small area the severity of likely food shortage could vary very widely. The local variety of maize proved unexpectedly resilient in places, and often survived when judged to be completely dead. Areas of floodland produced a yield of late-planted maize, and some hardy crops such as ratooned sorghum gave a normal crop. It was fortunate, perhaps, that the Department of Agriculture's campaign against the cultivation of this crop (on grounds of its disease-spreading capacity) had met with only limited success in the preceding years.

Another important variable was the extent to which the population of a given area had resources available to it other than their own-produced crops. The District Commissioner's (DC) report from Zomba for February 1949 indicated how this variation could affect the projected 'famine picture' in one district:

> Reports from field officers indicate that food supplies actually stored will last for two months in five Native Authority areas of old Zomba district. The one exception is NA Mlumbe's area where villages on the western slopes of the mountain are existing on purchased food already . . . In Liwonde section, NA Kawinga's area has food for two months, with the exception of Sub. NA Mposa's area near Lake Chilwa. Their rice crop was almost a complete failure in 1947 and the maize is never good. They can however probably keep going for two months with the barter of fish. NA Msamala's food stores should last for two months. Worst reports come from NA Liwonde's area where existing food stocks are not expected to last for more than three weeks . . . Considering the district as a unit the food position is better than first anticipated. There are scattered villages with food stores which will last for as much as 5 or 6 months. There are *dimba* gardens with maize ripening already. There are large quantities of sweet potatoes, their growth retarded by the drought, but which should sprout quickly now. Cassava and millet are fairly plentiful in most areas suitable for their cultivation. On the debit side there are smaller areas where the population is postponing the day of famine only by the purchase of food and the barter of fish. (MNA, MP 12352 DC Zomba to PC Southern Province, 8/2/49)

The crisis was thus a patchwork one, varying in intensity over a small area. This same phenomenon was reported from Port Herald District in the Lower Shire Valley, where it was said in February that food prospects varied not only between different areas, but also 'as regards individuals within the same district'. This variation was attributed to the 'improvidence' of some, and the foresightedness of others (MNA, MP 12352, Port Herald: Food Prospects, n.d.).

The most worrying area for government officials was Blantyre District, though here again there were considerable variations. In February 1949 the Blantyre District Commissioner produced a map showing the relative crop prospects of different parts of the district, under hypothetical conditions of rain falling or not falling. By his estimation (based on village-to-village surveys of the contents of grain-stores), there were three distinct areas in which famine conditions would prevail by March, *whether or not* any rain fell (MNA, MP 12352, DC Blantyre to Provincial Commissioner (PC) Southern Province). These were firstly the townships of Blantyre and Limbe with 12,000 inhabitants; secondly the sections of Native Authorities (NA) Kuntaja, Somba and Kapeni with 40,500 inhabitants, and lastly the Shire–Lisungwe area with 7,000 inhabitants and incorporating the sections of NA's Symon, Chigaru, Lundu and Mlauli. Even within the predicted 'famine areas', however, there were variations in food availability when the Blantyre District *ulendo* reports were written in March (MNA, NSB 7/4/1, Blantyre District Ulendo Reports, 1946–9). In NA Mlauli's area it seemed that villagers would be able to live on the crops they had harvested, without buying food, until at least mid July. In the neighbouring area of NA George, new gardens had been opened during the year, a reasonable crop had been harvested, and villagers had seed in reserve to be planted in the event of late rains falling. In NA Kuntaja's area, however, the situation was much more serious. The first and second plantings of maize had failed completely, wild pigs, baboons and hippos had devastated remaining crops, and there was an estimated six weeks' supply of food in the area as a whole. In the heavily populated areas around Chileka people had been purchasing food for some time from Chikwawa district to the south, and Ntcheu to the north.

In these parts of Blantyre District drought was not a new phenomenon, and food shortage was for some an annual event. But when the rains failed in 1948–9 there was a general feeling that this was an eventuality beyond most people's experience. In Blantyre District, the very old people who lived through a severe famine in 1922, now claim that all the signs were there indicating a major crisis in 1949. 1947 had been the 'year of the locusts' when many crops were destroyed, and in consequence there had been few full granaries in the area in 1948.[7] Furthermore, the rain had failed in December 1948 in a way which indicated that the drought was not going to be amenable to traditional remedies. In December, when it was apparent that the rains had really stopped, people gathered in many villages to pray for rain. They sang the songs they had always sung to call the rain and appease the ancestors:

Koke Kolole	Pull, pull hard, pull the clouds.
Koke kolole	Why does the rain not come?
Kamtambo mvula pano sibwera?	Pull, pull.
Koke.	
Makolo munapita	Our dead fathers
Tatani ife wanu wanu?	What have we done?
Tikhululukireni chonde! chonde!	Forgive us, please, please!
Timvereni ife chifundo	Have mercy on us,
kodi mukufuna tife?	Do you want us to die?
Tinizani mvula.	Please, send us rain.[8]

But despite the prayers, and the taboos and sanctions which accompanied them, the rain did not fall. Christians, meanwhile, were exhorted by their churches not to join the the heathen prayers in the villages, but to pray for rain in the church instead. In Catholic and Protestant missions throughout Blantyre District rain-calling ceremonies were held. The Protestants served tea and biscuits after theirs.[9]

When prayers of all types failed, some people looked around at their neighbours to see who might be 'holding the rain' for their own ends. The usual suspects were old men with grey hair or bald heads, but people who were making bricks were also in line for accusation – after all, their work would suffer if the rain fell.[10] One man working in Blantyre at the time heard stories of such accusations being made in his home village in the Middle Shire. The people accused there were those who had long been labelled as 'lazy' and who, even in favourable conditions, never had enough food to feed their families. The accused were made to drink water and hot pepper, and if they were men (and they generally were) they had chilli powder rubbed into their testicles. Some were taken to see the famous Doctor Bwanali, a soothsayer and healer who lived in the heart of the drought-stricken area at Lunzu. But Bwanali looked into his divining glass and found them innocent, saying that this drought was beyond human intervention.[11] Others in the area were taken prisoner by their neighbours and led to the office of the District Commissioner in Blantyre, but he took a similar line on this to Doctor Bwanali and sent them home. Quite quickly the consensus had emerged that this drought, unlike less severe ones, was the work of 'God' and could not be attributed either to human action or to the anger of the ancestors. One man explained how this was understood:

No black cloud could be seen, and no thunder was heard. According to our belief, when people are 'holding the rain' an expanse of dark cloud is seen and thunder heard, but suddenly all the clouds get swept away and the sky clears. This did not happen in '49. The drought was too serious to blame on any human being. Some believed that the territorial spirits were angered and needed a sacrifice to cool them down. Some believed that it was God's work. The two camps used their means to ask for rain – but still no rain came.[12]

Drought for the European population of Blantyre meant the inconvenience of not being able to water the garden. The *Nyasaland Times* announced the cancellation of the usual annual round of gardening competitions. But as employers of labour, Europeans soon became more centrally involved in the crisis. All employers were instructed to encourage their workers to concentrate on replanting their crops, and to plant new root-crop gardens (*Nyasaland Times*, vol. 52, no. 3, 13/1/49, p. 1). Urban employees, by February, were spending much of the working day chasing the increasingly scarce and expensive foodstuffs in the town. A government-controlled shop was set up in Blantyre market, where maize was sold to urban workers at 5d. per lb, a price described by both African and European observers as 'extortionate'. The usual price for maize was around 1d. per lb. Very soon sales from this shop fell off as people could no longer afford to pay 5d. per lb, and as accusations of corruption and inefficiency abounded. Beer brewing was prohibited in all urban and rural areas of the Southern Province deemed at risk of famine, with a view to preserving precious foodstocks (MNA, MP 12348: Famine Precautions: Beer Brewing). Light rains fell in parts of the Southern Province in February, and people were generally busy cultivating a plot, even within the Blantyre and Limbe townships where cultivation was normally prohibited.

By March the crime rate in the town had increased considerably and the small police force was stretched to capacity (MNA, POL 5/2/2, Police Monthly Reports, Blantyre, 1949). The increase was accounted for mainly by petty thefts of food. Having closed down the stall in the market, the government decided that food would be issued to 'legitimate' workers only, and directly through their employers (*Nyasaland Times*, vol. 52, no. 12, 14/2/49, p. 5).

Meanwhile in the rural areas of the Southern Province and the smaller drought-stricken areas of the Central Province, the predictions of January remained unfulfilled. District Commissioners were amazed by the way in which whole populations continued to feed themselves, despite apparently possessing no food stocks at all. By June the District Commissioner of Zomba District (to the north of Blantyre District) was of the opinion 'that it may not be necessary to ask government to supply food before the end of the year', and remarked that a 'well organised internal distribution system' had so far functioned satisfactorily (MNA, MP 12352, D. C. Zomba to Chief Secretary 3/6/49). Interviews with survivors of the famine in Blantyre District disclosed what this 'system' was.

By March or April, according to these sources, in the Lirangwe and Lunzu areas of the Middle Shire food shortage was beginning to look really serious; as one man put it, 'The situation had started as a small joke, but it turned into a bad joke, and a serious issue'.[13] The main features of this period were, firstly, the extreme mobility of the population (especially the men) in search of food to buy, earn, beg or gather; secondly, the gradual increase of what was known as *ubombo*, a concept embracing greed and lack of community solidarity and the practice of mutual aid. Some aspects of this stage of the famine are recalled in the pounding songs of women in the area. These songs and their meanings will be discussed at more length in Chapter 5, but their main message seems to have been that available food supplies were not always distributed evenly within families, and that marriage ties often proved weak.

As things got worse and as local supplies of food finally became completely exhausted, people began looking further afield for places where they could obtain food either with cash, or in return for goods or labour.[14] In the highland areas of Dedza and Ntcheu Districts to the north of the Middle Shire, and in the highlands which bordered Mozambique to the west, more rain had fallen and a larger crop had been harvested. Men (and less often women), from the drought area went off in groups to search for food in these areas, and also in the Mulanje mountain area to the south-east where some cassava was available. Many of the men who went on these expeditions were making use of kinship ties. There had been a long history of Ngoni men from Dedza and Ntcheu marrying into Yao and Nyanja families in Blantyre District. At a time of crisis these men went back to their families expecting, and usually getting, help there.

In Southern Malawi, although much cultural emphasis was placed on the brother–sister link, it was nevertheless seen as a *husband's* duty to find food for his wife and immediate family in times of crisis, and those men who did not do this were chided in the women's songs:

Iwe ndi mwamuna wanji	What type of husband are you
Wokhala pakhomo ndi azimayi?	Staying at home with the women?
Amuna ku Mwanza awo	The other men are off to Mwanza now
Nanga iwe, watani?	Why not you?
Nchito kugwira munchiuno basi.	You just stay here and your only 'work' Is to fondle women.[15]

Communities in this area practised matrilocal marriage, whereby a husband lived in his wife's village with her relatives, and strains in this system seem to have come to the fore at this stage of the famine (see Chapter 5 for full discussion). Men were aware of the praises they could earn if they succeeded in finding food for everyone in the village. Women sang the praises of their husbands to their sceptical mothers, and the men replied realistically that they didn't expect this new-found popularity to out-live the famine:

Pamudzi pano mundikonda	You in this village, you love me now
Chifukwa cha njalayi	Because of the famine, [Because I brought food here]
Koma ikatha	But when it ends
Mudzinena zambiri.	You will start saying many things.[16]

The journey on foot to the highlands or to Mulanje was long and arduous and some people died on the way. Whilst travelling they lived on wild foods which they gathered in the bush, and of which there seems to have been a communal knowledge. There were varieties of yam-like tubers, wild cassava, banana roots, edible grasses, funghi and fruits.[17] Collecting and processing these foods was time-consuming and had to be done with extreme care as many of them were fatally poisonous if not cooked correctly. The women and children left at home also collected these wild foods, and often grandmothers would take their grandchildren off into the bush to collect them. As time wore on many people developed severely swollen limbs, and this condition they attributed (wrongly as it happens) to the eating of these wild foods.[18]

The migration of men in search of food was a widely observed phenomenon in this, as in many other famines. Research in the Cameroons has suggested that this behaviour could be used as an indicator of the increasing seriousness of food shortage (Campbell and Trechter, 1982). Officials in Malawi were rather more complacent about it. They were clearly relieved that communities had their own ways of dealing with shortage, which put off the necessity for government action by many months. The District Commissioner for Dedza District, where the lakeshore areas were badly affected, described his astonishment at the ability of people to stay alive and apparently healthy when there were no food stocks left in the villages:

> a census at the end of June showed that 30 were already without food, and were either buying or borrowing from friends locally or in the highlands, or subsisting on wild fruits and roots, . . . as the food in the *nkhokwes* was used up, more and more people were observed in the bush collecting fruits and roots, and what was at first a dribble became a procession of people along all the paths leading to the highlands . . . In connection with the hidden source of foodstuffs, it should be emphasised that these could not be hidden or hoarded stocks as every hut was searched during the survey, and when calculating the food availability note was made of all rice, millet, groundnuts etc. in addition to maize . . . It would appear that the various roots, fruits and leaves must have sustaining properties much in excess of those usually attributed to them, and in support of this it should be mentioned that on two separate occasions, Drs Watson and Bourke were taken into the villages in the evening, just as meals were being prepared. They examined each meal, which consisted almost entirely of green stuff or roots, together with in one or two cases, a handful of maize . . . Owing to the general fair condition of these villagers when examined, both doctors expressed great surprise at the obviously high food content of these wild foods and leaves. (MNA, AFC 7/2/1, DC Dedza to African Foodstuffs Commissioner, 25/4/50)

But in lakeshore areas of Dedza, as in Blantyre, people were not surviving on wild foods alone, but also on foods which they could procure from other areas. Men from Blantyre District went back to their homes in the Ntcheu and Dedza areas and were usually met with generosity. They were given a meal to revive them and a place to stay, and then they either bought food for cash or worked for it. Sometimes they exchanged beads, plates or clothing for maize. In the early months of the famine they also sold their domestic livestock (mainly chicken and goats) but the supply of animals was quickly exhausted. One of the main markets for livestock was Mwanza, near the Mozambican border, and the people of Mwanza began to refuse to accept the animals in exchange for grain because of their disturbing tendency to turn into snakes as soon as their owners had departed.[19]

Men bought food in varying quantities, according to their means. The price they had to pay in Dedza and Ntcheu was comparable to that paid by urban workers in Blantyre at the time, and is usually quoted as three shillings for a four-gallon tin. The demand was high and little bargaining was possible. One man who had money remitted from a son working in Southern Rhodesia, walked to Ntcheu and bought two bags (each containing 200 lbs) which lasted him and his family for about two months. He returned to Ntcheu several times during 1949.[20] Another man was a tailor from Blantyre for whom business had dried up, but who did have some money saved up. He walked to Ntcheu as well, diverging into the hills on the way to collect wild foods.[21] A woman whose husband was insane and incapable of travel, joined a group of people going west from the valley to Neno and Mwanza. She had no money so she worked in other people's gardens in order to earn a small basket of maize.[22]

Not everyone met with immediate sympathy in the areas to which they went to find food, and some encountered downright scepticism:

> One day I went with my friends to look for food in Ntcheu, but when we got there a certain woman asked us rudely to 'produce the serious famine for her to see' and after failing to produce it she told us to go back to Lirangwe and wrap the famine in big leaves and bring it to her.[23]

At home the women waited for their husbands to return, which they usually did at night so that their neighbours could not see how much food they had with them. But, both written sources and oral testimonies indicate that often the men did not return at all, but stayed away in their home areas until the famine was over, or took extra wives in the places to which they had gone to find food. 1949 is thus remembered as the year of 'many divorces',[24] and this aspect of the famine features prominently in women's songs:

Chako chino tabvukita	We have suffered this year
Amuna akutileka maukwati	Our men are divorcing us.
Titani ife njala-imeneyi?	Oh, what shall we do with this hunger?[25]

Those marriages which survived the famine were said to be 'good and strong ones' which could outlive any disaster, but for many women the famine proved the fragile nature of marriage ties, and especially those with men from other areas with different customs. Many of the songs sung by women during and after the famine were critical of men and cynical about marriage. For those women whose husbands were labour migrants in South Africa and Southern Rhodesia, the famine also proved a test of their marriages. Some of these women were better off than the majority – if their husbands sent regular remittances then they had a steady source of cash with which to buy food. But if their husbands sent nothing they had to rely on the help of relatives, usually those within their matrilineal group, the *mbumba*.[26] Whilst such help was generally forthcoming at first, it became more difficult to obtain as the famine worsened.

The destitution of women and children was widely reported by officials in the accounts they wrote at the end of the famine. The District Commissioner for Dedza attributed much of the suffering along the lakeshore to the 'absence of a great many men at work in South Africa, and the failure of remaining men to give effective aid to their wives', adding that the 'men appear to treat their homes in this area purely as resting places upon their return from work elsewhere pending their departure for another spell of work' (MNA, AFC 7/2/1 DC Dedza to African Foodstuffs Commission). In Fort Johnston District at the southern end of Lake Nyasa, it was remarked 'how many children and young mothers were neglected and without any means of support – one saw cases of children with no parents or relatives to turn to in times of distress, and of females deserted by their husbands, who had gone off to find food and employment for themselves' (MNA, AFC 7/2/1, DC Fort Johnston to African Foodstuffs Commissioner 24/4/50). In Blantyre District where things got worse more quickly, destitution was blamed on the same factors. Firstly there were men who were no longer able or willing to support dependants *other than* their wives and children, so that step-children and aged parents suffered; secondly there were men who deserted their wives and children (MNA, AFC 3/2/1, DC Blantyre to PC Southern Province, 30/1/50).

As well as being remembered as a year of divorces, 1949 is also recalled as a year of few marriages and few conceptions. Women did not conceive, and this they attributed to a lack of desire for sexual intercourse (though amenorrhea probably also played a part).[27] In one song a young woman laments the fact that she is without a child:

Mulera dzuwa	I am the nurse of the sun
Ine ndilera dzuwa	I am nursing the sun
Anzanga alera mwana.	While my friends are nursing babies.[28]

Those babies which were born in 1949–50 were said to be sickly and weak, and nursing mothers were anxious that, without enough food to feed themselves, they would not have enough milk for their babies. One woman recalls how her milk supply became insufficient to feed her three-month-old baby, and how she had to make her drink a thin porridge instead.[29] But it was probably the small children who had already been weaned who suffered more than the babies, and their constant wailings were heard everywhere. Stories are told of how some mothers, unable to quieten their children or to find food for them secretly murdered them. Others were simply abandoned, along with some of the very old and disabled:

Kaja kamwana kulira kulirambo eee	I can hear the crying of the child He is crying continuously
Pakuti kulilira chelicheche	He is crying like a bird.
Kwagona mwana, kuswakwagona.	He has slept out there in the bush Because he has nowhere else to sleep.[30]

As the custom of sharing broke down, so increasingly each nuclear family, and then each individual paid attention only to his or her own food supply. European officials reported this phenomenon and saw it as indicative of a more general breakdown in 'community life', not confined to the period of famine. E. C. Barnes, the Provincial Commissioner for the Southern Province, had this to say about what he saw happening in parts of Blantyre District:

> There were people in the villages very nearly dead and village communities doing nothing to assist . . . this came as a great shock to me. I have been 26 years in this country and I never imagined for a moment that the African village community had ceased to look after its own people, and that points to the fact that your old customs of community life are breaking down very fast. (MNA, MP 12655, Address by E. C. Barnes, 17/4/50)

Oral testimony, however, views behaviour during the famine as definitely abnormal. People today recall with embarrassment how they ate inside their houses and not in public as was usual and how children had to be kept inside at mealtimes otherwise they would go and beg at every house.

In general it was the women who had the strongest ties at home and who were more or less tied by their child care duties. But some women decided that the only way to obtain food was through prostitution in the towns. According to male informants, there were many women from the famine-stricken areas who went to the towns of Blantyre and Limbe and slept with any man who could assure them of a meal. Some of the women's songs also associate the famine with recourse to prostitution.[31] But there are other songs which indicate that even at the height of the famine people were half-conscious of how their behaviour might be judged afterwards. One song, for instance, warns young girls to behave with propriety during the time of hunger, or afterwards they might be faced with harsh judgement:

Ziyankhulani bwino asungwana	Be careful girls when speaking
Njalayi idzapita dede	This famine will one day end,

Tiwone kunyada kwanu.	And then we will see (recall) your pride.[32]

Whilst most families were managing to feed themselves in one way or another, the government was arranging for the importation of food into the country. These arrangements were made as early as January 1949 when the failure of the rain was apparent, but they were supposed to be strictly secret for fear that Africans would come to expect the government to supply food, and would therefore not make the efforts required to grow and obtain it themselves.

In February 1949 the Governor, Colby, instructed District Commissioners in the Southern Province that 'it should be taken for granted in all conversations with Africans that no imports will be made' (MNA, MP 12352, Governor to DCs 7/2/49). This caution was partly explained by worries over the expense of any famine relief exercise. The original estimates of import requirements carried with them alarming financial implications. Colby estimated in February that maize from the United States, which might become available, would cost no less than £40 per ton, or 5d. per lb. To import 5,000 tons a month for twelve months would therefore cost the country £2,400,000 (MNA, MP 12352, Governor to DCs). Furthermore, the Colonial Office in London, whilst expressing concern about the situation, did not seem willing to help directly in easing the financial burden. At worst their attitude seemed callous:

> We note that you expect to recoup from sales to the public very little of the expenditure involved. We appreciate that the price of food to African consumers will be expensive but we are given to understand that owing to a lack of consumer goods Africans have preferred to hoard rather than spend and have large sums salted away . . . Please do not think that we are unsympathetic. (MNA, MP 12385, Secretary of State to Governor, 29/2/49)

The government in Zomba then turned for help to its immediate Central African neighbours, with whom it had long had both formal and informal arrangements over food supplies. In February a conference was held between the representatives of governments of Southern Rhodesia, Northern Rhodesia and Nyasaland (MNA, MP 12355, II Salisbury Conference Report 8/2/49). One of the major problems to be considered was transportation, for the capacity of the railway was limited and this meant that maize could only be transported at the expense of other requirements. It was decided that as Nyasaland needed food so quickly, it would be best to obtain this from Southern Rhodesia, with a guarantee of replacement, preferably from sterling sources such as Kenya or the Union of South Africa. Ultimately, however, it became necessary to import from both the United States and Argentina, and the three territories made these arrangements jointly.

At the same time as government officials were arranging imports they were also attempting to build up any available surplus within the country. Much of the surplus came from the Central Province, and we have seen in the stories of the men from Blantyre District how some of this was distributed informally. But the government Maize Control Board, which had been set up in 1947, also purchased 5,483 tons, and this mostly from Lilongwe District in the Central Province (Maize Control Board Annual Report 1949–50). The price paid to producers was 1d. per lb, a fact which immediately caused much comment amongst urban Africans who were buying from the government store at 5d. per lb.

By March the government had found it necessary to drop the price to consumers to 3d. per lb in Blantyre, Limbe and Zomba townships, but it was still not providing any supplies to rural areas (MNA, AFC 2/1). In the drought-affected villages 'Operation Njala' continued with the aim of keeping these areas self-sufficient for as long as possible. Operation Njala involved the replanting of gardens and the planting of root crops, enforced by agricultural officers in the field, and by compliant village headmen and chiefs (MNA, MP 12324, Department of Agriculture, Operation Njala, 6/1/49). It was not always popular, and sometimes brought to the fore more deep-rooted resentments against the Department of Agriculture and its officials. In a letter to the District Commissioner in Zomba, one E. J. Kapinji, clearly a relatively wealthy peasant, complained at the treatment he had received at the hands of a representative of the African Protectorate Council, Charles Mlanga. Mlanga had been given the task of enforcing Operation Njala in his area. Entitling his letter 'Compulsory Hoeing Torments Humankind', Kapinji described how his wife had been caught pounding maize, when she was supposed to be hoeing:

> In this part of the country people have replanted the second time and the result of the rain falling is just the same as which has spoilt the first maize. To compel people for gardening is to torment humankind! . . . From Monday to Friday my wife and I went to our garden. On Saturday she gave ample time for pounding. Failing to give this time up the whole family during hoeing periods has to live on boiled maize and chew like donkeys. Is this the living condition the government wishes people to stay? . . . These compulsors have never spared their times to see peoples' gardens! How badly scorched and hopeless they are! (MNA, MP 12324, E. J. Kapinji to DC Zomba, 28/2/49)

Despite the discontent felt by some villagers, the government was largely pleased with the results of Operation Njala, though it is difficult to assess how far it was this operation which kept whole areas alive, and how far people were still relying on migration and famine foods.

A number of other government measures were taken at this stage. Beer brewing had been prohibited as early as January, but this prohibition was not without its rational opponents (MNA, MP 12348, DC Zomba to PC Southern Province, 28/3/49). In February representations were made by chiefs, administrative and agricultural staff to the Provincial Commissioner for the South, arguing that the prohibition on beer brewing was having a detrimental effect on the planting campaign in areas where normal practice was to assemble work-parties at the start of planting and to reward these parties with beer. A very practical consideration, and one of which the government was well aware, was the fact that many people (especially single women) relied on beer sales in order to pay their taxes, and also that the treasuries of the Native Authorities depended heavily on funds raised through the sale of beer-brewing licences. The ban was not finally removed until April 1950, but the government did allow flexibility in its enforcement. Lacking beer, many urban Africans had taken to distilling increased quantities of *kachasu*, a form of gin, and a drink much less compatible than beer with work in the fields (MNA, MP 12348, Chief Secretary to Controller of Essential Supplies, 24/10/49). Beer was definitely the lesser of two evils in the view of some officials.

The supply of fish was another area of government intervention. Already in January a Greek fisher and trader, Mr Yiannakis, had requested permission to start fishing increased quantities from Lake Nyasa, and saying that he would be prepared to catch, salt, store and hold the proceeds solely at the disposal of the government (MNA, MP 12354, Note of Meeting at Government House, 29/1/49). New licences were duly extended to him, and to two other non-African fishing enterprises, one owned by another Greek, N. Tratаris, and the other by an Indian, Ibrahim Osman. By May, however, the Controller of Essential Supplies was issuing a permit for Yiannakis to export twenty-five tons of salted fish to Southern Rhodesia 'as it appears that this fish is not required for consumption in the territory and will not keep any longer' (MNA, MP 12359, Controller of Essential Supplies to African Foodstuffs Commissioner, 17/5/49). It seems that the market for fish decreased rather than increased at a time when staple cereals were in short supply. The reduced market was already well supplied by fish from Lake Chilwa which was traded by African fishermen on bicycles, while in the Lower Shire Valley a fish glut had already become evident as a result of the government's ban on food exports. Ultimately most government officials concluded that it was best to let the internal market for fish operate unhindered (MNA, MP 12359, Chief Secretary's minute, 19/4/49).

Perhaps a more significant area of government intervention during the famine concerned the recruitment of emigrant labour. In January the government had decided to extend the normal 'closed season' for recruitment by the South African mine recruitment agency, the Witwatersrand Native-Labour Association (WNLA), and the equivalent Southern Rhodesian organisation, the Rhodesian Native Labour Supply Commission (RNLSC) (MNA, MP 12353: Acting Labour Commissioner to RNLSC 14/1/49). This ban on recruitment was designed to ensure that as many men as possible remained at home to take part in the replanting campaign. By February, however, the government was being wooed by an alternative suggestion from the Governor of Southern Rhodesia:

> in view of the serious position of native food supplies in Nyasaland, Ministers suggest that your Government may be prepared to alleviate the position in the Southern Province by extending to that area the Governor's permits now granted to the RNLSC for recruitment in other Provinces of the Protectorate. The Commission consider that it could absorb a number of natives accompanied by wives and dependants, and would be glad to accept as a condition of recruitment in the Southern Province that a definite proportion of any recruits must be accompanied by dependants . . . it is suggested that 'dependants' be defined as being wives and small children of recruits and we would also accept adolescents who might be capable of light agricultural work . . . it would not be desirable for this Colony to accept dependants who are aged or infirm as such people would accentuate the drain on our own food supplies. (MNA, MP 12353 Govenor, S. Rhodesia to Governor Nyasaland, Telegram, 7/2/49)

The scheme was agreed to and in March the Commission was authorised to recruit 500 men accompanied by their families from the Lower River District (in the Lower Shire Valley), and 500 from Fort Johnston District (MNA, MP 12353, Governor Nyasaland to Governor, Salisbury, 31/3/49). Extending labour recruitment was repeating a response to famine in these areas first exercised by the government in 1912 (Vaughan, 1981, p. 182).

As the famine worsened, so crop thefts increased, and there was more and more concern about the possibility of riot and disturbance, especially in Blantyre and Limbe. Feeding the urban populations thus remained a priority for political reasons, and the Governor warned of the problems that would ensue if the 'scallywag' element was allowed to get out of control (MNA, MP 12375, Governor's meeting in Blantyre, 19/1/49). Although the police in Blantyre did prosecute on average 130 cases of crop theft a month between January and December 1949, at the same time their powers were limited by the practical difficulties of feeding prisoners. The Chief Justice suggested making prison conditions less attractive, and introducing caning and flogging as alternative punishments for food theft offences (MNA, MP 12375, Discussion with Chief Justice 19/1/49). A number of culprits in Blantyre were sentenced to six months of public work, and in one case the father of a juvenile was sentenced as it appeared that he had instructed his child to steal (MNA, POL 5/2/2).

Another political worry for the government was with its public image amongst migrants outside the country, and the fear of some kind of nationalist insurrection resulting from its handling of the famine. As early as January 1949 the editor of the *Nyasaland Times*, Mr Hess, had expressed his concern to the Governor over the importation of *The Guardian*, a communist-financed newspaper published in South Africa. In May an extract from this paper was sent to the Nyasaland Public Relations Officer by a Malawian student at Fort

Hare University in South Africa, Mr Bwanausi. The report quoted another publication, *New Africa*, and linked the drought to European moves towards political union in Central Africa, pointing out that 'no concern for this grave famine condition was manifested by the white leaders of Southern Rhodesia, Northern Rhodesia and Nyasaland at the Victoria Falls conference recently, when plans for the unification of the territories were agreed upon'. The loyal Mr Bwanausi, in a covering letter, warned that 'This may not be the first time that these Communists have eyed our country with the aim of causing unrest. We shall not stand it, and I wish the Government take a serious view of this' (MNA, MP 12324, Extract from *The Guardian*, 9/5/49).

From then on, strict censorship was enforced on reports of the famine leaving the country, and even the ultra-cautious editor of the *Nyasaland Times* fell foul of government exertions (MNA, MP 12932, F. Withers to Chief Secretary 1/3/49). This did not stop stories spreading amongst migrants outside the country, however, many of whom recall the distressing letters they received from home, and who recount their efforts to send food back jointly to the country from Southern Rhodesia.[33]

In general the country remained calm, and it was only in the Lower Shire Valley, an area renowned for its 'superstitions', that the spectre of unrest grew real. In March a wave of rumours swept the Ngabu, Tengani and Mlolo areas to the effect that small children were being taken and retailed by Indian shopkeepers to Europeans who used them for food and for the preparation of 'powerful medicines'. Before long crowds had started behaving in a threatening manner by brandishing spears, bows and arrows and knives, in the presence of European officials and their own chiefs and headmen. Chiefs Mlolo and Tengani were given the task of averting any real riot, which they apparently accomplished within a few days (MNA, NS 3/1/18, Annual Report for the Lower River, 1949). Indeed, as the famine worsened, so the worst problems of unrest receded, especially as the government came to assume a more central role in supplying food.

In May and June some areas of the Southern Province had a harvest of sweet potatoes, and in August those who had earlier in the year planted the fast-maturing variety of cassava called *chilingano* began to reap some of this (Interviews and MNA, MP 18690: Director of Agriculture's Report, 18/10/50). But these small root-crop harvests were a drop in the ocean, and could in no way replace the failed maize crop. By September it was obvious that the 'internal distribution system', the functioning of which had so surprised officials, was finally breaking down in some areas. Food distribution centres were gradually opened up in the worst hit rural areas, at which maize was sold to those without any other sources of supply.[34] Such purchases were rationed by family, and the task of enforcing the rules and regulations was entrusted to local headmen and chiefs, usually overseen by a European official. The whole relief campaign became a testing ground for the capacity of the local Native Administrations. As time wore on, so in some areas the ability of the population to purchase food was exhausted, and increasing numbers of free issues of food were made. Finally, by the beginning of 1950 it became necessary to open up feeding camps for the worst affected cases, where cooked meals were provided and medical treatment given (MNA, AFC 7/2/1).

In the first instance individuals were allowed to buy maize from the centres once a week, and the amount they were allowed to purchase depended on the number of dependants they had, and the amount of food available at the time at the centre. All married women were classified as dependants, and this later caused problems, as we shall see. Each village was allocated a day for attendance at the centre, and the village headman was required to attend when food was being allocated to his people. Then the procedure began:

> The maize to be sold was removed from the store, and placed ready for sale, by men waiting to buy first, and this had to be done without payment. The maize was spread in a heap with the two watchmen to fill up the measures. The local Native Agricultural Instructor was employed in levelling off the measures and giving purchasers the correct quantity of maize. The Distributing Officer sat in a position which enabled him to watch the issues directly and made every purchaser pass before him. On one side of him stood a scrutineer, a forceful councillor or the Native Authority himself. Another councillor and the Native Authority's clerk were also in attendance . . . (MNA, AFC 7/2/1, DC Dedza to African Foodstuffs Commissioner, 25/4/50)

When everything was ready for the issues to commence, the headman of the village farthest away from the distribution centre was called up with his people, who formed a line, women first. The headman took his position beside the scrutineer, a Councillor took position at the head of the line with the NA's clerk between him and the Distributing Officer. The headman was warned that he must say immediately if any person buying maize was not from his village, or if any person had entered twice, and he would be punished on the spot by fine if he was found to have failed in either of these duties. Each man in line had to produce his hut tax receipt, which was checked by the five responsible people there – the Native Authority, two of his councillors and his clerk, and the Native Agricultural Instructor – all of whom were well enough acquainted with the villagers to be able to check on the headman. Next the money and maize changed hands:

> The Councillor at the head of the line accepted money from the leading purchasor, and called out the amount, and passing it to the NA's clerk who checked it and repeated the amount, and handed it to the scrutineer, who repeated to the issuing Native Agricultural Instructor the amount, and, after the purchasor had received the correct quantity of

maize, handed the money to the Distributing Officer. Meanwhile the Distributing Officer was entering the amount of maize sold in a book kept for this purpose. (MNA, AFC 7/2/1, DC Dedza to African Foodstuffs Commissioner, 25/4/50)

It was usually assumed that 1 lb of maize kernels per person per day was sufficient to maintain health, and it was also assumed that the average family consisted of four people, so the maximum weekly ration for a family was set at 28 lb. Survivors of the famine remark that larger families were discriminated against by this system and had to find other ways of making up their deficit. But the lack of cash resources in the famine areas acted as the most efficient form of rationing, with the majority of recipients taking less than the maximum allowed. The price at which the maize was sold varied from area to area. In most of Blantyre District it was 3d. per lb, but in the lakeshore area of Dedza District it was sold at 2d. per lb, reflecting the shorter distance over which it had to be transported. Even at this price (which was more than double the normal price in the area), it was not always easy to sell the maize and recipients muttered that 'when in their turn they were in a position to sell maize, they would remember this price' (MNA, AFC 7/2/1).

The government was determined to keep free issues to the minimum, and initially reserved these for the old and infirm. But cash resources everywhere dried up – very old banknotes were produced, coins discoloured by burial in the earth were proferred, chickens were brought in for barter (MNA, AFC 7/2/1, DC Domasi to African Foodstuffs Commissioner, 2/5/50). In order not to increase the number of free issues, District Commissioners began organising 'food-for-work' schemes, whereby able-bodied men and women could earn the food they required but were unable to buy. In the Lirangwe area, the building of the road to the railway line is well-remembered as the local 'food-for-work' project. The majority of participants were women, as so many of the men were away. In particular women who were married but whose husbands were away, took part in these schemes. Because of the government's policy in categorising all married women as 'dependants', such women were unable to claim rations in their own right, and could only gain direct access to food by working for it. Each woman collected ten large stones and carried them to where they were needed on the road, earning a gallon tin full of maize and a penny for milling fees.

When the rains commenced in October 1949, relief work could conflict with the vital preparation of gardens for the following season, as well as weakening still further a population already severely malnourished. In Dedza District road-building was also undertaken, but it was noted that women working alone often took three to five weeks to complete a task earning them a 200 lb bag of maize. Once the rains started they often did not complete the task at all, as all their remaining energies were invested in garden preparation, in finding seeds, and later in weeding (MNA, AFC 7/2/1, DC Dedza to African Foodstuffs Commissioners, 25/4/50).

Most extended families could, between them, employ a variety of different ways of obtaining food – some men would obtain it through employers, others would migrate; some women worked for food. If they had cash they could distribute this amongst a group of 'nuclear' families, thus limiting the effects of the rationing system. But women alone and without the support of either husbands or other male relatives found it much more difficult to feed their children. Some gathered at the few remaining working maize mills in Lunzu and desperately gathered up the flour which fell from the engine onto the floor. Some worked on the relief schemes literally until they fainted, as the rules were that they were not entitled to free food if they were married.[35] Eventually a number of village headmen made representations to the District Commissioner in Blantyre about the injustice of this rule, and more flexibility was introduced.[36]

By the time the rains of 1949 began to fall in October, signs of real malnutrition were becoming more apparent in Blantyre District. Those who had been living on a diet of wild foods supplemented by occasional maize rations, quite suddenly showed a marked deterioration in health. Survivors recount how physical appearances changed – legs became swollen with 'famine oedema', faces were haggard, and people were no longer able to speak. They developed sores, and many suffered from diarrhoea. The dating of this deterioration varied from place to place. In the affected areas of Fort Johnston District these signs were seen in January 1950, and the timing was about the same in Mulanje District (MNA, AFC 7/2/1, DC Fort Johnston to AFC, 22/4/50) where it seemed to coincide with the end of the mango harvest. People had survived for some time on green mangoes, but now these had come to an end, and the reversion to cassava leaves and banana roots precipitated a crisis (MNA, AFC 7/2/1, DC Mulanje to African Foodstuffs Commissioner, 3/5/50). In the Lirangwe area of Blantyre District, January was also a crucial month. On January 17th, the Provincial Commissioner for the Southern Province visited the Lirangwe Distribution Centre (MNA, AFC 3/2/1 Provincial Commissioner to Chief Secretary, 17/1/50). When he arrived there was a crowd of some 3,000 people waiting for food to be distributed to them. Out of these there were some three to four hundred children in a very advanced state of starvation and about two hundred adults in a similar condition (of whom only about six were men). Two of the children were moribund, and he doubted if they would survive the night: 'There were many others approaching the same condition, and I was really horrified at the state of these people' (ibid.).

At Chirangoma Distribution Centre near Lunzu there was a crowd of about 2,000 gathered to buy food, and amongst them some eighty old people and forty children showing signs of advanced malnutrition. At Lunzu itself people

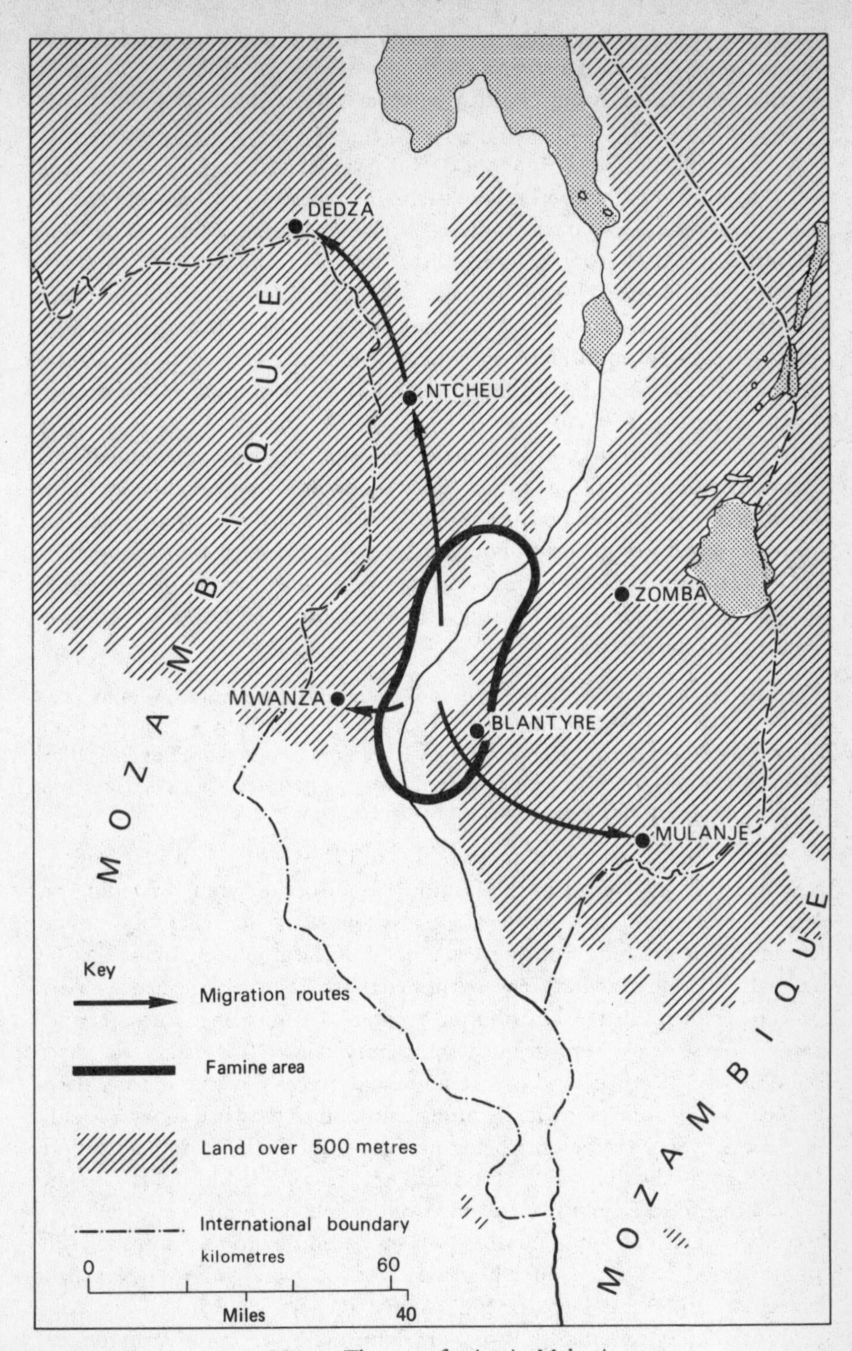

Map 2. The 1949 famine in Malawi.

looked in a better state, but the sub-chief said that there were many people in the villages who were in a very bad state and were too weak to walk to the Distribution Centre. A similar situation apparently existed in NA Ntaja's area (MNA, AFC 3/2/1).

A decision had to be made about the best way of adapting the famine relief policy to meet these worsened conditions. The idea of lowering the price of maize was mooted, but the officer in charge of the African Foodstuffs Commission, Mr Barrow, considered that this would be a mistake as 'such a reduction would only result in the maize falling into the hands of healthy people who would put it on the black market'. In his opinion, the solution lay in opening feeding camps to feed only those who were clearly starving, and this was the policy pursued (MNA, AFC 3/2/1, Extract from minutes of Executive Council Meeting, 19/1/50).

In Lirangwe from the end of January, free issues of food were granted in all cases of 'genuine destitution'; purchasers at food centres were no longer limited to specified days but could buy on three days a week at any centre, and finally a camp was organised to receive, house and feed the near starvation cases (MNA, AFC 3/2/1). An equivalent camp was set up in Lunzu, where Mrs Dorothy Kabichi, then a teenage girl, assisted the European Red Cross worker who administered the camp:

> Nearly ten people came every day – some in a state of collapse. The aged, who could not walk, were carried in *machilas* [stretchers]. They were given milk by government health officials. They were also given porridge and salt at 10 a.m. and at night. But *nsima* [thick porridge] was only given when they were showing signs of recovery . . . There were about 300 people in this acute condition in January 1950.[37]

Receiving relief was not without its humiliations. Mrs Mandauka (and others) remembers being slapped in the face by the European woman handing out supplies at Lirangwe Distribution Centre. As one man said, relief food was not distributed 'like manna from heaven'.[38] Mrs Kaulembe remembers that her disabled uncle and grandfather were entitled to free food, but she had always to accompany them to the Distribution Centre to ensure that they got their share.[39] Those who were deemed sufficiently starved to qualify for direct feeding, were placed behind a wire fence and given 'government necklaces' (likened to dog-licences, by many informants) which they had to wear around their necks.[40] Some remember being made to 'dance' after eating, apparently with the aim of distributing the food through the body.[41] Most of the inmates of the direct feeding camps were either old people or children aged between three and twelve. The total number of people admitted to the camps over the famine period was 4,575, of whom nearly 3,000 were children (Nyasaland Protectorate, Medical Department, Annual Report for 1950, p. 5). Most showed typical symptoms of advanced malnutrition – the 'hookworm tongue',

1. A withered maize crop at Likwenu, 1949

loss of fat and dullness of skin. The very young were especially vulnerable to famine oedema, and a number of the older children suffered from kwashiorkor as well as marasmus, showing reddish hair, stunted growth and liver enlargement.

Only 71 deaths were reported in these camps, [42] but all oral accounts stress that many more people died without coming to the attention of the authorities. Old people, who were too weak to make their way to the Distribution Centres, were often left to die. Their relatives, ashamed at the neglect they had shown, covered up these deaths. Young children were abandoned by their mothers. Countless numbers of people died on their long journeys to find food, and many more succumbed to the normal round of diseases – malaria, dysentery, tuberculosis. A smallpox epidemic broke out in Ntcheu District, in the areas to which many famine victims had gone to get food. Because of the mobility of the population the outbreak was difficult to control, though its severity lessened as it moved south where a large percentage of the population had been vaccinated (Nyasaland Protectorate, Medical Department, Annual Report for 1950, p. 5).

The time of the worst suffering thus occurred a year after the initial failure of the rains, and it coincided with the busiest period of garden cultivation. Fortunately the rains were good in the Southern Province, but people were weak and most had eaten their stores of seed. Although the government offered to distribute free seeds from their stock of imported maize, most people spurned this in favour of finding local seed, and they went to great lengths to obtain it (MNA, MP 12379, Director Agriculture to Chief Secretary, 11/1/50). They walked again to Ntcheu and Mulanje to obtain maize seeds, and also the fast maturing cassava seedlings which had proved so useful during the famine.[43] In some areas the government distributed root crop seedlings, and agricultural officials encouraged people to plant more of these crops to supplement the maize. Many were in any case inclined to plant more cassava, and this was probably the major agricultural adaptation they made as a result of the famine, combined with the greater use being made of the wet *dimba* land which had yielded a crop even in the absence of rain. The Department of Agriculture took advantage of the disaster to press home its message on conservation, and to enforce more energetically the ridging and bund-construction they had been advocating for so long. When in 1950 a famine tax was levied locally to help pay for the costs of the relief programme, many people saw this as the government 'punishing' them for their infringements of the agricultural regulations.[44]

Ironically, and tragically, many people died at the beginning of the 1950 harvest. When the maize crop began to ripen, green cobs were boiled and eaten. This was the first 'real' food that many people had had for months, but some who had survived a whole year of deprivation died when they ate the new food from their gardens. Survivors say that this was because 'their bodies had got used to bad food, so that when they started eating good food again this caused reactions in their bodies, and with fatal results'.[45]

As the crop ripened, so many of the 'lost' husbands, who had disappeared during the famine, reappeared at their wives' homes in Blantyre District. Some were turned away. People looked around them at their fellow survivors. Communities and families assessed how each member had behaved during the crisis. People tried to forget the abandoned children and aged parents who had been left to die. The ban on beer brewing was lifted (MNA, MP 12348). Life began again – new grain-bins were built, new marriages contracted, and new pounding songs composed.

The retrospective analysis began. Some people in the famine area felt that God must have been annoyed and offended to have made them suffer so much. Perhaps it had been the Second World War, in which many Malawian men had participated, which had offended him.[46] European observers had other theories. The first, and probably the most common of their explanations was that the famine had been a Malthusian 'check' on population growth, and it is this theory which I explore in the following chapter.

2

Famine as a Malthusian crisis

Most European observers in Malawi claimed not to be at all surprised by the advent of the 1949 famine. For them this was the predictable climax to a crisis in food production which had been gathering momentum in the 1940s. The theory that the famine was due first and foremost to ecological deterioration brought about by population pressure and destructive African farming practices was a popular one amongst government officials both in the districts and in the Department of Agriculture. This chapter examines the applicability of that theory to the 1949 famine, in the light of historical evidence of changing agricultural systems, population movements, and the notion of 'subsistence'.

As I indicated in the Introduction, neo-Malthusian theories are popular in explaining Africa's present-day food supply problems. In colonial Malawi such theories had been current since the imposition of colonial rule in the 1890s. William Beinart (Beinart, 1984) has described in detail the origins of these ideas and their application to Southern Africa in the first part of the twentieth century, and in particular has pointed out how they provided a rationale for greater intervention in peasant agriculture in the 1930s and 1940s. David Anderson has described a similar process for Kenya (Anderson, 1984); and Paul Richards has examined the same ideas and their use in 'development thinking' in Africa as a whole (Richards, 1983).

In colonial Malawi a commonplace of European thought since the 1890s was that African farming practices were dangerously destructive of the environment. In particular, the practice of 'shifting cultivation', the burning of rubble at the end of the season, the lack of manuring and the superficial nature of hoe cultivation, were all cited to prove that the African was no agriculturalist at all.[1] In the 1920s and 1930s these ideas received added weight from scientists working in Malawi, and were also given more urgency by the evidence for increasing population densities in the south of the country. Throughout the 1920s, 1930s and 1940s, colonial officials in the Southern Province were amassing evidence for a coming Malthusian disaster. In order to assess the correctness of their theories, we need first to examine the functioning of pre-colonial systems of production in the area, the distribution of population, and the ability of these systems to withstand natural disaster.

Change and mobility were central features of the history of Southern Malawi in the century leading up to 1949. It would not be possible or valid to attempt to describe any 'natural' pre-colonial ecological system for this area, and to this extent I cannot prove or disprove colonial theories of ecological crisis. Written sources for the pre-colonial history of the area consist of travellers' accounts dating from the mid to late nineteenth century, and they describe a social and economic system which was anything but static. As elsewhere in East and Central Africa, the second half of the nineteenth century was a period in which the direct and indirect effects of the region's involvement in international trading systems became most acutely felt (Alpers, 1975). It is only against the background of the ivory and slave trades that we can understand the dynamics of local agricultural economies in this area. There are, however, some broad patterns in the systems of agricultural production in the nineteenth century which can be delineated and which may help in understanding subsequent developments.

The broadest geographical division within Blantyre District is between highland and lowland. The Shire Highlands, of which the higher areas of Blantyre District form part, is a ridge lying at between 2,000 and 4,000 feet and acting as a watershed between streams draining westwards to the Shire Valley and east to the Chilwa plain and Mozambique. In the nineteenth century this area was inhabited by the 'original' Nyanja people, under a decentralised political system based around matrilineal kinship ties and loose notions of chiefly territoriality. As the nineteenth century progressed, so more and more immigrants, calling themselves Yao, moved in from Mozambique (Vaughan, 1981, ch. 1).

Although the evidence is indirect, it seems that by nineteenth-century Central African standards, Southern Malawi was relatively densely populated. The highlands were favoured by reliable rainfall and iron-ore deposits. By the middle of the century a bush-fallow system of agriculture was practised here, employing an iron hoe. This was a more labour-intensive system than the forest-fallow cultivation it was gradually superseding but which was still practised in some areas. In the 1850s Livingstone travelled through the area and described two systems of agriculture operating in the highlands – a 'woodland' system in the less densely populated areas where frequent shifting of villages was still possible, and a 'grassland' system in the more densely populated parts (Livingstone and Livingstone, 1865, p. 110).

The 'woodland' or forest-fallow system involved an initial heavy input of labour as trees needed to be felled or burnt, but subsequently it required less labour than the grassland system as seeds were planted directly into the ashes without further land preparation and without the need for any tool except a wooden digging stick. In the 'grassland' system the hoe was vital and land preparation was lengthier as the secondary forest growth had to be removed. Although Livingstone does not indicate which of these two systems predominated in the Shire Highlands, by the 1870s the observations of other Europeans imply that some kind of bush-fallow system involving the clearing of grass was the dominant agricultural system of the highlands. John Buchanan, an early planter, described this system in some detail, and his account accords with oral testimonies (Buchanan, 1885; Vaughan, 1981, ch. 1).

Early in the dry season men marked out the ground they intended to cultivate, and with axes they cut down any standing trees to about three feet from the ground. The branches were lopped off, piled into heaps and burnt. These heaps, or *matuto* (later to be the object of vigorous hostile campaigning by the colonial Department of Agriculture) were then covered with vegetation and soil and left to smoulder slowly into ashes. Planting began once the first rains had fallen and maize, sorghum or millet seeds were planted directly into the mounds, along with pumpkin and bean seeds. In the case of maize cultivation, the field was hoed when the maize plants were about six inches high, and again when they were about three feet high. Maize had probably been known in this area since before the eighteenth century, but did not become the main crop until early in the twentieth (Vaughan, 1981, ch. 3). Both finger-millet and sorghum were widely grown (and bulrush-millet in places) and these were more drought resistant than maize. Where rainfall was reliable, however, as on the highlands, maize could yield a higher return and was being grown in increasing amounts when these nineteenth century accounts were written.

In the Middle and Upper Shire Valley, to the north and west of the highlands, a rather different agricultural system was practised. It was in this area, one hundred years later, that the famine hit with most severity. In the nineteenth century, as in the twentieth, the climate of most of the valley was hot and dry, the area lying within a partial rain shadow. The agricultural disadvantages of vulnerability to drought were partially offset by the fact that patches of fertile alluvial soils could be found here, along with *dambo* land which retained moisture all year round. The people of the valley, also predominantly Nyanja, grew finger-millet as their main staple and supplemented this with sorghum (Vaughan, 1981, ch. 1). Both crops were well suited to conditions there due to their low moisture requirements and wide range of temperature tolerance (Acland, 1971, p. 27). The natural vegetation of the valley was grass and shrub, interspersed with patches of *mopane* woodland, and this vegetation implied the early use of the hoe in these areas and a variant on the 'grassland' system which was becoming common on the highlands. Livingstone noted that maize was also grown in small quantities on the *dambo* land of the valley. River sand was placed on top of waterlogged *dambo* mud and the maize seeds planted into it. As the plant grew, so the roots could take what moisture it required from the clay below, while the layer of sand prevented waterlogging and saturation. In addition, Livingstone described how in the dry season maize was grown by making holes in a sandy depression through which a stream flowed, and sowing the maize into the bottom of these holes (Livingstone and Livingstone, 1865, pp. 457, 498).

As well as growing a wide variety of food crops, the people of the valley also cultivated patches of cotton, the product of which was a thick handwoven cloth. By the mid nineteenth century there were two distinct varieties of cotton being grown – one an indigenous plant, *tonje cadja* with a short staple, and the other an exotic perennial called *tonje manga* (Livingstone and Livingstone, 1865, pp. 110–12). The spread of this exotic variety along with the spread of maize, highlights the fact that by the nineteenth century the agricultural economy of this area was undergoing change, and much of this change was related to the region's involvement in a system of exchange centred on the East African coast.

Exchange of products within the area had probably always been a feature of this pre-colonial economy, and was founded on the fact that there was much ecological variation within a small area, and this variation was associated with specialisation in human skills. Some crops, such as beans, grew better on the highlands than they did in the valley. When rain failed in the valley it often fell on the highlands, and food could be obtained from there, as well as from the watered riverside gardens of the valley itself. Cotton was woven by men in the valley and exchanged for iron products manufactured on the highlands, where deposits of iron ore were widely scattered (Vaughan, 1981, ch. 1). The valley was tsetse-infested and therefore unsuitable for cattle-keeping, while the highlands were free from tsetse until the twentieth century and small livestock were more commonly kept there. Fishing was an important industry in the valley, and fish were exchanged for other products from the highlands. Women made salt from the grasses which grew along the river banks, and traded this for food from other areas (Vaughan, 1981, ch. 1).

Whether or not this had once been a harmonious and balanced system of production and exchange can only be a matter for speculation as our first written sources were produced during a period of rapid change. All that we can say with any certainty is that the agriculturalists of what was to become Blantyre District had evolved a system of exploiting the environment which attempted to minimise the inevitable risks involved.

It has been said of Southern Malawi as a whole that the rich variation in environments which occurs within relatively small areas has made the region a 'secure' one and a refuge for populations fleeing from drought elsewhere. Certainly by the nineteenth century the Nyanja of this area were renowned for their agricultural success and ability to avoid major food crises. The in-coming Yaos remarked on this, as did later immigrants. Most stories of pre-colonial famine told in the area refer to famines which took place elsewhere and which were responsible for driving populations into the Malawi region. The only recalled famine which took place in the region itself was that of 1862–3, and the peculiar circumstances of this famine will be described later.

To say that the region does not appear to have suffered major famine in the late pre-colonial period, is not of course the same thing as saying that everyone was adequately fed. There were doubtless periods of scarcity, and 'hungry seasons' at regular intervals. The system of local exchange may not always have functioned smoothly, and as a form of insurance it was liable to be upset by war or political disagreement between groups. The fact that religion and chiefly authority in pre-colonial Southern Malawi were so firmly based around rain-making powers is an indication of the ultimate vulnerability of the entire system to natural disaster (Schofeleers, 1972; Rangeley, 1953; Amanze, 1980). All one can say is that the evidence of the nineteenth century points to a *relative* immunity to famine which was based on careful use of micro-environments, and which in some years was translated into a surplus.

The social organisation of production was of course integral to the system, but is even more difficult to describe with any certainty than are production techniques. Oral testimony has two contradictory but often co-existent tendencies. One is to contrast 'then' and 'now' very starkly indeed; the other to project backwards present-day social formations. Neither of these tendencies is testable, but one has to be aware of them. Written sources have similar problems. European observers either squeezed their observations into a familiar mould by describing a pre-industrial family idyll, or they became obsessed with certain alien features of the societies they confronted. The near obsession of many European writers with polygynous marriage forms is the main example of this. More often than not, however, they seemed hardly interested at all in the domestic economies of the areas they passed through. Livingstone was something of an exception to this, and produced a characteristically idealised account of Nyanja family agriculture:

> All of the people of a village turn out to labour in the fields. It is no uncommon thing to see men, women and children hard at work, with the baby lying close by beneath a shady bush. (Livingstone and Livingstone, 1865, p. 110)

Nyanja agriculture, according to Livingstone, was intensively practised and organised around a nuclear household of man, wife and offspring. Men cleared the land initially, women hoed the grass into *matuto*, and men, women and children worked side by side in hoeing the crops at various stages. Livingstone had his own reasons for portraying the Nyanja as hard-working, home-loving agriculturalists, for such a picture was necessary to highlight the ravages of the slave trade which he was campaigning against, and also to encourage British investment in African cotton production. We need not accept his picture in entirety, but much of it accords with the testimonies of Yao immigrants and of the Nyanja themselves (Vaughan, 1981, ch. 1). These indicate that agricultural production in the pre-slave-trade period was organised around the household of women, husband and children, while consumption may have involved a wider kin-group. Men and women both contributed considerable agricultural labour, and whilst some tasks were sex-specific, many were not. The Nyanja kinship system was based around the *mbumba* or sorority group, and marriage was usually matrilocal and inheritance matrilineal (Mitchell, 1956; Vaughan, 1984; Vaughan, 1983a; Vaughan, 1982; Vaughan and Hirschmann, 1983). The *mbumba* group was sometimes co-extensive with a village settlement, but more often a village would comprise several such groups, usually related. Rights to land passed through women, but were directed by the responsible men at the level of the *mbumba* or village. Each group of sisters was 'overseen' by an elder brother or sometimes an uncle, and it was to this man that women were supposed to turn for help, advice and protection. Each adult woman had her own field, and her husband gained access to this by virtue of marriage to her. She was expected to grow enough staple food to feed her immediate family, and she had her own grain-bin or *nkhokwe* which her husband built but to which only she had access. On some tasks she would cooperate with her sisters and other female relatives. Harvesting was one of these, along with processing of the food (especially maize pounding), and the brewing of beer. Although each woman would cook every day on her own hearth, she would usually eat with her female relatives and children in a group, while the men ate in their own separate group, pooling the pots of food produced by their wives and sisters. Whilst emphasis was placed on the ideal of each adult woman and her household being self-sufficient in staple food, the custom of communal eating meant that in practice disadvantaged households could be helped without too much embarrassment. If a woman had been ill, if her husband had died or left, or if she had a large number of young children, she might find herself unable to produce enough food. In such a case her relatives, and especially her sisters, were likely to share some of their food with her, and usually this sharing took place at the stage of eating.[2]

Population in the early nineteenth century was dispersed. This enabled the best use to be made of the land, and especially of the scattered *dimba* land which was so valuable in enabling the cultivation of dry-season crops. Livingstone tells us that settlement was strung out along the Shire River banks, and other observers noted the relatively dense population of favoured parts of the highlands. There was very little centralised political control in this period. The Nyanja did have chiefs and their traditions speak of the existence of the 'Maravi Empire' in the eighteenth century, but by the nineteenth century chiefly power was limited and territorial boundaries vague.[3] The authority of individual chiefs rested more on their relations with ritual leaders than on anything else, but it hardly impinged at all on the organisation of agricultural production.

Non-agricultural production was, however, sometimes organised around larger units and thus more amenable to political control. Most iron-ore sites were small and scattered, but a few were larger and more closely controlled by local political leaders. Likewise the best fishing grounds and salt pans had their use regulated by political leaders, often through the form of ritual control. In general, however, economic activity was dispersed along with skills, and control was very limited beyond the village (Vaughan, 1981, ch. 1).

The picture I have drawn here is necessarily tentative and simplified, and to some degree misleading. As I have already indicated, whatever the nature of the Nyanja agricultural economy in this area, it was undergoing profound change by the middle of the nineteenth century. These changes initially consisted in alterations in the use of products, but they increasingly affected production itself and the social organisation of production.

In the course of the eighteenth century a complex, multi-ethnic society which we will label 'Yao' had evolved in northern Mozambique. This society was based on a dominance of valuable long-distance trading networks, and especially control over the ivory trade (Alpers, 1975; Vaughan, 1981; Webster, 1977). The original Yao were probably a small group, but they had absorbed communities of other tribes – Lomwe, Makua and Eastern Nyanja – into their ranks and bound them together with a common trading language, culture and economic interest. In the eighteenth century the main item of their trade was ivory, and Yao traders moved progressively westwards in quest of new reserves. Yao caravans travelled to and through the Shire Highlands and Shire Valley, into present-day western Mozambique and the Luangwa valley in Zambia. In Southern Malawi Yao hunters negotiated deals with Nyanja chiefs, whose rights to ivory had previously been rather vaguely defined. In return for ivory, imported beads and cloth were exchanged. More important, perhaps, than the exchange of luxury goods, was the intermediate trade which developed around the caravans themselves. The Shire Highlands was known as a good source of foodstuffs for travellers, and agricultural production was probably stimulated and intensified in response to this. Other items of Nyanja production also entered the trade. Fish, salt and iron goods were bought from the Nyanja and used as exchange items along the caravan route. Nyanja salt from Lake Chilwa was apparently highly prized and won fame far afield. As the volume of intermediate trade increased, so the Nyanja economy became drawn more into a wider circuit of exchange. It would be misleading, however, to exaggerate the effects of this slow penetration of merchant capital. Caravans were seasonal and sporadic affairs, and whilst the Nyanja may have valued the imported cloth which came with them, the fact remains that in the 1860s they were still making their own cloth out of cotton and bark. Production of foodstuffs, salt and iron goods may all have been stimulated by this trade, but there were no radical changes in the organisation of production of any of these items. The real changes came to be felt from the middle of the nineteenth century onwards. As the slave trade supplanted the ivory trade, so shifts took place in the political organisation of the area which went much further than anything experienced in the eighteenth century. At the same time, disruption to the system of agricultural production created a greater vulnerability to famine which was only partly compensated for by increased political centralisation and economic control.

The earliest Yao traders in this area had not established their own settlements, but from the last decade of the eighteenth century onwards Yao groups began migrating into the southern half of Malawi to settle amongst the Nyanja (Vaughan, 1981). The first groups to settle were probably of Nyanja ancestry, having 'become Yao' in Mozambique during the previous century. They were fleeing from famine and warfare there, and they settled peacefully amongst their Nyanja hosts who welcomed them for the potential wealth accruing from their trading activities. Oral traditions emphasise that these first immigrants were initially very dependent on their hosts. They had brought no seeds with them; they didn't know how to fish or make canoes. They showed signs of being a group over-specialised in trade who had left their homes in a great hurry. Gradually, however, their initial disadvantages were outweighed by their valuable trading contacts. They slowly established an economic dominance over the area and a degree of centralised political control.

In the 1870s another, much more militarised group of Yao moved into Southern Malawi. This group, known by their clan as the Mbewe Yao, possessed firearms, which they had used to capture the slaves they sent to the east coast and also to fight off other militarised groups such as the Maseko Ngoni who had simultaneously moved into the region from Southern Africa (Vaughan, 1981, ch. 1).

The decades of the 1860s to 1890s can be characterised as a period of extreme economic and ecological distortion in the whole of the south of Malawi, but perhaps especially in the area we are dealing with. The southern Shire Highlands and the middle Shire Valley were criss-crossed not only by trade routes but also by the migration paths of warring groups. Yao and Ngoni battles took place on the highlands, and Nyanja chiefs were 'bought out' in return for their support. Travellers' accounts of this period indicate how both human and animal populations became more concentrated than previously. The movements of population were those associated with fear and warfare rather than with the exploitation of natural resources. Agriculture was severely disrupted, and when a drought struck in 1861–3 a massive famine resulted. When they could, people fled to the banks of the Shire River where crops could be grown on the wet land, but the level of physical insecurity was such that many people did not dare move that far for fear of exposing themselves to the slave-raiders (Livingstone and Livingstone, 1865; White, 1987). In 1903 the mission journal *Life and Work* published the accounts of people who remembered the 1860s well, and all referred to the retreat to the river banks as a well-tried reaction to drought.[4]

This was the first serious famine in the area recorded in oral tradition, and it was clearly a famine created in part by political circumstances. Both the Mbewe Yao chiefs and the Ngoni attempted to organise and intensify food production in this period in order to feed the concentrated populations of their stockaded 'towns'. Yao testimonies tell of harvest ceremonies organised by the chiefs, at which each villager was required to donate a basketful of maize or millet (Vaughan, 1981, ch. 1). This grain was stored by the chief and used both to feed visitors and as a reserve in the event of a drought and crop failure the following year. Another Yao account describes how the names of exceptionally good farmers were noted down by the chief, so that their surpluses could be commandeered when necessary. Both Yao and Ngoni agriculture in the stockaded towns was innovative, and impressive to European eyes accustomed to intensive cultivation. For a while this strategy of intensive cultivation and control appears to have staved off disaster, but crucial to the system was the availability of slave labour, coupled with raiding of Nyanja settlements.

Gomani's Ngoni, who settled in the highlands of Ntcheu, and who feature prominently in the story of the 1949 famine, adopted such a strategy. The highlands were tsetse-free, and therefore suitable for their cattle-rearing economy. Travellers reported the area to be densely populated in the 1870s, with large villages concentrated on the hilltops. Maize and millet were cultivated intensively using Chewa and Nyanja slaves operating in work parties, and in this way the Ngoni seem to have often produced a surplus. But the Ngoni economy of the late nineteenth century was in fact a war economy, relying on force to maintain its level of production. Furthermore, the concentrated population and intensive agriculture were ultimately damaging to the environment. By 1878 one traveller was noting how part of the area was completely denuded of trees, and that people had to rely on maize roots for fuel (Laws, 1879). Nyanja populations, meanwhile, were also taking defensively to the hills, and as early as 1862 Livingstone remarked on how this unnatural population distribution was affecting agricultural production and increasing vulnerability to famine. After the Ngoni raid of 1884, which extended over the whole of the Shire Highlands as well as the middle Shire Valley, population distribution was more distorted than ever. In the 1880s many travellers reported on how an increasing game population was invading areas now abandoned by human settlement (Drummond, 1888; Hetherwick, 1887). This development had been proceeding for some time. In the 1860s Livingstone had reported that tsetse was prevalent in the Middle and Upper Shire and that abandoned villages there were full of the tracks of buffalo, elephant and antelope, concluding that 'wild animals have now taken possession of what had lately been the abodes of men living in peace and plenty' (Livingstone and Livingstone, 1865, p. 685).

This is a picture familiar in the histories of many parts of East and Central Africa in the nineteenth century, and provides a necessary background to any analysis of economic and social change in the colonial period which followed (Vail, 1981; Kjekshus, 1977). Whilst in some ways this story of slave raiding and warfare might seem rather remote from the analysis of the 1949 famine, I would argue that it is of direct relevance in discussing the causation of the famine.

The neo-Malthusian theory employed in explaining the 1949 famine refers implicitly to some 'natural' state of affairs existing in pre-colonial times, when there was assumed to be a balance between population and resources. Such a balance may have existed to some degree in the early part of the nineteenth century, but our evidence for this is indirect. What is clear, however, is that by the late nineteenth century, when the first Europeans arrived, the economy and society of this area had undergone rapid transformation, and that the scene which greeted the first European arrivals was anything but 'natural'. Not only was population distribution very skewed (an important factor when Europeans started to alienate land), but the area was probably experiencing an absolute population decline. Though we have no direct evidence for demographic trends, there is plenty of indirect evidence. Mortality was increased directly through the violence associated with the slave trade and the Yaos' possession of rapid-repeating firearms. But there were also important indirect effects on mortality of these late nineteenth-century conditions. Violence not only disrupted agriculture, and thus affected nutritional standards, but it also brought about the concentration of population in areas where water supplies were not optimal, and this could precipitate a higher incidence of water-borne diseases. Not only would mortality increase in this way, but in all likelihood fertility and fecundity were adversely affected, and this especially as women were the most frequent victims of the slave trade.[5] The relatively centralised authority of the Ngoni and Yao chiefdoms attempted to accommodate to this situation by organising food production using slave labour, by distributing seed, and by enforcing quarantine measures through ritual sanction. But these efforts were only temporarily and marginally successful. The evidence for minor famine, and epidemics of both human and animal disease at the end of the century is overwhelming, and indicates that this was a disastrous period for communities of this area (Vaughan, 1981, ch. 1).

Any assessment of the neo-Malthusian theories popular in the 1940s needs to take account of this pre-colonial background. The immediate pre-colonial period – the 1860s to 1890s – was, as we have seen, a highly abnormal time, but there was little recognition of this on the part of the early European administrators. Throughout the 1890s they were involved in 'pacifying' the country and putting an end to the slave trade. In the Middle Shire this process took some time, and accounts of the 1890s show a continuation of violence and destruction, compounded by the actions of the new administration. Although a Protectorate was declared in 1891, the Ngoni continued to raid throughout the Middle and Upper Shire Valley. After the death of a leading Ngoni chief, Chikuse, the raids were transformed into seasonal migrations of Ngoni labourers, coming south to work on estates or as head-porters (Vaughan, 1981, chs. 2, 3, 4). Often they ran off with their loads around Matope, or were raided by Yao bandits. There were outbreaks of smallpox, jiggers, and measles in this period. Cattle died from rinderpest, and there were invasions of locusts which had bred in the vast areas of bush deserted by human populations. The valley was not an attractive place in which to live.

Gradually population began to disperse from the hilltops onto the more favourable areas of the plains and the valley. People were attempting to re-establish patterns of settlement closer to those that had prevailed before the major disruptions of the late nineteenth century. They said that they were 'tired of hoeing among stones', and moved down from the hills (Vaughan, 1981, p. 143). But when they moved down they found that much land, both in the highlands and in the Shire Valley, had been assigned to individual European speculators. Abandoning the imposed intensive cultivation of the hill stockades, they attempted to resume their land-extensive grass-fallow system of agriculture, but this was viewed with extreme alarm by European officials, and by the planters who now owned vast tracts of land.

The obsession with the 'destructiveness' of African agricultural techniques begins in the 1890s and gathers force as population increases from the third decade of the twentieth century. It must always be viewed, however, in the political context arising from the alienation of much of the better land in the south of Malawi to European settlers. A second consideration when assessing the neo-Malthusian theory is one which relates directly to our discussion of the nineteenth century. We have seen that the economy and society of this area in the earlier part of the nineteenth century were predicated on exchange. Whilst food production was the most important occupation, there were wide variations in the pattern of economic activity as a whole. Colonial writers tended to view exchange as a totally new phenomenon, and one imposed on a subsistence base in which each family was seen as providing itself with all its needs. Yet our speculative picture of the early nineteenth century shows a regional economy in which many communities calculated their subsistence with the certainty of trade in mind. When colonial agricultural officers painstakingly calculated the carrying capacity of the land in this area, they failed to bear in mind the fact that never in the accessible past had villages, let alone households, provided all their needs from their own labour on their own plots of land.

Blantyre District was the first area of European economic activity in the Protectorate. Initially the objective of this activity was to redirect the trade in ivory and other 'collected' items such as rubber, away from Yao and Swahili traders and into the hands of European trading companies. This process was taking place prior to the official establishment of colonial rule in 1891, and was largely accomplished through the agency of the African Lakes Corporation. In Blantyre District this company's main impact was as an employer of labour for head-porterage or *tenga tenga*. Employment of labour was also one major impact of the presence from 1876 of the Blantyre mission of the Church of Scotland, but a third major influence on the district was the British Central Africa Company. Its founder, Eugene Sharrer, claimed two large areas of land in the Middle and Upper Shire – the Kupimbi estate, comprising 68,000 acres and the Chelumbe estate of 150,000 acres. Throughout the 1880s and 1890s other settlers arrived to take up coffee production in Blantyre District, and were given certificates to legitimate their land claims by the first Commissioner, Harry Johnston (Vaughan, 1981, ch. 3). The European land-grab gathered pace, and was taking place at the same time as African communities were attempting to re-establish a more normal pattern of settlement and cultivation. Furthermore, the land-grabbing itself was facilitated by the political discord and social upheaval of the late nineteenth century which had set one community against another. Chiefs and headmen still refer back to this period when involved in present-day land disputes, arguing over where the guilt lay for alienating so much land, and fruitlessly attempting to establish claim to 'original' occupation. The chiefs and headmen who 'gave away' the land however, were not the ones to feel the real effects of their actions. The full impact of loss of land was seen with population growth from the 1930s, and accentuated by the increasing profitability of estate agriculture in the 1940s.

Although colonial census data is notoriously unreliable and difficult to use, it does provide an indication of the concerns preoccupying those who collected the figures. On this basis it seems that the issue of population pressure became prominent in the minds of colonial officials in the 1930s. National population censuses were carried out with varying success in 1911, 1921, 1926, 1931 and 1945. In the 1920s much space was given over in the reports to the issue of the apparent slow rate of increase of the African population. In 1931 however, there was an abrupt change, with the first alarm being sounded over population increase (Nyasaland Protectorate, Census Report, 1931). This new concern with overpopulation was almost entirely a Southern Province concern, and in particular it reflected conditions in areas of European settlement and economic activity – in the districts of Mulanje, Thyolo, Blantyre, Chiradzulu and Zomba.

If we accept that the official census figures provide a rough indication of demographic trends, then it is clear that the decades of the 1930s and 1940s witnessed a considerable growth of population in the Southern Province, and in Blantyre District particularly. The 1931 census report gave a figure of 73,650 Africans resident in Blantyre District with a density of population of 85.64 per square mile. The corresponding figures for 1945 were 102,208 and a density of 118.85. Even allowing for the probable underestimation in the 1931 census, it would still seem that population density had increased in the inter-censal period (Nyasaland Protectorate, Census Report 1945; MNA, LB 14/3/3). How far this growth was due to immigration and how far to natural increase, is not immediately obvious.

Immigration into Blantyre District and other districts of the Southern Province had gone on throughout the early colonial period. In the case of Blantyre District two main groups were involved. These were the Ngoni from the highlands of Ntcheu and Dedza districts in the Central Province, and the Lomwe (known throughout most of this period as 'Nguru') from Mozambique.

The opening of coffee estates in Blantyre District in the 1870s and 1880s had attracted immigrant labour even before the start of official colonial rule. But movement into the district gathered momentum in the 1890s when a hut tax was imposed throughout the Protectorate. By now the precarious Ngoni slave-raiding economy described earlier had come to a point of collapse through the subjugation of Ngoni chiefs, the ending of the slave trade and continued environmental decline. Groups of Ngoni men travelled south to work on European estates in the Shire Highlands and earn their hut taxes. To begin with they came as seasonal migrants, returning to their homes in the agricultural peak season. By the turn of the century, however, many were already marrying into Yao and Nyanja communities in the area and becoming permanently resident in Blantyre District. By the 1920s this influx of Ngoni men as labourers had died down, but the practice of inter-marriage between Ngoni men and Yao or Nyanja women persisted. In 1931 people identifying themselves as Ngoni constituted the second largest group in the district, as Table 2 indicates.

The second group of immigrants, the Lomwe, began coming into this and other districts of the Southern Province in large numbers at the turn of the century. Their immigration was part of a desperate escape from the harshness of colonial and company rule in Mozambique, and has been described in detail by Landeg White (White, 1987). Subsequent waves of immigration continued into the 1930s, their timing reflecting a balance of conditions on the other side of the border and fluctuations in economic opportunities in colonial Malawi. By 1931 there were 12,391 people resident in Blantyre District who identified themselves as Lomwe, and the vast majority lived as tenants on European-owned estates (MNA, NSB 7/1/2). This figure does not, however, provide an accurate estimate of the total volume of Lomwe immigration up to this time. Many of the earlier Lomwe immigrants had been absorbed into the Yao and Nyanja communities of the district and identified themselves by one or other of these ethnic labels (Vaughan, 1981; White, 1987). Their offspring were even less likely to have identified themselves as 'Nguru', an offensive and disparaging

Table 2 *Blantyre District: African population by tribe and residence*

	Number	% of total on private land	% of total on Crown land
Yao	27,996	28	42
Ngoni	18,537	20	26
Nguru	12,391	37	6
Mang'anja	8,811	7	14
Miscellaneous	5,945	8	12
	73,680	100	100

Source: MNA, NSB 7/1/2, Annual Report, Blantyre, 1931.

term. The volume of Lomwe immigration then, was likely to have been much greater than indicated in these census figures.

On the other hand, the population increase resulting from the immigration of both Ngoni and Lomwe people was probably partly offset by the poor health conditions which prevailed in the first two decades of the twentieth century. Communities which had only recently been decimated by the slave trade now fell prey to new diseases. Smallpox had occurred in this area in the last half of the nineteenth century, but now a new and much more virulent strain became common. Totally unfamiliar diseases such as measles, influenza and cerebro-spinal meningitis also took a large toll, and need to be seen as acting in conjunction with the poor nutritional standards prevailing particularly amongst the immigrant population (Medical Department, *Annual Reports*, 1912–56 and Iliffe, 1985). Medical services were in their infancy and statistics very unreliable, but there seems little reason to disbelieve the view expressed generally by contemporaries that this was a period of exceptionally poor health amongst the African population of Southern Malawi, and that the rate of natural increase was low.

There are indications of a change in this picture occurring in the mid 1930s. Medical services, whilst still very limited, had had some success with smallpox vaccination campaigns, thus controlling one of the major killing diseases of the region. The control of the epidemic killers, above all else, resulted in the reversal of the demographic trend. As immigration into the area slowed down in the 1930s, so much more of the population growth of the 1930s and 1940s must be accounted for by natural increase.

By the early 1930s population pressure was already being seen as acute in some parts of the Southern Province, including Blantyre District. The Lomwe were held largely accountable for this. It was said that their preference for millet over other staples, and the shifting system associated with the production of this crop, compounded the general problem of congestion in the highland areas. In 1932 the Chief Conservator of Forests advocated halting any further influx of Lomwe people and returning some of the more recent immigrants to their homes in Mozambique (MNA, AGR 3/2/156, Conservator of Forests to Chief Secretary, 2/9/52). By 1933 it was said that African chiefs and headmen were themselves discouraging the settlement of people from other districts (including the Lomwe), and although numbers of Ngoni and Lomwe labourers still came to work for both Europeans and Africans in Blantyre District in the planting season, very few of them remained for more than three months (MNA, NSB 7/1/3). Despite the slowdown of immigration, most European observers remained pessimistic about long-term prospects for the area. The Manager of the British Central Africa Company (still the largest land-holder in the district) reflected this opinion when he said that 'if the natives of this country are left to their own devices they will *starve themselves* in a very few years – soil erosion, deforestation, poor husbandry and complete disregard of soil fertility will completely impoverish the land of this country' (MNA, A3/2/156, Kaye-Nicol's memo on the Development of Nyasaland, 27/10/33).

The prophecies of doom increased in urgency in the 1940s, and emanated more and more from the Department of Agriculture (Department of Agriculture, *Annual Reports*, 1940–50). The agricultural experts' concern over erosion had reached fever pitch, and for most officers the evidence of their own eyes seemed indisputable – there was an ecological crisis around the corner. In the following paragraphs I summarise the evidence they produced to support this view.

In 1939 there was an acute shortage of maize in some parts of Blantyre District. Close to Blantyre township, on the densely populated hill areas of Ndirande, Soche and Mpemba, the soil was said to be played out, and the crops very poor. But maize yields were also low in some of the more recently colonised land of the Middle Shire Valley, around Lunzu and Matope (MNA, NSB 7/1/5, 1939). In 1940 again crops were reported to be poor in Mpemba, Soche, Ndirande, Matope and in the Neno hill areas to the west, though they were satisfactory elsewhere and there was no overall shortage (MNA, NSB 7/1/6, 1940). Meanwhile a circular from the Secretary of State for the Colonies gave rise to a whole series of reports by District Officers in the 1940s concerning the nutritional status of the people in their areas (MNA, MP, Secretariat 14399; MNA, NS 3/3/3). The more closely officials examined the health and nutritional problems of the African population, the more they were drawn to the conclusion that there was an imminent crisis of health in the making. The District Commissioner for Chiradzulu reported that there was now a population of over 30,000 in an area of only 270 square miles, and that the average garden size per household was only two acres. Cassava was being planted in increasing quantities on areas of poor soils, and the nutritional disadvantages of this crop were well-known. Reporting on the steps taken in his district to improve nutrition he outlined three measures: soil conservation by contour ridging; the manufacture and use of compost; and lectures on mixed farming and husbandry (MNA, NS 3/3/3 DC Chiradzulu to Provincial Commissioner, 30/1/40). In Mulanje District the District Commissioner reported that the average diet was deficient in fats and vitamins, but that overpopulation in the district made it impossible to increase gardens to the size necessary for an improvement in diet to take place (MNA, NS 3/3/3 DC Mulanje to Provincial Commissioner, 3/2/40). When a meningitis outbreak had occurred in this district the Medical Officer had expressed real doubts about the wisdom of controlling it, arguing that by doing so a natural 'Malthusian check' was being prevented from operating (MNA, M2/5/6 Cerebro-Spinal Meningitis, 1937). The Blantyre District Commissioner reported that each year there was a 'hungry season' from November to February, when much of the population had insufficient to eat (MNA, NS 3/3/3 DC Blantyre to PC 12/3/40). The District Commissioner for Liwonde, in the Upper Shire Valley, reported the same phenomenon and advocated the greater enforcement of soil conservation measures as the only remedy (MNA, NS 3/3/3 DC Liwonde to PC 7/2/40).

In 1941 there was a general food shortage in all four sections of the newly created Blantyre Administrative Unit (comprising Blantyre, Chiradzulu, Chikwawa and Neno Districts (MNA, NSB 7/1/6). As early as October (six months after the harvest) the shortage was acute in the northern part of Chikwawa District, the Matope area of Blantyre District and the Kambalame area of Neno District (MNA, AGR 4/10 DC Blantyre to PC, 30/10/41). In other parts of the Southern Province the situation was equally acute. In Native Authority Nazombe's area of Mulanje district the people were largely existing on cassava bought from Chiradzulu. Nazombe's being an area of poor, sandy, porous soils, the cereal crop had been disastrously affected by the light rainfall. Even in better years these areas were said to be often short of food (MNA, AGR 4/10 Agricultural Supervisor, Mombezi, 20/12/41). In the Lower Shire Valley there was an annual shortage of food in the area to the south of Chiromo, brought about primarily by the flooding of the richest soil by the rising river, and the consequent crowding of the population onto the foothills (MNA, AGR 4/10 Provincial Agricultural Officer to PC, 16/6/41). Reporting again in 1943 on the probability of food shortages in the Lower River, the Senior Agricultural Officer said that 'the threat of famine, which increases yearly, can only be averted by thorough and compulsory conservation' (MNA, AGR 4/10 Lawrence to Director of Agriculture, 25/1/43).

Around the same period a series of village surveys was conducted in the Southern Province which brought to light further the problem of land shortage and the insufficient production of food (MNA, AGR 3/7 1944). In Zomba

District a survey was conducted in the village of Ntaja, in Chief Chikowi's area. Out of a total of 95 acres at the disposal of the village, there was none under fallow except four acres of uncultivable swamp and one acre of rocky outcrops. There were thirty families in the village, and on average each family cultivated 3.17 acres. Maize was their main food crop and the average yield was 943 lb per acre. The survey showed that on average each family produced 1415 lb of maize a year, while their ideal consumption was calculated to be 1600 lb. The deficit of 185 lb per family was made up through the purchase of food from wages. In Blantyre District the area chosen for the survey was one lying very close to the town boundaries. Out of a total of twenty families, fourteen farmed an area of between 0 and 1.5 acres (with a mean of 0.75 acres), and the remaining six farmed between 1.5 and 2.5 acres (with a mean of 1.82 acres). Here the average production of starch food per family was 617 lbs, and the average deficit of this food amounted to 2,663 lb per family. In fact most villagers relied on buying their food from Blantyre market, and, as the officer conducting the survey remarked, 'should the market fail, the plight of the villagers would be very serious' (MNA, AGR 3/7 Survey of Matope village, n.d.).

The village surveyed in Blantyre District was recognised not to be 'typical', lying as close as it did to the biggest urban concentration in the country. However, reports from other parts of the district were no more optimistic about the possibilities for food self-sufficiency. The Department of Agriculture's *ulendo* reports for 1946–7 described production throughout the district, as observed by Agricultural Officers travelling on foot from village to village (MNA, NSB 7/4/1, 1946–9). These reports are most complete for the area of the Middle Shire Valley which was later to be severely affected by famine. In the areas of Chiefs Kuntaja and Somba there were complaints regarding the shortage of food in 1947, and the officer reported that there was no scope in this area for further settlement – everywhere suitable for cultivation had already been occupied. Further west into the Shire Valley was the area of lowland and erratic rainfall which had been progressively settled since the 1930s. During the 1930s the government had installed wells here to allow for the movement of people from the most congested environs of Blantyre township into this traditionally underpopulated area. Further north and west was the valley of the Lisingwe River, which ran into the Shire, and here new gardens were still being opened up in the late 1940s, though the Agricultural Officer considered that no further opening up of gardens should be allowed here. According to him, agricultural practices in this area were 'backward', yields were low, and erosion a serious problem. Everywhere he went in this area in 1947 the Agricultural Officer stressed the need for ridging and boxing fields, and for 'putting their backs into it', if a serious shortage was to be avoided (MNA, NSB 7/4/1, 16–24/10/47). It was apparent, he wrote, that unless soil conservation policy was carried out to the full, 'land shortage' would become acute.

In order to evaluate these observations, and thus to judge the plausibility of the neo-Malthusian theory of the famine, we have to take into account some of the assumptions behind the Department of Agriculture's thinking at this time. Successive Directors of Agriculture in the 1940s provided what they saw as evidence of impending crisis with their estimates of the carrying capacity of the soil. Reviewing the food position of the Protectorate as a whole in 1946 (MNA, MP 35/26, Director of Agriculture to Chief Secretary, 3/5/46), the Director, G. Nye, prefaced the presentation of his calculations with the view that any estimates had to take into account three facts: that population was increasing rapidly; that yields were declining; and that land was becoming short. Assuming there to be 480,000 families in the Protectorate, he calculated their annual basic food needs to be 388,560 lb of maize, 54,720 lb of groundnuts and 109,440 lb of beans. Estimating the average maize yield in the country to be 800 lb per acre, he calculated that approximately one million acres were required to be cultivated in order to provide the staple food of the *present* population. But one needed to add into this equation the implications of the Department of Agriculture's policy of introducing a system of resting leys. This would mean that the acreage required would be *double* that under maize annually. In terms of the average peasant household this meant that each would require 9.75 acres of land, divided as follows:

House, etc.	0.25	acres
Maize	2.00	,,
Groundnuts	0.50	,,
Cassava	0.25	,,
Cash crops	1.00	,,
Village woodland	2.00	,,
Fallow	3.75	,,

(MNA, MP 35/26)

To allow for a further expansion of cash-crop production (upon which the family would rely for any increase in their standard of living), another two acres would have to be reserved, bringing the total up to 11.75 acres per family. As the Director of Agriculture pointed out himself, in many parts of the Protectorate the land simply did not exist to enable this scheme to be put into operation. To many officials the outlook was both depressing and alarming:

> The rapid increase in population and the expansion of the area devoted to economic crops, combined with the steady loss of soil fertility, can only lead eventually to a failure to produce sufficient food to feed the population. There is already ample evidence that we are proceeding towards this dreadful end point, and I believe that if matters are allowed to remain as they are it will not be many years before the country is faced with serious food shortages and the concomitant political unrest. (MNA, MP 35/26, Director of Agriculture's Memo on Food Position, 3/5/46)

Only radical solutions were likely to have any effect on a problem of the proportions perceived. Most officials believed that in the long run the strain on the land could only be relieved by a total social and economic remodelling. Some proposed that a proportion of the population be forced off the land into total dependence on wage labour, so that the remaining land could be divided into larger peasant plots. A few officials favoured collectivisation (MNA, MP 4/68, Smalley to PC Northern Province, 13/11/48), but by the late 1940s more favoured the development of a progressive 'yeomanry'.[6] Kettlewell, later to become Director of Agriculture, was a major proponent of this idea. In a despatch to the Director of Agriculture, Nye, in 1947 he expressed the view that individual ownership of land would have to be introduced to facilitate the creation of a class of 'yeoman' farmers. Through this a measure of depopulation could be achieved and the 'evils' of the matrilineal system overcome (MNA, MP 3/2, Kettlewell to Director of Agriculture, 28/5/47). Nye concurred with this analysis, remarking that he believed the present system of land usage and tenure could not lead to any increased standard of living. In his view, acreages had to be increased, and the only way to do this was to remove some of the people from the land. He proposed 'siphoning off' excess population into agricultural wage labour and secondary industry (spinning being one suggested industry), leaving the land to be divided into holdings under one or a combination of systems: peasant holdings of 20 to 25 acres; larger African holdings of up to 100 acres; European estates; and finally (and only possibly), communal farms. Each of these proposed systems would necessitate the creation of a landless class living by wages alone (MNA, AGR 3/2).

One attempt at social and economic engineering along these lines was the Domasi Community Development Project, which was started in Zomba District in 1949 (Vaughan, 1983b). For the most part, however, the Department's ideas for radical solutions remained untried owing to a chronic shortage of funds for ambitious undertakings. Instead they concentrated their limited human and financial resources on what they saw as the most pressing problem of all – that of soil erosion. Agricultural officers everywhere in the Southern Province attempted to enforce the construction of ridges to replace the traditional *matuto*, and in places they also enforced the building of box-ridges and bunds (Beinart, 1984). This exercise was not without its problems, and met with considerable resistance in some areas.

The fact that the Department of Agriculture was unable to pursue many of its ideas in practice is perhaps less important than the fact that these ideas remained very influential in the formulation of wider government policy. But how correct were they in seeing a Malthusian crisis around the corner, and how far was the 1949 famine a confirmation of their views?

Much of the Department of Agriculture's analysis in the 1940s rested on the notion of 'carrying capacity'. Officials in colonial Malawi were heavily influenced by the work of Allan in Northern Rhodesia (Allan, 1949), but there are many problems with the kind of calculations which Allan and his followers made.[7] Calculations of carrying capacity rely on only one variable in determining the limits of population which can be supported in a given area, and that variable is land. Critics have argued that not only is there immense variation in the productivity of land over small areas, but also one needs to consider as an active variable the level of labour input. Calculations at a national level such as those made by Kettlewell for colonial Malawi verge on the meaningless – they consider neither the variation in productivity of land, nor the variation in labour inputs over this vast area. They cannot, then, be used to determine critical population density in any given area. Another, and perhaps more serious problem with the model is that it assumes an economy in which all households strive for subsistence through their own production on the land. In fact, 'subsistence' in this area had for at least a century, and probably for longer, included a large element of exchange, and so this model bore little relation to economic reality. As the Department's own surveys had shown, and as will be demonstrated in more detail in Chapter 4, many households in the Southern Province did not expect to grow their own food needs, even in a favourable year. If these households suffered from poor nutrition, or if they starved during a famine, this could not be said to be caused by the failure of their own production, though this may have had a part to play.

Another aspect of these calculations was that they took no account whatsoever of the ability of local agricultural and social systems to adapt, adjust to, and survive changing circumstances. There was no room for optimism in the Department's thinking on the future and no respect whatsoever for the agricultural abilities of the communities of this area. Whilst we might agree that in a predominantly agricultural society population and land resources are crucial factors, the really central question is how far they are seen to be *determinant* or to what degree they are flexible (Ellen, 1982; Berry, 1984). This means taking into account the previous experience of the community itself, and examining its history of modification of the environment. As far as the Department of Agriculture was concerned, the only modifying influence these communities had had on their environment was a damaging one. This brings us to another point about their calculations, and this is that they always had built into them a prescription for a modification of the agricultural system which involved fallowing and the utilisation of livestock manure. Paul Richards has recently shown that this Eurocentric obsession with manuring was totally inappropriate to many parts of Africa (Richards, 1983). African farming systems pay more attention to the preservation of the physical properties of the soil than they do to fertility, and this is because physical deficiencies are much less easily repaired than infertility. Hence the farmer is more likely to concentrate on heaping, ridging, intercropping, minimum tillage and the deliberate neglect of weeds at certain stages of the cultivation cycle. It is true that in their campaign to promote ridging and boxing the Department was also emphasising the preservation of physical properties, but the ultimate aim was to produce a 'mixed farmer', and it was with this in mind that the calculations included such a large area of fallow, and thus led to such depressing conclusions about the possibilities for agriculture supporting a growing population.

Finally, despite the evidence of their own surveys, government officials based all their calculations of food availability solely on the availability of *maize*. Jane Guyer has recently criticised a similar tendency on the part of the World Bank and other agencies to concentrate on trends in cereal production whilst ignoring the figures for root crops (Guyer, 1983). Officials in Malawi in the 1940s had the same tendency, and this was in part determined by their view of root crops as nutritionally inferior. Interestingly, after the famine in 1949 they encouraged the cultivation of greater quantities of root crops, but in their 1940s calculations they ignored the contribution such crops made to the nutrition of whole communities. In the Department of Agriculture's own survey of Ntaja village in Zomba District, which has already been cited (MP 3/7 Village Surveys), the conclusion was that on average each household had a deficit of 185 lb of maize per year. But apparently no account was taken of the fact that within the village considerable quantities of other starch crops were grown. On average each household cultivated 1.61 acres of maize, but it also cultivated 0.82 acres of sorghum, 0.26 acres of cassava and 0.09 acres of sweet potatoes. Both cassava and sweet potatoes had high yields per acre – 1,514 lb in the case of cassava and 3,512 lb in the case of sweet potatoes, compared with 943 lb for maize (MNA, AGR 3/7). This is not to say that the surveys were wrong to indicate nutritional deficiency and poor health in much of the Southern Region, but the Department's blinkered view may have led them to reach the wrong conclusions about the causes of these problems. Adding root crops into their calculations would have produced a less pessimistic view of the availability of starch foods, if nothing else.

Even if there were any validity in the calculations of 'carrying capacity' produced by the Department, and in the prediction of ecological crisis, their approach to the problems ignored the most important fact of all. This was that population was unevenly distributed, and the unevenness of this distribution was due not only to 'natural' environmental variation, but more crucially to the existence of large areas of privately owned land. If there was a Malthusian crisis in the 1940s, it was one structured around this pattern of land ownership, and thus one with an important political dimension.

Blantyre District, for instance, was divided between Native Trust Land (formerly Crown Land) held under a traditional but evolving matrilineal land tenure system, and private land largely in the hands of European companies and partly occupied by their tenants. In order to assess the perceived problem of land pressure and ecological deterioration in Blantyre District, we need to examine the history of this pattern of land-holding and its effects on population distribution and on agricultural production.

In the 1940s about fifty per cent of the total land area of Blantyre District was privately owned (MNA, NSB 7/1/6, Report for 1940). Much of the alienation of this land had taken place in the 1870s to 1890s, and although there had been some changes in ownership in the intervening years, the amount and location of the alienated land remained mostly unchanged. In 1939 there was a total of sixty-nine estates in Blantyre District, but most of the land was divided between two companies – the British Central Africa Company and the Blantyre and East Africa Company. Of the 9,000 African tenants on private estates in 1939, fifty per cent resided on land owned by the British Central Africa Company, about 1,000 lived on the estates of the Blantyre and East Africa Company, 400 on land owned by the African Lakes Corporation, and the rest were distributed over the remaining, smaller estates (MNA, NSB 7/1/5, Report for 1939).

Not only did private ownership account for about half the total land area of the district, but private land also comprised most of the agriculturally favoured land. Blantyre District could be divided into three ecologically distinct strips. The first was the eastern strip of the higher elevations of the Shire Highlands; the second was a central strip of 2,000 to 3,000 feet above sea level; the third a western strip of lowland adjoining the Shire River. The eastern strip, which included the immediate environs of Blantyre and Limbe townships, had the best soils and rainfall, and was mostly held by private owners. Sandwiched between the private estates were small areas of heavily congested Native Trust Land. In 1931 a survey had shown that the land lying within a ten-mile radius of Blantyre township was divided into 222 square miles of privately held land and 92 square miles of Native Trust Land. There were 25,096 Africans living on this Native Trust Land, giving a density of population of 273 per square mile. The overall density of population for the area was 85.64 per square mile, so it is clear that the private estates were much more sparsely populated, and that population distribution as a whole was very skewed. One chief, Native Authority Machinjili, found himself presiding over an area in this eastern strip in which only five per cent of the land was held under customary tenure, the rest being privately owned. By contrast, the central and western strips were almost entirely given over to Native Trust Land (MNA, NSB 7/1/2, Report for 1931).

The western strip was that area of land bordering the Shire River, for which Livingstone described the 'lowland' system of agriculture operating in the nineteenth century. During the period of disruption at the end of the nineteenth century many communities from this area fled to take refuge on the hilltops of the highlands, but some returned at the end of the 1890s and the first years of the twentieth century, to re-establish their agricultural economy. Away from the river banks it was not an easy place to cultivate, as a report in the *British Central*

Africa Gazette of 1896 indicated. From just north of Matope going westwards to the Lisungwe River the land was almost totally uninhabited and judged as 'probably uninhabitable' except close to the Lisungwe River itself, for 'the ground is stony and ungenerous, bringing forth puny shadeless trees and, with dog-in-the-manger perversity, an undergrowth which, when it is not thorn, is bramble' (*BCA Gazette*, July 1896, p. 1). The early nineteenth-century pattern of river bank cultivation was probably the only viable one here, but by the 1930s the Department of Agriculture was actively discouraging settlement close to the river banks, and in the 1940s was prosecuting individuals for river bank cultivation (MNA, NSB 7/4/1).

Just to the east, on what was known as the central strip, however, the government had been actively encouraging settlement from the mid 1930s (MNA, NSB 7/1/5). This area included the chieftaincies of Kuntaja, Kapeni and Lundu, and the settlements of Lirangwe and Lunzu which feature so often in accounts of the 1949 famine. As far as we can judge, this strip of land had been very sparsely populated in the nineteenth century. The 'lowland' system of agriculture described by Livingstone was that practised on the western strip bordering the river, while the 'highland' system applied to areas further east. This central strip lay in a rain shadow, the soils were poor, and the lack of domestic water supplies had compounded its problems. But from 1934 the government began establishing wells and boreholes in this area to encourage the settlement of people from the most congested parts of the eastern highland strip (MNA, NSB 7/1/5). Considerable immigration had resulted. In the fifteen years leading up to the famine there was continuous movement of population in Blantyre District, and most of this movement was away from the congested highlands into the less crowded but more agriculturally marginal areas. Although European observers made the easy equation between congestion and vulnerability to food shortage, it was in fact in these newly colonised and less crowded areas that the 1949 famine struck with most severity.

The availability of land in the central strip and the provision of water supplies there may have enabled people from the congested areas of the highlands to avoid moving onto privately owned land as tenants. According to the 1945 population census, of the total population of 101,218 in Blantyre District, 30,209 lived on private estates, and the remaining 71,009 were on Native Trust Land (MNA, NSB 7/1/6, Report for 1940). As we have seen, this skewed distribution of population had existed in the 1930s, and had probably existed to some degree ever since the alienation of land had taken place. But in the course of the 1930s and 1940s it took on a new significance as a result of the more rapid natural increase in population, combined with a change in policies towards tenants on the part of the major land-holders. These changes are outlined in the following paragraph.

As a result of the Land Commission set up in 1948, histories of the two major land-holders – the Blantyre and East Africa Company and the British Central Africa Company – were produced by the Protectorate's Lands Officer, H. V. MacDonald (MNA, MP 12258; MP 12405). These studies were written with a view to recommending which areas of privately held land might be compulsorily purchased by the government to relieve the congestion of Native Trust Land. Both companies had long histories of non-exploitation of their vast land reserves, of 'wasted opportunities', and the non-enforcement of rental obligations. The British Central Africa Company had 372,500 acres in the Southern Province at the turn of the century. By 1924 it had sold 17,345 acres and leased out another 59,432 acres. Out of the remaining 295,723 acres, only just over 6,000 were under any direct cultivation in 1924. By 1947 the company held 329,353 acres, of which about 29,000 were being actively worked. The rest of the land had been settled by tenants, most of them Lomwe immigrants from Mozambique. The Department of Agriculture was unhappy about the 'haphazard' nature of this settlement, and about the farming practices of the tenants. The Blantyre District *ulendo* reports of this period showed that there was very little enforcement of the anti-soil-erosion measures on privately held land. The contrast between this '*laissez-faire*' attitude on the part of estate owners and the strict enforcement of regulations on Native Trust Land was causing resentment amongst inhabitants of the latter. The Blantyre and East Africa Company had a similar history. By 1947 this company held a total of 111,529 acres, and none of the 47,258 acres held in Blantyre, Chiradzulu and Chikwawa Districts were being directly worked. Most of this land was under tenant cultivation and the company was said to have a very casual attitude to its tenantry. In 1947 total cash receipts from *all* the company's land only reached £1,662.

The British Central Africa Company had taken a similarly relaxed approach to its tenants up to the mid 1930s when the financial pressures induced by the Depression, and new managerial control, combined to produce a change in policy. Even before this change, however, people seem to have preferred to live on Native Trust Land, despite the overcrowding. Successive District Commissioners in Blantyre described this tendency, and most thought it was explained by the fact that residence on Native Trust Land offered greater security. Even if rent was rarely collected on the estates there could be serious drawbacks to living on privately owned land. To begin with, the owner might always change his policy, or the land could change hands and rental obligations (in the form of cash, *thangata* labour, or cash crops) might then be enforced. Evictions could, and did, take place when rent had not been paid. Another oft-cited drawback to estate residence concerned marriage, in the context of a matrilocal system. If a female tenant married a man from Native Trust Land, and if he came to reside with her, as was the custom, then he immediately became liable to rental obligations and subject to restrictions on his mobility.

But it was a change of policy on the part of the British Central Africa Company which added to these disadvantages from 1937 onwards. The aim was to raise revenue through the enforcement of tobacco production by its tenants, and at the same time to prove to the government that it was making fuller use of its land now that the threat of compulsory sale was becoming real. Tenants who did not fulfil their obligations were now liable to eviction. In 1937 the company applied to evict 1,200 tenants on these grounds. Of this number only 150 eventually received notices to quit, but the new approach created a greater feeling of insecurity amongst those who remained (MNA, NSB 7/1/4, Report for 1937). In 1938 the company again applied to evict 1,112 tenants from their Lunzu, Lirangwe and Mikalongwe estates, and 359 orders to quit were eventually issued (MNA, NSB 7/1/4, Report for 1938). This policy continued through the 1940s, but it did not go unresisted by the tenants, and especially by the more educated amongst them. In 1948 five tenants on one British Central Africa estate refused to be evicted. They argued that they had been born on the land and that they had never once failed to pay their £1 rent in lieu of working. All five were members of the nationalist organisation, the Nyasaland African Congress, and had whipped up considerable support in the area in the course of their resistance (MNA, NSB 7/4/1). The government was obliged to settle evicted tenants on Native Trust Land, and even in the 1920s District Officers had found this a problem. In 1924 one District Commissioner in Blantyre had made the following prophetic observation:

> Educated natives are still grumbling at their inability to acquire land on a tenure sufficiently secure to justify them planting trees etc. . . . while the uneducated native who is being turned off private land as a result of its development is complaining of the impossibility of finding a holding on Crown Land sufficient to support him and his family. Owing to the fact that a large portion of this district is kept by the B.C.A. Company in its own hands, and that at present their policy is to retain their native tenants, the position is not so acute here as it is in other parts of the highlands – but the fact that it was found impossible to find room for about 600 natives whom it was proposed to move in order to form a Forest Reserve at Soche, shows that the position might become extremely acute should this company decide to change its policy. (MNA, NSB 7/1/1, Report for 1924)

It is clear from this evidence that the division of Blantyre District (and indeed much of the Southern Province) into private and customary land must be considered when assessing the argument for a Malthusian crisis in the 1940s. The allocation of much of the best land to private owners, and the disadvantages of residence on that land, resulted in a very skewed distribution of population and one which could hardly be regarded as 'natural'. After the disruptive years at the end of the nineteenth century the population never re-established its old patterns of settlement because hard on the heels of the slave trade came the European invasion. Furthermore, as time went on, increasing government intervention meant that resettlement of people from the crowded areas of the highlands took place into the central strip of the district which had previously been sparsely populated, and in which a new kind of farming system had to be tried out and established. Some of the pre-colonial insurance mechanisms which might have aided new immigrants in an uncertain environment were now being actively discouraged as the Department of Agriculture prosecuted those who cultivated along river banks, or grew the hardy perennial sorghum.

If there was severe population pressure in parts of this district, it was due less to natural increase than it was to the non-availability of much of the land for ordinary settlement and production. To this extent, the ecological crisis which appeared to be mounting in parts of the district can hardly be seen as inevitable, or the result of short-sighted African farming methods. Population pressure can only rightly be viewed within the context of the political economy of colonial Malawi and the position held by European landowners within this. A second and related point, but one which is hard to validate, concerns the perceptions of African cultivators. It is possible that the existence of large areas of uncultivated, privately held land in the district, lying side by side with crowded Native Trust Land, affected African perceptions of the environment and altered their responses to growing land shortage. We have plenty of evidence from the nineteenth and early twentieth centuries for the successful adjustment of African farming systems to changing circumstances in this area. It could be argued that there are limits to the possibilities of adjustment, without far-reaching technical change, and that these limits may have been reached by the 1940s. On the other hand, we must bear in mind that when an African cultivator, struggling to produce food on a small overworked plot, could see large acreages of under-used land next door, she or he may have reasoned that the 'crisis' was an artificial one, and that sooner or later more land would be made available. If we add to this the intervention of the Department of Agriculture in banning or discouraging some long-held practices, then it is plausible to argue that in some parts of Blantyre District and in parts of the Southern Province as a whole, the normal processes of adjustment, change and adaptation within African farming systems were being inhibited at this time.

The Malthusian crisis theory is thus open to a number of criticisms, falling within two broad areas. Firstly, the assumptions behind the calculations used to establish this crisis 'scientifically' are themselves open to question. Secondly, although areas of Blantyre District were undoubtedly experiencing population pressure, this cannot be viewed as a 'natural' linear development, given that so much of the district was given over to private ownership.

One important fact does however emerge from the Department of Agriculture's documentation of this period, and this is that within the Southern Province there were many families which were unable to feed themselves from their own production. The majority of them relied to some extent on the purchase of food. Some of this was produced by other families within the community who were better endowed with land, labour and capital; some came from other parts of the Southern Province, and an increasing proportion came from the Central Province. How these families earned their 'entitlement' to this food is obviously crucially important to understanding the famine, and this will be the subject of Chapter 4. Also important, however, is an understanding of the mechanisms operating to supply this food, and here we have to move away from a purely local perspective to view the production and marketing of foodstuffs at a national level. In the next chapter I examine the theory held by some contemporaries that deficiencies in pricing and marketing mechanisms were responsible for the famine.

3

Famine as a failure of the market

Although the theory of Malthusian crisis was the most influential in explaining the 1949 famine, there were two other theories (quite closely related to one another) which were put forward by European observers and expounded at length in the planters' newspaper, the *Nyasaland Times*. One held that the famine was due to a shortfall in maize production nationally, and that this could be accounted for by the high tobacco prices of the post-war period and the consequent shift into tobacco production on the part of many African farmers. This shift was seen to be at the direct expense of food production. The second theory also saw a shortfall in maize surplus production as being responsible, in this case caused by inappropriate government intervention in the marketing of foodstuffs. Over a period, it was argued, this had had an inhibiting effect on production, village food stocks had been run down, and one bad season was enough to topple the country into disaster. Sometimes one or other of these explanations was used alone, sometimes in combination with each other or with the Malthusian theory. Both were critical of government policies on African agriculture, and both relate to wider debates outlined in the Introduction. In this chapter I discuss the two theories and assess their relevance to the analysis of the famine.

A positive aspect of both these theories is that they treated the events of the famine in the context of an economy wider than that of the local area in which the famine struck. In this respect they have many advantages over the ecological crisis theory, which as we have seen, was notable for its lack of contextualisation and which treated the economy of the famine area as a 'pure' subsistence one, isolated from larger economic influences. But when European observers put forward these theories they also had vested interests involved, and for that reason the evidence provided needs to be closely examined.

The theory that the famine was due to the substitution of a cash crop for food crops is one which received wide support, not only from the European estate owners, but also from officials within government. As I have argued in the Introduction, it is also a theory which in more general terms has received much attention in current debates on the economic history of Africa, and in the literature on food supply and famine. I shall argue here that whilst there was an important relationship between the cultivation of cash crops and the supply of food, the application of the theory requires caution. The argument for substitution is one which might possibly be applied at the level of a survey of the colonial economy as a whole, and when related to a discussion of pricing policy. However, it can be totally misleading when applied at the level of individual households and communities in the famine area, and in this respect it does not help us to understand why people starved in 1949.

The *Nyasaland Times*, published in Blantyre, paid scant attention to the famine itself, though it had reported the drought in some detail. It was only on the letter page that the subject received attention. Most of the letters used the food shortage as an occasion for individual members of the European community to voice their own economic grievances and long-standing disagreements with government policy towards African agriculture. One 'Junius' was typical in seeing a close association between the government-sponsored production of tobacco by Africans on Native Trust Land, and the coming of the food shortage:

> It is astounding how many folks there are who attribute the current lamentable shortage of foodstuffs to the present drought. Apart from the few tons of maize now required for re-seeding gardens already planted, there is no link whatever between the two disasters. The whole cause of the present hunger lies snugly tucked inside the Native Tobacco Board's 'Cushion'. The Native has received every encouragement and no restraint in the growing of tobacco – to the detriment of his own food. (*Nyasaland Times*, vol. 52, no. 16, 28/2/49)

In a similar vein, the Chamber of Commerce pronounced that:

> The famine is not a crisis of this year, it is a crisis of last year and the preceding years. Government has seen fit to encourage the growing of tobacco by Africans, without any action to keep up food production. (*Nyasaland Times*, vol. 52, no. 16, 28/2/49)

In truth, the history of African cash-crop production in colonial Malawi had been much more chequered than was implied by the European letter writers.

Since the beginning of the century the impoverished colonial administration of Malawi had been juggling with the economy in an attempt to maintain the country as a viable entity, and this story has been described in detail by John McCracken, Leroy Vail and others (Vail, 1983; McCracken, 1983 and 1986). The first sector was that comprising large-scale European-owned agricultural enterprises, producing at various times coffee, tea, cotton, tobacco. This sector was originally concentrated in the Shire Highlands in the Southern Province, but by the 1920s and 1930s was extending significantly into the Central Province. The second sector comprised the African peasant economy. At various times the government encouraged the production by Africans of cotton, tobacco, groundnuts and other crops for sale and export, but the encouragement had not been geographically uniform or consistent. Finally, there was the important sector involving labour migration outside the country. Some of this was official and controlled, and thus susceptible to changes in policy. Some was virtually uncontrolled and autonomous.

The relative importance and weight of these three sectors varied at different times. The colonial state stumbled from one plan to another in attempts to solve its economic problems and generate revenue. Hampered by impossibly high rail freight rates, the problem was always one of finding a profitable export crop, and beyond this the political problem of who should grow it – Europeans or Africans (Vail, 1983).

By the 1940s the major cash crop, and one receiving high prices on the world market, was tobacco (McCracken, 1983). Tobacco production had started on the large estates of the Shire Highlands in the early years of the century. The tobacco grown here was of the Virginia variety, which was flue-cured in large barns and exported to Britain and South Africa. Flue-cured tobacco production declined with a collapse in prices at the end of the 1920s, but production of fire-cured tobacco by African tenants on the same estates increased. This tobacco was grown and processed by individual African families, who then sold the product to their landlords, and a portion of the crop was taken as rent. In the mid 1920s this form of production was extended into the fertile plains of the Central Province, and from then on the focus of tobacco production began to move north from the Shire Highlands. At the same time, African families resident on Native Trust Land in both the Southern and Central Provinces took up tobacco production and sold their crop independently to European estate owners acting as buyers. Before too long this independent production was seen as a threat to the more closely controlled tenant production and attempts were made to control it through the Native Tobacco Board. These efforts finally brought about a collapse in the independent African industry in the 1930s, when European growers were particularly concerned to protect themselves against the effects of the Depression. With the high prices of the 1940s, however, the Board embarked on a policy of encouraging the expansion of production on Native Trust Land, and this reached a peak in 1947 (Nyasaland Protectorate, Department of Agriculture, *Annual Report*, 1947). After 1947 there were attempts to reduce acreages and to restrict the price paid to the African producer. Many Europeans still insisted however, that the prices paid to Africans were too high. The Native Tobacco Board 'cushion', referred to by Junius the letter writer, was in fact a price assistance fund created out of the profits of the Board (McCracken, 1983).

The letter writers of the *Nyasaland Times* were thus constructing their arguments around a perceived threat to their own economic interests in the era of high tobacco prices after the war. For other reasons the Department of

Agriculture was also concerned by the volume of African tobacco production. In particular there was concern over its effects on food production, and its contribution to soil erosion. In 1946 the Director of Agriculture articulated the problem in the following terms: high prices ruled for tobacco, and the production of this crop was increased only at the expense of food production; furthermore, the high prices paid for tobacco in Southern Rhodesia would force up wages there and result in an increased flow of migrants from Malawi. This in turn would compound the problem of food production at home by withdrawing labour from the 'subsistence' sector (MNA, MP 35/26 Director of Agriculture to Chief Secretary, 3/5/46).

As we shall see, there was some truth in the argument that an increase in differentials between maize and tobacco prices contributed to bringing about a famine. It is essential, however, to establish the level at which this analysis can work, and the limitations to its application. Most observers assumed that there was a direct substitution of tobacco for maize in the peasant household. The picture was quite simple – people grew tobacco when prices were high, and consequently neglected their food crops. Ultimately they starved. This view was put forward again and again in government despatches of the 1940s, and belies the European settlers' accusation that the government was unconcerned about food production. Department of Agriculture propaganda was built around the fear of a shortfall in food production. An article published in 1943 in the vernacular newspaper *Nkhani za Nyasaland* was typical:

> Many people are now feeling hunger because their maize is short and until next maize harvest many people will remain hungry. In Lilongwe district and in other places this is well known. Last year the maize crop was poor and now there is *njala* [hunger]. Nobody wants *njala* next year . . . Money cannot buy food if there is no food. Many people have money and want to buy food, but they are not able to do so, because the wise people who have enough maize wish to keep it for themselves and their families to eat so that they may be comfortable and strong. (MNA, MP 11000, Director of Agriculture to Information Officer, 10/11/43)

The argument rested on the assumption, belief or hope that the people of the country were organised into self-sufficient subsistence households which might be extended for a small amount of cash-crop production. As Chapter 2 has shown, this assumption also underlay the Malthusian crisis argument. But in the 1940s it was a model becoming less and less appropriate, for two reasons. Firstly, because much African cash-crop production took place under a tenant system on estates, supervised and controlled by European estate owners, and production decisions were therefore not entirely in the hands of the producers; secondly, because of the very uneven distribution of land within the country and within villages, which meant that there were some households which did not have the option of becoming surplus producers of any crop. Looking in

2. An African market at Blantyre in the 1950s

more detail at the history of cash-cropping in Blantyre District it is apparent that the 'substitution' argument cannot be applied in any mechanistic way.

Chapter 2 outlined how in the nineteenth century communities in what was to become Blantyre District had grown both food and non-food crops for exchange. The most important of the non-food crops was the cotton described by Livingstone and others. Indigenous cotton production and weaving were early casualties of the penetration of foreign goods – firstly through the trade to the East African coast, and then through early European trading companies which set up their retail stores along the river and in Blantyre township. However, the opening up of European-owned estates on the Shire Highlands in the last two decades of the century afforded new opportunities for cash-crop production to the people of Blantyre and surrounding districts. From the very beginnings of their enterprises European estate owners complained at the unwillingness of local people to work as wage-labourers, and resorted to importing Ngoni labour from the centre and north of the country, and then Lomwe labour from Mozambique. It was this latter flow of labour which, as Landeg White has described, allowed the estate sector to function in the early part of the century (White, 1987). Meanwhile, many of the local inhabitants of the Shire Highlands attempted to re-establish their agricultural systems to provide them not only with foodstuffs but also with a surplus to sell to enable them to pay hut tax, and to provide them with the cash to buy imported hoes and cloth. Although many people in this area were eventually dragged into wage labour, and although tenants frequently had no choice but to perform labour service, a substantial proportion survived as independent surplus-producing peasants. Some became rather more than this. In Blantyre District there were several examples in the early years of the century of mission-educated Africans who secured leases on land from the government and established their own labour-employing estates (Vaughan, 1981, ch. 3). Kumtaja was the most famous of these, gaining recognition from the government and establishing a chieftaincy in the Middle Shire Valley. Kumtaja was a Nyanja and said to be an escaped slave. In the 1870s he had settled on Blantyre Mission land and hunted elephants but had found himself in trouble with local chiefs through disregarding their traditional rights to the ground tusks of elephants slaughtered in their territories. He moved to another site within the township and worked as an elephant hunter for the African Lakes Corporation. He was then granted a large area of land at Michiru by the first Commissioner, Harry Johnston, and established a coffee plantation there. In 1897 he was growing forty-four acres of coffee, had four houses of his own, and was headman of two large villages (Blantyre District Notebook, vol. 1). There were others like him, and though they were often not entirely successful in the long-term, they nevertheless established positions for themselves and their descendants in the eyes of the colonial government.

Even in the 1940s, when pressure on land was becoming acute in some areas of Native Trust Land, there were still communities of independent cash-croppers around Blantyre, growing for the urban market and increasingly for a rural market as well. Even in the most crowded parts of the Southern Province, such as Chiradzulu and Mulanje Districts, maize and vegetables were produced for sale. However, it was not this kind of cash-crop production which European observers had in mind when they argued that African producers paid insufficient attention to maize in the 1940s. What they had in mind was the organised production of tobacco and cotton both by independent producers on Native Trust Land and by African tenants on estates.

After the failure of estate coffee production on the Shire Highlands at the turn of the century, and under pressure from the British Cotton Growing Association, the government began sponsoring African cotton production (Vaughan, 1981, ch. 4). Initially this project was confined to the Upper Shire District, but was soon extended to Blantyre District by an enthusiastic District Resident, Hector Duff. The enterprise foundered even before the First World War, partly because of pressure from European estate owners who claimed that Africans were stealing their cotton and selling it as their own, but also because of the poor prices paid, inadequacies in the marketing system, and severe pest problems. However, the industry survived in patches and by the 1930s African cotton production was again being actively promoted in Blantyre District

(MNA, NSB 7/1/4). Cotton was also grown by tenants on the massive estates of the British Central Africa Company in the western part of the district. The poor infrastructure and organisation of these estates meant that tenant production was the only viable method of producing cotton (MNA, MP 12258). Tenants used family labour to produce the crop, which they then sold to the company, which processed it in its own ginneries within the area.

The extent of cotton production in Blantyre District – both independent and tenant production – should not be exaggerated. In the early days of the industry pests and disease wiped out whole crops. In 1926, 151 tons of cotton were produced by independent African growers in Blantyre District, and this production was almost entirely concentrated in the western and central strips of the district – the very areas in which famine was later to strike most severely (MNA, NSB 7/1/1 Report for 1926). It would be difficult to argue, however, that cotton was being produced here at the expense of food. Cotton production seems always to have been unstable and somewhat half-hearted, and the Department of Agriculture's efforts to promote it as a cash crop in the 1930s and 1940s met with only partial success.

In 1931 there were 384 registered growers in the district, and most were concentrated in the Matope area on the Shire. They produced 57,875 lb of cotton and received an average return of 6s. 3d. (MNA, NSB 7/1/2, Report for 1931). This compared with an average return in 1930 of 14s. Despite the low Depression prices the Department of Agriculture continued to encourage production of the crop in these drier areas of the valley, but increasingly the focus of the industry moved to the Neno area to the west of the Shire. In 1932–3 there were 852 growers in Neno and 196 in Blantyre District itself, producing 146 and 13 tons respectively (MNA, NSB 9/1/3). Fluctuation in cotton production continued in the late 1930s and 1940s. The 1938 report for the district, for instance, noted that cotton was on the decline, but by 1943 there was an increase, with 193 tons being purchased (MNA, NSB 7/1/6, Report for 1943).

What evidence we have points to cotton being an occasional cash crop of communities in this area, and one which was experimented with by the new immigrants who had moved from the highlands into the valley in the course of the 1930s. When prices were high these people planted cotton, and when they were low it was abandoned. The evidence does not show, however, that this was an industry competing significantly with food crops for either land or labour.

In fact European observers paid no attention at all to cotton when they put forward their arguments about substitution. Unlike tobacco production by Africans, the growing of cotton was not perceived as any threat to their own interests. It was the 'tobacco boom' which received all the publicity and attention from European estate owners and government officials.

In Blantyre District tobacco was grown by Africans living on Native Trust

Land, and by tenants on estates. Production on Native Trust Land was, from 1926, regulated by the Native Tobacco Board. As John McCracken has shown, this was essentially a device in use by European tobacco producers to restrict and tax the African industry (McCracken, 1983). Their fear was that any extension of the independent African industry would compete with their own needs for direct labour and tenants.

Discontent with low prices led to a near collapse of the African industry in the late 1930s, but a spectacular revival took place during and after the Second World War, and there was a steady increase in prices up to 1958. By the mid 1940s, as the Department of Agriculture's figures show, tobacco had become by far the most profitable cash crop to grow. By 1946 the District Commissioner for Blantyre was expressing concern over the effects of high prices for tobacco in depressing the production of surplus food. His table of the comparative returns of different crops on a two-acre garden makes clear how attractive tobacco was as a cash crop (see Table 3). The price quoted for maize was the official marketing price, and this may have been exceeded on the open market in Blantyre at some times of year, but even bearing this in mind the figures indicate quite clearly the advantages of growing tobacco.

The question remains as to whether tobacco was being grown at the expense of maize, and the answer to this depends in part on who we think was growing the tobacco and how production of the crop was organised. In Blantyre District, as we saw in Chapter 2, Native Trust Land became increasingly crowded in the 1930s and 1940s. As this happened so African tobacco production shifted slowly from being predominantly an occupation of Native Trust Land dwellers to becoming more and more common as an industry practised by tenants on European estates. In 1926, for instance, there were 1,302 registered tobacco producers on Trust Land and 734 on private estates. By 1936 there were 669 growers on Trust Land and 466 on private estates, and by 1939 the figures were 123 on Trust Land and 503 on estates (MNA, NSB 7/1/1; NSB

Table 3 *Comparative return to a two-acre garden, Blantyre District 1946*

Crop	Return	Price	Reward
Tobacco	400 lb	8d. per lb	£13 6s. 8d.
Groundnuts	600 lb	2d. per lb	£5 0s. 0d.
Wheat	800 lb	1½d. per lb	£4 3s. 4d.
Beans	1,000 lb	1d. per lb	£4 3s. 4d.
Simsim	600 lb	1½d. per lb	£3 15s. 0d.
Cotton	500 lb	1¼d. per lb	£2 12s. 1d.
Maize	1,600 lb	3lb per d.	£2 5s. 0d.

MNA, NSB 3/2/1, D C Blantyre to PC Southern Province, 10/7/46.

7/1/4; NSB 7/1/5). The Blantyre District Commissioner explained this shift by pointing out that the congestion on Trust Land left little room for tobacco production, and had forced a number of former Trust Land tobacco producers to migrate to the newly opened up tobacco producing areas of the Central Province. Others had given up tobacco production altogether and had become labour migrants in South Africa and Southern Rhodesia. He might have added that the attempts by large estate owners to make their enterprises pay in this period (as outlined in Chapter 2) also partly accounted for this shift in the location of production. Under an agreement of 1943, for instance, tenants on the Bruce Estates in Chiradzulu District were obliged either to pay a rent of 12s., or to work for five to six months, or to redeem rent through the production of a cash crop. For every 12½ lbs of tobacco produced, the tenant's rent was reduced by 1s. (MNA, LB 4/2/1, Agreement 1943). The Bruce Estates had long been exceptional in enforcing these rental obligations, but by the late 1930s both the Blantyre and East Africa Company and the British Central Africa Company were pursuing similar policies. In Blantyre District, then, the European estate owners had little to fear from the increase in African tobacco production since more and more of it was being channelled through their own hands. Tobacco production by tenants presumably did compete with food production for limited family labour, and thus placed a number of tenants in a potentially vulnerable situation as regarded their food supply. For Trust Land growers, however, the supply of land was probably a more important constraint.

We have no detailed figures which would provide a picture of the organisation of tobacco production in Blantyre District, but a survey in neighbouring Zomba District conducted in 1944 gives some indication (MNA, AGR 3/7, Carroll Wilks to Senior Agricultural Officer, 8/11/44). In the village surveyed there was a total of thirty families, of which twelve were growing tobacco. All the labour on the tobacco gardens was provided by the families themselves, and an estimated 390 man-hours a year were spent on the tobacco crop, compared with 730 on maize. The average total garden size was 3.17 acres and the average tobacco garden measured 0.65 of an acre, but these averages disguised considerable variation in garden size between families. Tobacco is best seen in these areas as a crop grown by those with a disproportionately large amount of land, and with access to adequate family labour. In Mulanje District, for instance, one Agricultural Supervisor had investigated closely the question of whether or not tobacco was being grown in direct competition with maize:

> In conversation with the D.C. Mlanje recently he suggested that the increased tobacco production might be partly responsible for food shortage. I have been to some pains to investigate this, but can obtain no evidence to support it. In fact, all the evidence goes to show that the industrious tobacco grower still has food and is now helping to feed the district. He obtained his money from the sale of tobacco, so it was not necessary for him to sell his maize. (MNA, AGR 4/10, Agricultural Supervisor, Mombezi to Agricultural Officer, Mlanje, 20/12/41)

If the Agricultural Supervisor was right, then in Mulanje District at least the substitution argument would not hold, as the tobacco producers were also those most likely to be self-sufficient in food.

By the 1940s the profile of societies in the Southern Province was a complicated one. Some families were almost landless and relied heavily on wage labour to earn their food supplies. Others had enough land to grow both tobacco and maize for sale. Added to this already uneven distribution of land was the presence of the estates, and the varying conditions of tenants on these. It is because resources were distributed so unevenly that the substitution argument cannot be applied simply. This is not to say, however, that there was no truth in it at all. When we come to look at crop pricing policy at a national level it appears to hold some weight, and it is here that the argument merges with that concerning marketing.

The theory of the famine which I outlined at the beginning of this chapter held that the famine was due to the effects of government policy in attempting to regulate the marketing of maize, and this argument relates closely to a body of literature on marketing boards which I described briefly in the Introduction. European letter writers in the *Nyasaland Times*, like British officials in India in the nineteenth century, were highly critical of government interference in free trade mechanisms. Those who did not blame the famine directly on African tobacco production blamed it instead on government intervention in maize markets, and in particular on the operations of the government Maize Control Board:

> It is no exaggeration to say that but for the operations of the Maize Control Board, what otherwise would have been merely a shortage of maize for the industrial interests and a hardship for the villager, has become for industry a most serious situation, and for the villager, famine. (*Nyasaland Times*, vol. 52, no. 14, 21/2/49, p. 5.)

This was a popular analysis, and we shall examine later the workings of the Maize Control Board. But the issue went well beyond this, and related to circumstances beyond the boundaries of Malawi.

The apparent imminence of an ecological crisis in the Southern Region was one of the major forces leading government to intervene in food production and marketing in the 1940s, and this perception has been outlined in Chapter 2. Adding urgency to this concern, however, were two other factors operating in the 1940s. Firstly, the war itself and circumstances of the immediate post-war period which resulted in pressure from the Colonial Office and from the Ministry of Food in London for colonial territories to produce food for export or, failing this, to ensure their own food self-sufficiency (Cowen, 1982). The second factor was the increase in the wage labour force within Malawi, and in the Southern Province in particular. This growth was to some extent the outcome of the growth of the tobacco industry and the spin-offs from this.

Employers in the south of the country were anxious to secure cheap food supplies for their labour, and pressured government to act in support of this aim (Vaughan, 1984).

Examining British colonial economic policy as a whole in this period, Michael Cowen has described the political and economic pressures on the Labour government to increase colonial production (Cowen, 1982). This drive to expand production in the colonies followed directly, according to Cowen, from an ideological resolve to counter the apparent United States domination of the British economy, and this ideological resolve was underpinned by the material necessity to overcome shortages of goods, including foodstuffs. The desire to reduce dependence on the United States was made more urgent by the imperatives of the post-war dollar shortage. Ministers hoped to resurrect the triangular trade of earlier mercantilist periods. Raw materials, produced in the colonies, would be exported to the United States; capital goods would go from the United States to Britain; and Britain would complete the triangle by exporting manufactures to the colonies. In this scheme, commodities produced in the colonies would be both dollar earners (as exports to the United States) and dollar savers (as substitute imports from the dollar area) (Cowen, 1982, p. 144).

The overriding concern over material shortages in Britain, and the necessity to alleviate these as far as possible by imports from the colonies, was allied with a Fabian-inspired belief in the internationalisation of welfare. Colonial production was to be increased, not through the extension of capitalist relations within the colonies themselves, but under the supposedly paternalistic auspices of state corporations. As Cowen shows, increased intervention in the colonies, and the neo-mercantilist economic practices of the post-war government, were not always easily compatible with the welfarist strand of their policy, particularly in the face of new political demands on the part of the new colonial elites. Even in such a colonial backwater as Malawi, these conflicts and contradictions can be seen at work in the late 1940s, in the area of food production and supply.

The Second World War and its aftermath produced a greater awareness and heightened concern about problems of food supply at an international level (Poleman, 1977; Vaughan, 1984). Post-war Britain experienced food rationing, parts of Europe suffered severe famine, harvests failed or were drastically reduced in the Far East, Argentina, Australia and South Africa, as well as in Europe itself. The Food and Agriculture Organisation of the United Nations was established and its international bureaucrats got to work on global food supply sums. This was the beginning of the trend towards analysis of hugely aggregate figures which I described in the Introduction.

Colonial Malawi had long been a supplier of occasional food surpluses to the neighbouring territories of Northern and Southern Rhodesia, and this role had been further developed in the war years. Although the government in Zomba had withdrawn from a formal inter-territorial agreement on food supply,

Table 4 *Major Food Exports to Northern Rhodesia, Southern Rhodesia and Mozambique, 1940–53* (lbs.)

Year	Rice	Potatoes	Fish	Beans	Soyabeans	Broken pulses	Maize	Groundnuts
1940	53,348	41,217	234,439	—	—	—	612	—
1941	—	168,659	266,897	—	—	—	—	—
1942	—	598,409	191,076	347,258	—	—	7,805,917	—
1943	85,966	218,054	178,051	95,890	—	—	3,006,021	—
1944	43,408	205,924	479,669	110,790	—	—	210,200	396,448
1945	—	705,083	498,870	6,451,348	—	—	8,556	2,286,316
1946	501,247	107,588	223,791	2,963,732	—	—	—	579,932
1947	101,970	122,346	134,536	22,266,694	23,678	360,573	287	—
1948	17,990	3,538	105,475	430,162	405	104,578	—	—
1949	90	2,380	144,720	100,858	800	100,858	2,480	—
1950	—	169	—	997,170	83,600	91,247	—	—
1951	40,000	12,523	9,791	1,041,353	68,285	295,094	29,628,385	97
1952	649,860	48,090	3,581	5,501,961	387,200	79,666	55,164,600	140,216
1953	1,243,053	840,948	1,959	1,072,759	88,904	276,258	60,680,350	101,562

Source: Annual Reports of the Customs Department.

informally its links with the Rhodesias remained strong (MNA, MP 10797). Both Northern and Southern Rhodesia were in the habit of turning to Malawi for 'native foodstuffs' when their own supplies were inadequate. The major food exports to Northern and Southern Rhodesia from Malawi were fish, beans, potatoes, sometimes rice, and occasionally the staple cereal, maize. The figures in Table 4 are for foodstuffs which crossed the borders legally, and it can be seen that in the 1940s the volume of these exports was modest.

There was also an important unofficial trade in food across borders, however. This featured in particular dried fish from Lake Malawi which found a ready market in the urban areas of both Rhodesias. Although modest in volume, the official food exports were politically significant. This fact was demonstrated clearly in the immediate post-war period when London began putting pressure on the government in Zomba to redirect any food surpluses to those areas of the world deemed most in need (MNA, MP 10802). This caused some embarrassment in Central African government circles, as the Director of Agriculture explained:

> Both Rhodesias have become accustomed during recent years to turn to Nyasaland for their requirements of native foodstuffs and we have been only too glad to have such a nearby outlet for the surplus produce . . . We have now drifted into a position of being unable to meet demands by the Rhodesias without dislocation of other commitments which were unilaterally entered into and without reference to the Rhodesias . . . We have the closest economic ties with both countries. We have built up a connection with them for the disposal of our surpluses which might well become permanent and is of the utmost value to us . . . In view of trade relations [in foodstuffs] with the Rhodesias in the past years it may be that they feel we have let them down somewhat unceremoniously. (MNA, MP 11000 Minute by Director of Agriculture to Chief Secretary, 18/6/46.)

In the immediate post-war period the FAO attempted to calculate world food supply needs and to develop an efficient system of food flows from one part of the world to another. This plan involved the stabilisation of prices and the centralised direction of surpluses (FAO *Survey* 1946, p. 11). The spur to this was the occurrence of serious food shortages and famine in parts of Europe. For the first time peasants in colonial territories like Malawi were called upon directly to feed the starving of Europe.

A 'Food for Britain' campaign was launched in Malawi, the government calling for free donations of rice and oilseeds to send to the needy of Europe. It was hardly a resounding success. Only a few loyal chiefs responded, notably Chief Makanjira in Fort Johnston District, whose people collected together a few bags of groundnuts to send to Britain (MNA, MP 10802, Director of Agriculture, 18/6/46). But a spin-off from the post-war crisis was an increased awareness of the fact that many parts of the world were inadequately fed even in 'normal' times.

The FAO's World Food Survey of 1946 covered 70 countries. It was assumed by the nutritionists of the day that a daily calorie intake of 2,550 to 2,640 *per capita* was the minimum requirement, and on this basis it was calculated that in the pre-war period in areas containing half the world's population, food supplies at the retail level (i.e. not actual intake) were insufficient to meet these requirements. The fact that the experts subsequently lowered their figures for minimum requirements (see the Introduction) is less important than the fact that these calculations generated much concern at the time. This concern filtered back to Malawi through both official and unofficial channels. Readers of the *Nyasaland Times* were treated to many alarming editorials on the subject, and the paper also published the speech made by a South African expert on his return from the FAO conferences, warning that 'the world's increase in population is too great for the food the earth can produce' (*Nyasaland Times*, vol. 52, no. 17, Editorial).

Ignoring its own centralising tendencies, the FAO saw the problem as lying in the failure to adhere to a free market in foodstuffs. In an historical overview of the inter-war period, restrictionist policies were blamed for the failure to alleviate nutrition deprivation worldwide (FAO *Survey*, 1946, p. 26). The approach and outbreak of the Second World War brought a reversal in the economic policies of the 1930s. Surpluses had disappeared overnight and under the impetus of war technical efficiency in food production increased in the industrialised countries. A Combined Food Board was set up to allocate food supplies at the disposal of the United States, Canada and Britain, and in 1943 the Hot Springs Conference confirmed and continued the concern for food supply, which was carried over into the post-war period.

In the organisation of world food supply the British Empire had a potentially important role to play as an international structure capable of some centralised control. But what emerged ultimately from this internationally planned food policy was not so much the integration of the colonial territories into the world food market (though this took place to some extent), but rather a heightened concern for colonial self-sufficiency. By 1949 the crisis in cereal supply to Europe had already been alleviated and world cereal prices were falling as a result of the large stocks of North American produce which were building up (FAO *Report*, 1949). Few people really believed that areas such as Central Africa would become the bread baskets of the world,[1] but on the other hand it was important that they should not become net importers of food. In the market for oil-producing seeds such as groundnuts and sesame, however, there were more strenuous efforts to increase colonial production and to direct the surpluses produced because Europe remained short of vegetable fats for much longer than it was short of cereals. Surpluses of groundnuts from Malawi had long found a ready market in Southern and Northern Rhodesia, as well as in South Africa, but in the post-war period telegrams from the Secretary of State for the Colonies arrived on the Governor's desk almost every day, concerning the urgent requirement for vegetable fats in Europe (MNA, MP 10802). The peasant farmers of Malawi were exhorted to grow more groundnuts – no longer for feeding the urban workers in the Rhodesias, but to be made into margarine for Britons.

The colonial administration in Zomba made it clear that the production of groundnut surpluses and their transportation to Europe, would only be possible at a guaranteed fixed price. In 1946 the Governor wrote to the Secretary of State to say that the Ministry of Food's price of £25 per ton f.o.b. Beira was too low, bearing in mind the high prices being paid for tobacco in this period and the fact that there was a strong demand for oilseeds nearer to home, in South Africa. He argued that if it had not been for the fact that they were obliged to hold groundnut surpluses at the disposal of the Ministry of Food, the crop could have been sold to South Africa at £40 to £50 per ton (MNA, MP 11000 Governor to Secretary of State, 11/10/46). The Secretary of State then replied guaranteeing to purchase all exportable surpluses of groundnuts at the price of £27 7s. per ton, but also dictated that the trade in groundnuts with Northern and Southern Rhodesia be suspended (MNA, MP 11000 Secretary of State to Governor, 20/10/46). In the same year London ordered that all exportable surpluses of beans were required for Malaya, and rice surpluses should also be held at the disposal of the Ministry of Food (MNA, MP 10802, Secretary of State to Governor, 24/4/46). In the production and trade of these crops then – groundnuts, beans and rice – Malawi was more closely tied to world demand then ever before. But it was not a 'free international trade' in foodstuffs they were involved in, but rather a 'moral economy' imposed from London. The local government had a moral responsibility to inhibit speculation and free market racketeering in the interest of alleviating food shortages in the rest of the world; as the Director of Agriculture explained:

> I consider that the most rigid control should be established on locally-produced foodstuffs to ensure that every pound possible is available for assisting in the relief of food shortages elsewhere . . . along with control must go rigid price control for all foodstuffs exported – it cannot be correct morally to exploit world food shortages by allowing a few individuals who have not produced the goods to make enormous profits. (MNA, MP 10802 Director of Agriculture to Chief Secretary, 11/2/46)

The guaranteed prices, combined with the propaganda efforts of the Department of Agriculture did result in increased surpluses of some food crops – notably groundnuts and beans. In 1945, for instance, there was a 400 per cent increase in groundnut production over the previous year, and officials thought this largely due to the increased producer price. In the same year there was also a large increase in the sale of pulses. Much of this crop was grown by tenants on European estates who planted beans as a catch crop after their tobacco and winter maize (Department of Agriculture, *Annual Report*, 1945, p. 8).

International concern over food supply and pressure from London to produce surpluses and direct them to specified markets, was one of the major influences on government agricultural policy in colonial Malawi in this period. However, the staple cereal, maize, was not affected directly by the new situation as it was never considered seriously as an export crop. World maize prices had to be very high indeed for it to be worthwhile exporting from landlocked Malawi, and only briefly in the immediate post-war period did this seem a possibility.

Though the Metropolitan government attempted to dictate policy on food production and to exert control over surpluses, there were clear limitations to its powers. Probably more significant to food policy in the long run was the balance of interest groups within the country itself.

Throughout the 1940s the proportion of the population engaged in wage labour both inside and outside the country continued to rise.[2] Employment was generated within the country by the post-war tobacco 'boom'. Some of this growth in employment took place in the newer tobacco-producing areas of the Central Province (both on estates and amongst the peasant tobacco-producers there). Most formal wage employment, however, continued to be concentrated in the Southern Province – on tobacco estates, in tobacco-grading factories, on the tea plantations and in the construction of the railway. Table 5 indicates the distribution of what I shall call 'formal' wage employment in 1949. By formal employment I mean that employment which was outside the African peasant sector and which entered the statistics of the Department of Labour. The issue of how to feed the growing labour force of the Southern Province was a dominant one in the 1940s. The evidence indicates that whilst some parts of the Southern Province continued to produce surplus maize for the market *overall* the Southern Province was probably falling into food deficit in the 1940s and becoming increasingly dependent on the transfer of surpluses from the Central Province. I hope to show that this development was not a natural precursor of famine, and that the famine cannot be satisfactorily explained by it; but it is significant in other ways and a major factor influencing agricultural policy.

The evidence is difficult to disentangle as we only have figures for official maize sales. Just as in present-day analyses, so for the past the figures for foodstuffs marketed through official channels need to be treated with caution. Much of the internally generated Southern Province surplus probably was sold outside official markets. However, we do know that in the course of the 1940s employers in the south were becoming increasingly concerned over the problem of securing sufficient food supplies for their labour. In 1946 a Committee was set up to review the food situation in the Protectorate (MNA, MP 35/26 Foodstuffs Committee). This committee included representatives of the government and of both major groups of European employers – the tea and tobacco estate owners of the south, and the tobacco estate owners of the Central Province. The Southern Province employers put their case forcefully to the

Committee, for the provision of cheap and ready food supplies. The General Manager of the Railways expressed this view clearly:

The needs of the large labour force employed by the Railways rank equally with, if not in advance of, the needs of the inhabitants of a district. Because, having adopted an industrial mode of life, they are not able to grow their own food as can the villager. Their race is the same, they come in the same category of 'ward', and bellies get just as empty as do those of the villager. The foodstuffs resources of the Protectorate should be available equally to all its African inhabitants who are prepared to do a day's work. If a Railway African has to go short of food it is just as much a 'famine' as is a village *njala*, and it will as such, without doubt, get more publicity. (MNA, MP 35/26, Bucquet to Secretary, Foodstuffs Committee, 17/7/46.)

Most members of the Committee held to the 'substitution' argument which I have described above, and believed that high tobacco prices were responsible for the difficulties experienced by employers in the south in obtaining food supplies. With the Department of Agriculture already predisposed to see an agricultural crisis, and the government in general under external pressure to ensure national food self-sufficiency, the need for a new food policy came to be

Table 5 *Numbers in employment, 1949*

Southern Province	
Tobacco growing	9,657
Tea growing and manufacture	32,312
Tung	2,549
Mixed farming	4,524
Tobacco grading and packing	6,838
Brick-making	691
Building, contracting	2,584
Storekeeping, tailoring	877
Woodworking	169
Railways and lake transport	4,209
Road transport and garages	702
Engineering	153
Public and Municipal	900
Missions	200
Miscellaneous	1,265
Southern Province total	*67,630*
Central Province total	13,265
Northern Province total	2,159
Protectorate Total	*83,054*

Source: Labour Department, *Annual Report*, 1949.

expressed all round (MNA, MP 35/26, Minutes, 28/6/46). But the unanimous concern over food production was not accompanied by any agreement as to what should be done about it. A split developed between the employers of the south and those of the Central Province. Some representatives of Southern employers recommended that a guaranteed price should be established for maize in order to encourage increased production. Representatives of the Central Province employers, however, were anxious to avoid this. Operating in areas not experiencing land pressure and less uniformly covered by marketing systems, the Central Province tobacco estate owners had often established their own maize-buying monopolies and wanted above all to avoid any government interference which might raise the prices they had to pay. They argued that a guaranteed price for foodstuffs would not act as an incentive to increased production, as the African farmer would simply produce less (MNA, MP 35/26, Minutes, 18/7/46).

The Department of Agriculture was in favour of the centralisation of maize marketing through an extension of the Marketing of Native Produce Ordinance of 1938, which as yet did not cover maize. It was not, however, in favour of any narrowing in the differentials between the price of maize and that of tobacco, groundnuts and other cash crops. The agriculturalists argued, in an extension of the 'Malthusian crisis' theory, that any increase in the price of maize paid to the grower would result in a disastrous extension of maize monoculture, and a rapid increase in the rate of soil erosion.[3] At the back of the official mind also, was the consciousness that the country needed to produce export crops in order to secure its livelihood, and that a surplus of maize would be an embarrassment and not an exportable asset. Essentially the Department of Agriculture walked a tightrope. It wanted to ensure that the country would be self-sufficient in maize, but it didn't want a huge surplus; it wanted maize yields to increase, but without the incentive of a price rise and without the extension of cultivation.

Attention focused on the Central Province. It was here that land was available for the production of the maize surpluses upon which the south came to depend more and more. These surpluses, in the view of the government and the southern employers, had to be captured and controlled. Eventually the powerful lobby of Central Province Europeans had to be overruled and their maize-buying monopolies destroyed, to enable a government monopoly to function.

> with the exception of Lilongwe district [in the Central Province] all the main producing areas have been brought under the Ordinance and it is suggested that the time has now come to investigate more closely the claim of Lilongwe to resist incorporation . . . It is possible, indeed probable, that a continuance of the 'status quo' is advantageous to a minority of local residents of the district but it is suggested that a greater benefit to the majority and to the Protectorate generally would be secured by participation in the marketing organisation. (MNA, MP 35/26, Director of Agriculture, 14/7/46.)

Accordingly a Maize Control Ordinance was passed in 1946 and a Maize Control Board established. From the beginning of the 1947 harvest this organisation attempted to centralise the buying and distribution of maize surpluses nationwide.

In its first year of operation the Board fixed the price for maize to be paid to the producer at 3 lb per penny in the Central and Northern Provinces, and 2 lb per penny in most of the Southern Province (Maize Control Board, *Report*, 1947–8). In all, 7,671.6 tons of maize were purchased, falling far short of the estimated requirements of consumers of 17,496 tons. Of the total of 7,671.6 tons, 2,674.5 were purchased in the Southern Province for allocation to Southern Province consumers; 1,901.5 tons were purchased in the Central Province for sale to consumers there, and 3,095.6 tons were purchased in the Central Province for sale to Southern Province consumers. Most of the surplus maize was produced on Native Trust Land, with only 445 tons of the Central Province surplus having been produced on private estates, and only 39.7 tons of the Southern Province total. As the detailed figures reveal, much of the Southern Province total came from markets in Mulanje District,[4] and much less was bought from the immediate environs of Blantyre. It is possible that some of this Mulanje district maize was produced in Mozambique and smuggled over the border, but some of it also derived from areas which were relatively remote and less likely to be covered by unofficial marketing channels. The Maize Control Board had clearly performed one of its tasks, which was to divert Central Province surpluses to the south, but the overall volume of maize purchased was disappointing. The Board had not operated without opposition

Table 6 *Maize Control Board: Summary of markets and purchases in short tons, 1947–8*

Southern Province	
Mulanje District	2,189.6 tons
Thyolo District	402.7
Blantyre	82.2
	2,674.5
Central Province	
Lilongwe District	3,063.2
Dedza District	1,792.9
Dowa District	118.1
Kota Kota District	22.9
	4,997.1
Total purchases:	7,671,6

Source: Maize Control Board, *Report*, 1947–8, p. 6.

from vested interests. The 1947 Annual Report indicated this, the Board stating its 'appreciation of the loyal cooperation of its buyers and transport agents and of those members of the public who supported it in the performance of its unpleasant duties' (Maize Control Board, *Report*, 1947–8, p. 5).

The 1948 buying season was very disappointing. The prices paid to producers remained the same, but the volume of purchases fell (Maize Control Board, *Report*, 1948–9). Only 1,402.9 short tons were purchased in the Southern Province, where it appeared that producers were holding back their crop in the hope of receiving higher prices in the 'scarce' season. In the Central Province 5,753 tons were purchased, of which 3,613.6 were transferred to Southern Province buyers. Altogether then a total of 7,155.9 short tons were purchased, while estimated consumers' requirements amounted to 18,376.7 short tons.

When the famine struck in 1949 this unpopular organisation received much of the blame for the low stocks of food in the country and the consequent need to import. A typical expression of this view is found in the long letter written to the *Nyasaland Times* by a European estate owner who signed himself 'Sylva':

> The Board has failed to carry out its primary objective. This was . . . the stimulation of the production of maize, by preventing the exploitation of the grower in the less accessible parts of the Protectorate . . . In those days, that is to say when the MCB was first established, there was no shortage of maize, and this encouragement which was to be given to the maize grower – in what can be conveniently described as the Dead North – was to provide him with a cash economy, provide more food for Africans, and relieve the strain on the overworked lands of the Southern Province . . . When the MCB came into existence it became unlawful – as in the case of tobacco – for persons other than the agents of Government, to purchase maize from anyone but their own tenants. But unlike tobacco, maize is a crop that people are not very anxious to handle. It was performed by the Planter and the Indian Trader as a service to the African, and naturally the buyers endeavour to protect themselves from financial loss. Consequently, in the first year's operation of the MCB in districts where maize buying stations were few and far between, maize rotted in the villages . . . (*Nyasaland Times*, vol. 52, no. 14, 21/2/49, p. 5.)

In the Budget debate in the Legislative Council of January 1949 the Director of Agriculture acknowledged that there had been some faults in the operation of the MCB, but defended its overall record, claiming that without it he doubted 'whether the important consumers in the urban areas, such as the Railways, public utility undertakings and factories, would have obtained any supplies at all' (reported in *Nyasaland Times*, vol. 52, no. 1, 6/1/49, p. 2).

It was not only amongst European employers that the operations of the Maize Control Board were unpopular. In his letter 'Sylva' omitted to mention the increasing body of African maize traders who, along with the 'Planter and the Indian Trader' had performed the task of moving maize surpluses from one area to another. In the course of the 1940s reports indicate that this group of entrepreneurs had increased in number. Returning migrants and demobbed soldiers invested their earnings in maize mills, and some bought lorries to facilitate the purchase of maize from a wide area (MNA, MP 34/10, Director of Agriculture, 2/5/49). The shortage of consumer goods for sale immediately after the war, far from inhibiting economic growth as some observers claimed, may in fact have spurred investment by small capitalists in this kind of service industry.[5] Certainly the maize-mill owners and traders feature prominently in the stories of the famine told in Blantyre District.

The introduction of the Maize Control legislation must be seen against a background not only of pressure from European employers for cheap food supplies, but also of the intense government hostility to African maize traders. In the original drafting of the Maize Control Ordinance African traders had been excluded from the prohibition on private trading in maize, but this was later amended to include them. Some senior officials, the future Director of Agriculture, Kettlewell, amongst them, were especially worried by the practice of maize-mill owners of taking milling fees in kind (MNA, MP 34/10, Kettlewell to Director of Agriculture, 26/5/49). This constituted an invisible device by which they could accumulate large maize stocks which might otherwise have found their way to official markets.

How far the Maize Control Ordinance was effective in inhibiting the activities of African traders is not, however, easy to discern. If the legislation did inhibit independent traders, and if the Board's own operations were as inefficient as some observers claimed, then it could be argued that this government intervention in food markets was a major cause of the famine. The letter writer, 'Sylva' claimed just this: that because of the inefficient workings of the Board, and because of the absence of convenient markets for producers in many areas, the potential maize surplus producers cut back their acreages so that when a drought occurred in 1949 food stocks in the villages were already dangerously low.

Taken as a whole, however, the archival evidence is more ambiguous and presents a more complicated picture. In some parts of the country – particularly in border areas and in areas which were very close to the final consumers of maize – a black market appears to have operated successfully, and for such areas the operations of the Maize Control Board were marginal. This was indicated in the 1948 Annual Report for the Southern Province:

> the amount of maize and other foodstuffs sold through the native produce markets fell very considerably – the amount offered for sale was only 25% of the amount sold in 1946. These figures appear to show that the production of food crops must have deteriorated considerably in the course of two years, but it would be quite wrong to draw such a conclusion for there has been a very great increase in the inter-African trade in these foodstuffs resulting from the dissatisfaction with prices offered in Native Produce Markets . . . African-owned power-driven maize mills are now quite common in all districts except Fort Johnston and the Lower River, and the number of African-

owned mills now form quite a high percentage of the whole . . . An increasing number of Africans are concentrated in the trading of foodstuffs, and many of these men now own their own transport in connection with this trade. (MNA, NS 3/1/13, p. 6)

If informal markets continued to operate in much of the Southern Province, the complaints of African traders nevertheless indicate that in some parts control was effective. In 1947 the Blantyre delegate to the Nyasaland African Congress complained about the control being exerted over African traders:

He said he was not quite clear how this Board [the Maize Control Board] was established and its functioning, and that since it was established many African traders, whose only source of making an honest living was by selling produce such as maize in the township markets, are failing to obtain permits for the purchase of maize, and others who tried to purchase some without permits after failing to obtain the permits have been convicted and their purchased produce confiscated. (MNA, MP 34/1, Minutes of NAC, 26/9/47)

In order to assess the contribution of government intervention in food marketing in bringing about the famine, we need to look at a whole range of policies which may have inhibited surplus maize production in the period leading up to 1949. It is clear that the operation of the Maize Control Board was not uniformly effective, and therefore we must reject any simplistic explanation blaming this organisation for the failure of food supply. It would appear that in much of the Southern Province the informal markets for foodstuffs continued to operate and black market prices to dominate. If we consider, however, that in all likelihood the Southern Province was no longer able to feed itself entirely, then our attention must shift again to the growers of the Central Province. It is for this area that a combination of high tobacco prices, low official prices for maize and marketing uncertainties may have combined to militate against the production of maize surpluses in the late 1940s. It was here that more African farmers had the option of extending their maize gardens if conditions were right, but being more distant from the Southern Province consumers they were also more vulnerable to hiccoughs in the marketing system. A surplus maize producer in Chiradzulu District could take his own maize to the urban market, while a producer in a remote corner of the Lilongwe plain could not. The government was aware that the Central Province was where the potential surpluses were, and for this reason they overruled the European interests there in an attempt to establish an official buying monopoly. What the government was not prepared to do, however, was to raise the official price for maize.

No-one disputed that the price was low, and especially when compared to the prices paid in neighbouring countries. Occasionally officials outside the Department of Agriculture expressed some disquiet over this. In 1947 the Chief Secretary suggested that the differential between the price of maize and those for other crops be narrowed (MNA, MP 4/68, Chief Secretary to Director of Agriculture, 25/10/47). But as we have seen, there was a very powerful coalition of interests against this. Not only were the employers of labour, who sat on the Food Committee, concerned at the consequences of a price rise for their wages bill, but the Department of Agriculture remained vehemently opposed to a price increase for 'environmental' reasons. The Chief Secretary was persuaded of the unsoundness of his view.

The overall effect of government policies in pricing, marketing, and conservation, seems to have been to cause a general feeling of uncertainty and dissatisfaction amongst surplus-producing Africans. This is well expressed in a statement by the Mulanje Native Foodstuffs Growers Association, which argued that African producers were being asked to change their agricultural ways and to invest more labour for no return. Furthermore, the government was intervening in their right to obtain the best price from the consumer:

> The creation of Nyasaland Africans were created with loving kindness and modesty heart. Since the advent of the whiteman they had and still are showing their obedience and help the masters in many different ways and also loyal to the government. When they are employed the wages they get is insufficient it could only count as *posho*. They have big families to support and the wages they earn is very low for buying clothes, paying taxes, school fees and many more requirement . . . Some years ago Nyasaland Africans used to scratch on the top of the earth in hoeing their gardens according to their method without the Agricultural Officer's instructions and had to harvest plenty of maize and when sold had to get much money, £5 or £6 for one ton . . . People loose [*sic*] money and their energy exhausting now in following the new ways of hoeing their gardens but without benefit – both their money and power wasted for nothing. Taking the maize to the buyers they return home with only one penny in the hand for transport only for the basketful of maize which he or she carried. The people are greatly murmuring and discourage to follow the AO's instructions about the present scheme of tilling the gardens, because of the pay they receive by selling any of their produce, while the good soil vanished and the foodstuffs diminishing . . . the greatest desire of Nyasaland Africans is that they should arrange prices themselves for their produce etc. and if buyers want them they can buy them. (MNA, NS 1/3/9, Minutes, 20/4/44)

This plea for non-intervention was made on the part of growers in the south, close to a ready market provided by the tea estates. It was not echoed everywhere, as contemporary discussions in the African Provincial Council showed. In remoter areas growers sometimes viewed the possibility of a free market system with less enthusiasm, and welcomed the idea of government minimum prices for their produce (MNA, MP 34/1, Minutes of Southern Province African Council, 30/9/46).

Both the theories discussed in this chapter – the 'substitution' theory and the 'marketing board' theory – reflect the current debates on food supply problems discussed in the Introduction. One school of thought has argued that the growth of commercialisation in agriculture in the colonial period disrupted traditional economies and made them increasingly vulnerable to crises of subsistence.

According to this argument, communities of subsistence producers might be turned into cash-croppers, vulnerable to any fluctuations in world prices for their crops; or they might be turned into a reserve of labour, their families' food production jeopardised by the absence of male workers. Both of these arguments were used by observers in Malawi in the 1940s, but it should be clear from the evidence presented in this chapter that neither argument in itself can explain the failure of food supply in 1949.

To begin with, there is no conclusive evidence to show that individual farmers grew tobacco at the expense of maize, though at an aggregate level the differentials in price between the two crops did serve to undermine national food supply. It is crucial to understand, however, that it was not the tobacco farmers who suffered food shortages, for in general they were better endowed with land than the average, and they were also more likely than most to have the cash to buy food and make up any household deficit.

In the course of the 1940s Southern Malawi as a whole was moving into food deficit and becoming more dependent on the transfer of foodstuffs, through both official and unofficial channels, from Central Province growers. In order to understand the vulnerability of some communities in the south, then, we do need to analyse the workings of the national food market, and it is here that the arguments over pricing and the operation of marketing boards come in.

In a survey of Africa, Douglas Rimmer has drawn attention to the large extent of economic regulation, particularly in the period after the Second World War (Rimmer, 1983). He argues that this intervention muted the forces of capitalism and delayed the incorporation of African communities into wider economies. Michael Cowen has argued for Kenya that food supply problems arose from the insulation of internal food markets from international markets, and from the attempts of both colonial and post-colonial governments to segment local food markets in order better to control them (Cowen, 1983). He goes on to argue that food supply problems arise when local food markets are too little integrated, and when the development of a market in foodstuffs has not matched the growth of internationally determined specialisation in commodity production.

We have seen that in the case of colonial Malawi this argument has something to recommend it. At the same time, however, it has limitations. The Maize Control legislation was not uniformly or totally effective, and so government intervention cannot be assumed to be the cause of food supply problems in all areas and at all times. Furthermore, we cannot assume that without state control over food markets all would have been well, and Sara Berry has made this point for Africa as a whole (Berry, 1984). As we have seen, in the post-war period the world food market was anything but free – it was controlled and directed, prices were fixed at an international level, and political considerations were paramount. Following Sara Berry's analysis and that of Mike Watts for Nigeria

(Watts, 1983), however, we can argue for colonial Malawi that the uneven pattern of commercialisation in agriculture, and the uneven application of controls, contributed to the increased risks of food shortage experienced by some communities. This became especially significant when taken in combination with increasing intervention in farming systems on the part of the Department of Agriculture, the undermining of traditional insurance mechanisms, the pressure of population in some areas and the migration of communities to agriculturally marginal districts.

In the Introduction it was argued that some degree of separation was needed in the analysis of long-term food supply problems and the immediate problem of famine. In Chapter 2 and Chapter 3 I have attempted to analyse critically contemporary analyses of longer-term food supply problems in late colonial Malawi, and to build up an independent picture of how a number of factors combined to create a degree of national food insecurity in 1949. At this stage, however, it is necessary to return to an analysis of the famine itself, and to Sen's question of *who* starved, when and where. To argue, as I have done, that in the post-war period the Southern Province as a whole was moving into food deficit, is not in itself sufficient to explain the famine. We know from both oral and written sources that only some sections of the Southern Province African community suffered in 1949–50, and that available food supplies were not distributed evenly either within village communities, or within smaller family groups. To understand this we need to return again to the question of how different groups earned their entitlement to food in normal times, and how these entitlements were affected by the relative shortage occasioned by the drought.

Chapter 2 argued that over a long period people in the more crowded parts of the Southern Province had calculated their 'subsistence' needs with reference to the possibilities for exchange. By the post-war period the most common form of exchange was that involving the sale of labour. In the next chapter I analyse the structure of employment amongst the communities affected by the famine, and argue that this is a vital 'missing element' in the contemporary models. The analysis of employment also connects closely with the question of government famine policy and the nature of its intervention, and leads further to an examination of the role of gender in determining the structure of suffering in 1949–50.

4

Food entitlement and employment

ꙮ

The immediate post-war period in Malawi was one of quite rapid economic change. In Southern Malawi long-term changes such as population growth combined in this period with an increase in wage employment (both within and outside the country), the enforcement of government conservation regulations in agriculture, and the increased circulation of money within African communities. We certainly need to look beyond purely agricultural production factors if we are to understand the nature of the famine, because in the area hardest hit a large percentage of households depended for their livelihood on a combination of wage-earning, agricultural production, and what would now be termed 'informal sector' activity.

As we have seen, an important feature of the 1940s in this area was the growth of the towns of Blantyre and Limbe, and the increase in public works in the district. This growth was allied to the post-war 'tobacco boom' which resulted, not only in the expansion of estate and peasant tobacco production, but also in generally higher levels of investment in urban property. For the people of Blantyre District and neighbouring districts this meant that there was an increased demand for labour in the area – both skilled and unskilled – and wage-levels rose. To some extent, then, the increasing congestion on Native Trust Land around Blantyre may have been a response to the increase in employment opportunities in the area and to the demand for service industries. According to the Labour Department's report for 1949, in March of that year there was a total of 67,630 people employed in European or Indian-run enterprises in the Southern Province, the vast majority of whom were male employees in the tea and tobacco industries. The wages for unskilled labour had risen to an average of £1 2s. 6d. per month (inclusive of a food allowance) compared with an average wage in 1939 of 6s. to 10s. (Labour Department, *Annual Report*, 1949). Hand in hand with this growth in wage employment went the growth of craft and service industries – this group including butchers, dairymen, traders in fish and vegetables, knife-makers, charcoal burners, lime burners (supplying the building industry), carpenters, canteen-owners, shoe-repairers, and, most importantly, beer brewers. Beer brewing and *kachasu* distillation had become a major industry around Blantyre by the 1940s, and I discuss its implications for the economic position of women in Chapter 5.

Most villages around Blantyre, and most families, relied on a combination of different sources of income. Later surveys conducted in the 1950s give some indication of this. Bettison and Rigby's account of the patterns of income and expenditure in three peri-urban villages of Blantyre shows the diverse sources of income obtaining in the 1950s (Bettison and Rigby, 1961). These included within one village cash wages, agricultural produce sales, beer and *kachasu* sales, trading sales, meat and milk sales, 'services rendered', entertaining and gambling, credit received and loans repaid, gifts, and money from 'boyfriends'. A diversity of income was important, given the insecure nature of most employment and the low level of wages. For although in the 1940s cash wages had risen quite markedly, so too had the urban cost of living. Calculations made in 1947 estimated that in the years between 1939 and 1947 the cost of living for an African urban resident in Blantyre had risen by 100 per cent unless he was in a position to provide most of his food supplies, in which case the figure was 50 to 60 per cent (MNA, NSB 3/12/1, DC Blantyre to PC Southern Province, 2/1/47). This fact would also help to explain why, in the course of the 1940s, labour emigration from Blantyre District, and other parts of the Southern Province, had increased markedly. In 1941, 1,344 labour emigrants' passes had been issued to men from Blantyre and Central Shire Districts, and by 1944 this annual figure had risen to 2,116 (MNA, NSB 7/1/6). According to the Department of Labour's report for 1948, in the Southern Province as a whole 6.4 per cent of men over the age of eighteen were absent as migrants, and the incidence by district is shown in Table 7.

Table 7 *Percentage average exodus of males over eighteen years (Southern Province)*

Zomba	4.2
Liwonde	8.4
Fort Johnston	10.4
Blantyre	6.0
Chiradzulu	11.5
Mulanje	5.9
Cholo	3.4
Chikwawa, Port Herald	6.1

Source: Nyasaland Protectorate, Labour Department, *Annual Report*, 1948.

As estate owners effectively prevented their male tenants from emigrating (the penalty was family eviction), we must assume that most migrants came from Native Trust Land. Evidence from the 1950s indicates that absenteeism was most pronounced from the remoter areas of Trust Land in the valley, where agricultural production was hazardous and where the famine had its focus (Bettison, 1958). This evidence may, of course, reflect post-famine adjustments and so cannot be used to describe the 1940s. It seems quite likely, however, that migrants might come from areas most remote from local employment and trading opportunities, or from areas of very heavy congestion. This, at least, is what is implied by the Southern Province figures as a whole.

Side by side with Native Trust Land dwellers lived tenants on European estates. They generally enjoyed greater access to land and less crowded conditions, but, as we have seen, for many this did not outweigh the disadvantages of tenancy (White, 1987). The 1930s and 1940s had seen a shift in African tobacco production from Native Trust Land dwellers to estate tenants, but how far these tenants benefited from the high tobacco prices of the post-war period depended to some extent on the policies of individual managers. The fact that there had been no great shift to the estates on the part of the crowded population of Native Trust Lands indicates the disadvantages of tenancy agreements in normal times. When the famine occurred, however, many tenants found themselves privileged by virtue of their categorisation as 'employees'.

Within the broad category of Native Trust Land dwellers there were very significant economic divisions. One economic group consisted of skilled employees (artisans, teachers and clerks) combined with the wealthier self-employed craftsmen and businessmen (including maize traders). I have grouped these people together despite the variations in their occupations, because the evidence indicates that many of the wealthier self-employed had originally earned their capital through formal employment predicated on a degree of educational attainment. Teachers and clerks retired to become maize-mill owners, builders and traders, as did the wealthier of the returned migrants. Although this was a relatively small group, much of the analysis of the structure of the famine hinges on the development of this group in the 1940s. We have no figures for the self-employed of this group, but we do have some for skilled employees in the 'formal Sector'.

In 1949 of the total of 83,054 people employed by European and Indian enterprises in the entire country, 4,694 were clerks and artisans (Nyasaland Protectorate, Labour Report, 1949). This small group became increasingly economically and politically significant in the 1940s, providing the leadership of the new nationalist movement, and within a local area their activities could have a large impact. In the Domasi area of Zomba District, for instance, where a Community Development Scheme was started in 1949, there was a small group of clerks and retired clerks who were also involved in timber trading and brick-making. Their material standard of living seemed to be quite high 'judging by their clothing, the use of door and window frames and furniture, the possession of bicycles and gramophones, and the amount of money available for shopping, initiation fees, beer, court fees and compensation in civil cases' (MNA, MP 19376, p. 12). Such people had larger than average land-holdings as well as higher than average earnings through employment or trade. They were also employers of labour, hiring men and women to work in their enterprises and to perform casual *ganyu* labour on their fields. This form of employment, unlike the formal sort, does not show up in the official statistics, but was of great importance to the local economy.

There are a number of reasons for thinking that the fortunes of this group improved in the post-war period. Firstly, some of this group were peasant tobacco farmers benefiting from the rise in prices. If they were not themselves tobacco growers, as traders they could reap rewards from the increased prosperity of African tobacco producers in their areas. This money in the hands of cash-crop producers was combined with the earnings of disbanded soldiers who had fought in the war, creating what many Europeans regarded as a glut of money in African hands. Immediately after the war imports were restricted and expensive, with cloth and clothing in some places virtually unobtainable. A much smaller proportion of African earnings than normal was thus being spent on imports. The government concluded that money was actually being hoarded in mattresses and under floorboards (MNA, LB 5/4/1, 13/11/46). However, when Phyllis Deane investigated this question she came to the conclusion that money *was* being circulated, but circulated in the African sector where there was an increased velocity of trade. Unable to buy imported items, people instead spent what cash they had on building better houses, and eating a more varied diet, and these tendencies explain the growth of the African building industry and service sector around Blantyre at this time.[1] As we have already seen, officials also remarked on the increasing number of African traders who owned motorised transport and maize mills and who capitalised on the increasing demand for food from urban dwellers.

Income differentials within the formal sector of employment were very marked. A survey in 1948 produced the following figures for the distribution of income amongst Africans in one sub-sector of the economy which was important in the Southern Province – central government and mission employment. The same study argued that the income accruing to the wealthier members of society was distributed through the payment of wages for services:

> The family of an African clerk, earning an annual income of £30 or more, on average lives in the same village as the family of a shop assistant earning less than £15 per annum from all sources . . . One of the reasons why the standard of living in terms of the

consumption of material things would not vary greatly between one African and another is that the richer ones pay for services that the poorer ones would do for themselves e.g. thatching, (p. 12)

If this analysis is correct then it would indicate that increasing economic differentiation amongst the African population in this period was manifested above all in an increase in employment of Africans by Africans, and that this tendency was enhanced by the post-war shortage of consumer goods.

Although, as we have seen, the official price of maize was depressed in the 1940s, nevertheless this was a prosperous period for anyone involved in the marketing of foodstuffs, since the black market price in the Southern Province rose with the increase in demand.[2] The trade was particularly profitable for those with enough money to invest in motorised transport, who could thus bring cheaper maize from more remote areas to the market centres. It is not surprising that this group of traders resisted government attempts to centralise and control the trade in maize. Typically maize traders in the Blantyre District were retired government employees or returned labour migrants, who also had access to large plots of land and were themselves surplus producers. It was from amongst this group that aspirants to the Department of Agriculture's 'Master Farmer' scheme were drawn.[3] This scheme singled out the 'progressive' individuals for credit facilities and extension advice, in an attempt to create an elite of agriculturalists practising mixed farming and conservation measures, who would then act as a model for the rest of their community. The scheme was born partly of the Department's increasing frustration with the response of the 'masses' to its advice, and the growing pessimism (which I have outlined in Chapter 2) over the possibilities of peasant agriculture without far-reaching reform. As Kettlewell said in 1946, 'We have all been searching for years for the average native who will do exactly what he is told, when he is told, but we have

Table 8 *Government and mission employees: income distribution*

Income group	Numbers	Average earnings
£12 and under	19,844	£7.5
£13–£20	3,157	£15.7
£21–£30	759	£25.0
£31–	650	£46.2
	24,410	£18.4

Source: Great Britain, Public Record Office, CO 852/1035/2, Memo on Nyasaland Economy.

not yet found him. There are the more progressive native agriculturalists who might be relied upon to cooperate fully, but they are invariably larger farmers, employers of labour and scarcely "average"' (MNA, MP 3/2 Kettlewell to Director of Agriculture, 4/1/46).

As employers of labour the Master Farmer aspirants and maize traders had a critical role in structuring the famine. As was indicated in the Introduction, the extension of commercial relations in agriculture has been seen in different ways by the analysts of famine. In McAlpin's work on India (McAlpin, 1983), the extension of the labour market in particular is seen as a crucial factor ultimately leading to the decline of famine in India, and more recent evidence from Africa shows the importance of employment in rescuing communities from starvation. Other work, however, views the commercialisation of labour within rural communities as one factor dissolving the solidarity of the group, and undermining the traditional mechanisms of survival inherent in the peasant 'moral economy' (see Introduction). It would seem important here to separate national and local labour markets. McAlpin is discussing the development of a wider labour market, along with the extension of communications which enabled people to move easily from one area to another of India in response to employment opportunities. In the face of drought a local labour market could often collapse, and thus the wider market became crucial. The undermining of 'traditional' famine-averting mechanisms and the dissolution of the village community and its norms is seen in this model to be outweighed by the greater advantages afforded by specialisation in the wider economy.

The evidence of the 1949 famine in this respect is not easy to analyse, but provides some insights into the process of commercialisation of labour in a local community. This evidence comes almost entirely from oral testimony and it is hazardous to generalise from it, but nevertheless some interesting points emerge.

As we have seen, in the course of the 1940s a significant labour market had developed within the African communities of Blantyre District and the rest of the Southern Province, and was centred around the group we have discussed – the wealthier traders, farmers and entrepreneurs. Most of the labour demanded by this group was linked to agricultural production and was thus precarious in the event of a drought. The evidence of the 1949 famine, however, indicates that the demand for agricultural *ganyu* labour held up for a while, though it was insufficient to meet the needs of the whole community, and did eventually collapse. The fact that it held up at all was largely due to the fact that the larger farmers usually had access to *dambo* land, some of which remained productive even in the drought and on which labour continued to be employed in small numbers. Oral testimony is agreed that those with *dambo* land were extremely fortunate. Mr Chisale, for instance, lived in Chief Machinjiri's area. His dry-land crop of maize and groundnuts failed completely in 1949, but his vegetable garden in a wet *dambo* area continued to produce. He sold the vegetables, and with the money earned he was able to buy two bags of maize in Ntcheu which lasted him and his family two months. He repeated this several times during the year.[4] Mr Katsabola and Mr Diliza, both from Lunzu, both employed labour throughout the famine, some of this on their *dambo* plots, but more frequently in other activities which were less vulnerable to drought.[5] Mr Katsabola had a shop and farm in Lunzu, but was also in the business of moulding bricks. He employed people to cut trees (for burning the bricks), draw water and cut elephant grass for covering the bricks against sunlight. With the money earned the people who worked for him were able to buy maize from the government depots which opened in the area. Mr Kumpanda had a maize trading business in Lunzu and in 1949 he had a store of twenty bags of maize which he sold to people who came from Lunzu, Lirangwe and Chileka. Those who did not have cash did *ganyu* labour for him instead.[6] Mr Diliza also had a maize trading business and a truck which enabled him to buy from a wide area. At the end of 1948 he had a store of thirty bags of maize which he sold (on a rationed basis) in 1949. Those who had no cash worked for him in moulding bricks and cutting trees.[7] Mrs Damalesi, whose father was a prominent farmer in Lirangwe at the time, remembers that her family had a store of maize, and that people gathered in large numbers at their house to beg or buy maize. She says that her father gave a lot of maize away, but sold it to others.[8]

The behaviour of this privileged group during the famine is described in very contrasting ways by other informants. The evidence points to the fact that the maize traders made a killing in 1949, but that they were also involved in relationships of a non-capitalistic character, and that there was some strong social pressure on them to behave in a 'charitable' way. It seems that many of them did give maize away to their kin, and supported large groups of people both in this way and by employing labour. Patron/client relationships of a kind commonly described for an earlier period survived in one form or another. But these relationships were by their nature limited in scope, and towards the rest of the population they acted with commercial motives in mind. How they defined who would and who would not receive their 'charity' within a given community is of course the interesting question, but one which it is not possible to answer in detail from the evidence available. What is clear, however, is that many members of the communities affected by the famine felt that the maize traders' activities were in some sense immoral, and this is brought out in the widespread stories of their rapaciousness.

One of the most common stories of the famine is that recounted in Chapter 1 concerning its causation. According to this story, those who were engaged in moulding and burning bricks were first in line for accusation as being responsible for 'holding the rain'. Although the straightforward explanation for this was that their work would be spoilt by rain and so they had good reason to 'hold it', the accusation clearly had deeper connotations. The oral evidence is clear that the brick-makers of Lunzu and Lirangwe were also often the larger farmers and maize traders, and so this story reflects more generally on the jealousy and suspicion of this group. More explicit is the widespread account of how the maize-mill owners showed their greed as the famine wore on. This story is recounted by a man who worked as an assistant in a maize mill at the time, but is also widespread amongst women in the area.[9] At the beginning of the famine, the maize mills worked as normal. There were enough people in the community with cash to pay milling fees, and enough people with maize to mill. At this time those without any food and money would come to the mills and scrape up from the floor the flour which fell from the machine. As time wore on, however, so business became slacker, and so also the maize-mill owners became more conscious of the value of even the smallest amount of flour. Not only did they prevent women from scraping up the 'escaped' flour, but, as the story goes, they also collected this flour at the end of the day and sold it in the market.

The maize traders and mill owners were not only a significant group within their communities, but some of their representatives also had the ear of the government during the famine. I have described in Chapter 1 the government's concern about the unfavourable reports of the famine which were circulating amongst migrants outside the country. This group had close contacts with migrants, and were sometimes former migrants themselves. They were also politically influential within their communities, and though the government determined to work via the constituted 'traditional elite' – the Native Authorities and Village Headmen – it could ill afford to ignore the views of this other elite. The *Nyasaland Times* published letters by educated urbanites protesting at the price at which the government was selling maize in the early stages of the famine, and in the Southern Province Provincial Council there were complaints about the handling of the famine. In particular, Mr Charles Mlanga, who was an estate owner, protested over the government's attempts at the start of the famine to control the movement of people and food from one district to another. This policy had been pursued in earlier, less severe famines (in 1912 and 1922 for instance), but was probably counter-productive, as Mr Mlanga pointed out:

Mr Mlanga: In Olden Times those who were short of food went elsewhere to buy their requirements by performing *kasuma* [work for food]. Will Government explain why orders have been given prohibiting this practice? Is it Government's intention to take this 'trade' to itself?

The President (Provincial Commissioner, Southern Province) explained that it was not Government's intention to take this 'trade' to itself. When the emergency caused by the drought became acute, some District Commissioners wished to prevent the export of foodstuffs from their districts and issued orders under the Emergency Regulations prohibiting the movement of food out of their districts. It was soon realised that this prohibition caused hardship and the ban was subsequently cancelled. (MNA, MP 12655, Southern Province Provincial Council, 17–21/4/50)

The maize traders and mill owners were advocates of a 'free trade' policy during the famine, and for clear reasons. The government itself was torn between interventionist and non-interventionist inclinations, as we shall see when we come to examine the stories of less fortunate groups.

One such group consisted of the smaller self-employed artisans and traders in the service sector. Along with the businesses of the larger entrepreneurs, this sector had grown in the 1940s and was central to the economy of the immediate peri-urban villages, where land was in short supply. Such activities were also important in the more rural areas of Blantyre District, however, and this included the Middle Shire areas around Lunzu, Lirangwe and Matope. Around Blantyre there were the butchers, tailors, shoe-repairers, and other occupational groups which I have already described, as well as the women beer brewers and *kachasu* distillers whose case will be examined later in more detail. Away from the town, where the demand for such services was more limited, there were other groups of self-employed people who combined craftwork with agricultural production. Along the river at Matope, for instance, there was a large mat-making industry. There were people at Lirangwe who made barkcloth sacks for the lime-burners. One village in Machinjiri's area was said to be inhabited 'entirely by makers of knives which they fashion from old hoop iron and sell at 3d. each or more in the townships' (MNA, NSB 7/4/1 Ulendo in Machinjiri and Somba, April 1947).

Amartya Sen has described the vulnerability of such groups in other famines (Sen, 1981). In 1943 in Bengal, for instance, it was the community of barbers who dominated amongst the destitute. The experiences of members of this self-employed group in the 1949 famine were varied, but in general they were a vulnerable section of the population. While demand held up for some service industries, others collapsed entirely. In the description of the famine in Chapter 1, I described the case of the tailor whose business dried up, but who had money saved with which he could buy food in Ntcheu. Others were less fortunate in not having savings, and as the famine wore on, so demand fell for luxury food items and for services such as laundering and shoe-repairing. One informant had been a manufacturer and seller of mattresses until 1949 when the business collapsed and he turned his hand to small-scale maize trading.[10] Many women, whose entire livelihoods depended on the manufacture and sale of alcohol, were left completely destitute by the fall in demand and the government emergency prohibition of their activities in the famine.

As we have already seen, the demand for fish declined, to the extent that dried fish was actually exported from the country during the famine. Likewise, the market was flooded with meat, and when the people of Mwanza refused to buy goats 'because they changed into snakes when their owners left', this may have been reflecting a glut.

It took some time, however, for demand for services and luxuries to collapse, and so this group did not necessarily suffer immediately from the consequences of the drought on the local economy; but as the famine wore on, and as local supplies of food became more and more scarce, so this group also became more dependent on what was provided by the government. It was at this stage that some of them suffered as a result of the assumptions behind government relief policy. As self-employed people rather than 'legitimate employees' they were not given privileged access to government food supplies. Furthermore, those living in Blantyre itself could fall victim to the policy of sending back to their villages any urban dwellers who were unemployed or 'vagrant'.

The distribution of 'legitimate employment' is the key to understanding the structure of the 1949 famine. The interaction of existing economic structures and the biases of government famine relief policy must be understood if we are to make sense of who starved and why. The oral evidence indicates that those who were in 'formal' wage employment were privileged in the famine relief policy. By 'formal employment' I mean here that provided by European and Indian employers and by the government itself, as distinguished from the intra-African employment I have already described. Those in low wage formal employment in normal times may have been less well-off than the self-employed service workers, but during the famine their 'legitimacy' in the eyes of the government protected them against the worst effects of food shortage. Such 'formal' low-waged employees included tenants on estates, railway workers, agricultural labourers, road labourers for the government, tobacco factory workers, and they were almost entirely men.

As was described in Chapter 1, the initial response of the government to the drought and impending food shortage was to ensure a food supply to the urban workers of Blantyre and Limbe. The urban workers were seen to be potentially politically volatile, but also their employers were able to exert pressure on the government, just as they had throughout the 1940s on the matter of the maize price. In February 1949, for instance, the Chamber of Commerce voiced its criticisms about the running of the government maize stall in Blantyre market – criticisms which were more likely to receive the attention of the authorities than were those of the African buyers themselves. Mr Hess of the Blantyre Print and Publishing Company, described the inadequacies of the urban maize selling system:

As a townsman, I am chiefly concerned in the mismanagement of the feeding of urban Africans. As you know, there is an alleged controlled shop in the Blantyre market where, in theory, industrial and domestic labour receives daily 4 lb of maize for 6d. However, it works very differently in practice. At least 60% of the flour goes to spivs, who are not employed in, but just flock into the township. Having no responsibility towards any employer, they arrive early in the market and stay late, and there is no reason why the same African should not get in the queue on two or more occasions daily. And then, much of this flour is resold at blackmarket prices, as extortionate as 1 lb for 6d. to the legitimate unfortunates who have not managed to battle successfully in the queue before the limited day's stock is sold. (*Nyasaland Times*, vol. 52, no. 11, 10/2/49, p. 7)

In response to this pressure to protect the 'legitimate unfortunates', in mid February the government announced a scheme whereby rations would be issued to employees only through their employers, and the government shop in the market was discontinued. I have described the working of this system in Chapter 1. Its object was to ensure that the 'legitimate' worker did not go short of food, but where possible it was urged that his women and children 'should be returned to their outlying villages, where their houses are not situated in famine areas, and where, therefore, they are more able to maintain themselves' (Communiqué published in *Nyasaland Times*, vol. 52, no. 12, 14/2/49, p. 5).

The oral evidence indicates that even the poorest paid of the urban workers benefited greatly from this system, with employers often shouldering some of the cost of the food, and with plenty of opportunities existing for hoarding and re-sale. Government employees, for instance, could exaggerate the size of their dependent families and accumulate quite large stocks. Sometimes these stocks were distributed amongst their families in rural areas, but others sold them at a handsome profit. One man interviewed had been employed by the government as a driver, taking stocks of maize from one area to another. As a government employee he was able to buy maize at a price of 3s. for a four-gallon tin, and sell it in the villages for 6s. or more. On top of this was the fact that so much food passed through his hands that it was easy to 'play monkey tricks with it'.[11]

The advantages accruing to less strategically placed employees were fewer, but still considerable. The Forestry Department in Zomba surveyed all the gardens of its employees in 1949 in order to assess their food position. Both government and mission employees were given time off work to cultivate emergency root-crop gardens. A man who worked for the Blantyre Mission of the Church of Scotland told how each employee was given 5 lb of free maize per week, as well as credit to buy more.[12] The Malamulo Seventh Day Adventist Mission also gave its employees free food. In non-government and non-Mission enterprises the provision of food varied, but all employers provided food in some quantity, and either free or on credit. Even the lowest paid found themselves at an immense advantage, and almost everyone interviewed made remarks to the effect that food was always available in Blantyre and Limbe for those with the means to obtain it, and that 'the people who survived were those who were working'.[13] One man interviewed had been working at an Indian-owned store in Limbe and earning 10s. 6d. a month.

This was a low wage even by colonial Malawian standards, when we consider that the average wage for agricultural labour at this time was 30s. But in January 1949 his employer began giving him an advance on his salary of 7s. 6d. a month, to enable him to buy maize.[14] Another man was a store-keeper in an Indian-owned shop in Limbe, whose wife and children lived at home in Lirangwe and farmed there. During the famine his employer gave him a small basket of maize flour each Saturday which he took home to his family, and he was also able to buy food from the government maize depot at Chirimba, near Blantyre. The price was high, and everyone complained, he said, but they also recognised that they were better off than their relatives at home in Lirangwe and Lunzu, who could not get maize at this stage even if they had money.[15]

Those who worked as domestic servants for European or Indian families received food directly from their employers. One woman had worked as 'house-girl' for an Indian family for the miserly wage of 3s. 6d. a month. However, her job held the advantage of allowing her to eat with her employers, and during the famine this was worth a lot in real terms.[16] Amongst the other informants were three men who had worked as domestic servants in European households and one who had worked as a cook for an Indian family.[17] They had all received free food from their employers during the famine.

The other major group of people to benefit from their designation as 'legitimate employees' were employees in the tobacco industry. Both labourers residing on Native Trust Land, and tenants living on estates, had privileged access to food through their employers.

There were many different categories of estate labour in this period, and in normal times these different groups held varying 'entitlements' to food from their employers. The 1949 Labour Department Report listed five main types of estate labour:

(1) *chitandu* labour: workers housed on the estate in housing provided by the estate.
(2) labour on 'special agreement': allowed to occupy a house and cultivate a garden upon estate land usually upon payment of a rent which may be waived or reduced if the tenant works for, or produces crops for, the estate.
(3) resident tenants: those who have certain rights under law to permanent residence on estate lands.
(4) labour not resident on the estate – usually from adjacent villages.
(5) *ganyu* labour – casual labour normally resorted to when work urgently required to be done gets beyond the capacity of the normal labour force.

(Labour Department, *Annual Report*, 1949)

In normal times the sources of food supply amongst estate labour varied according to which category they were in, but for the *chitandu*, 'special agreement' and tenant labour, at least a proportion of the food would be provided directly by the estate owner in the form of *posho* (weekly food allowance). This allowance was usually inadequate, as contemporary surveys repeatedly showed. A survey of labour on a tea estate in Mulanje in 1942 found that the ration issued was usually 15 lb of maize meal per week, plus 2 lb of beans and $\frac{1}{4}$–$\frac{1}{2}$ lb of salt (MNA, M2/17/16, Report on visit to Mulanje District, March 1942). This provision was inadequate for anything like a balanced diet, but was usually supplemented by other foods provided by the labourer's wife or children. It was found that the men who lived on the estate without their families were those who were worst off in respect of their diet, as they were entirely dependent on the rations. Access to food supply on the part of tenants differed from one estate to another. When working for the owner, tenants would receive *posho* (rations) as other labourers did. More important, however, was the provision of land on which they and their families could grow their own food. Some had access to gardens which were large enough to provide most of their food needs, and perhaps a tobacco crop as well. On other estates their position might be more akin to that of *chitandu* labour, who lived in estate housing 'lines' with only very small plots of land around their huts. Such families were dependent on a combination of food rations and the purchase of food off the estates.

These differences in food entitlement during normal times were obscured when the famine occurred. Both resident and non-resident labour on the estates benefited from designation as 'employees' and received food, often free of charge. European estate owners, apart from having their own access to food supplies, were also often involved in administering the government food distribution scheme, and thus in a particularly advantageous position from which to help their employees.[18] At Lirangwe, for instance, Mr Binson's estate was the location of the food distribution centre and feeding camp for the area. Informants who worked on the estates at the time, or in tobacco factories, all say that they received food either free or on credit. When severe malnutrition set in in the district, the victims came from Native Trust Land areas and not from the estates.[19]

When attempting to understand the structure of the famine, then, it is important to bear in mind the direct effects of the government's relief policies. African employers did not have the legitimacy of European and urban Indian employers in the eyes of the government, and so were not given the privileged access to government food stocks enjoyed by the latter. Most people employed by other Africans were engaged in agricultural labour or rural industry, and did not appear to the administration to hold the same kind of political threat as did urban employees. Whilst some African employers did have access to food throughout the famine, the smaller ones did not, and so those who relied on this form of casual rural employment were left without support. It was these people who migrated to find work and food, and who were ultimately extremely dependent on the government's willingness to intervene in the rural areas to avert suffering.

This leads us to an analysis of the final group – those who suffered most severely from the 1949 famine in Blantyre District. These people can be identified in a number of ways – geographically, occupationally, and by age and gender. We need more than one classification, because the structure of the famine and the definition of who suffered were the result of a number of factors interacting.

Throughout the Southern Province, those whose crops had failed and who were not in formal, officially recognised employment, were extremely vulnerable. The worst hit areas of Blantyre District were those which were agriculturally marginal, lying in the valley, some ten to fifteen miles from Blantyre township. When food camps for the severely malnourished were finally established, details emerged about where the real victims of the famine were. Many came from the areas north of Lirangwe, in Native Authority areas of Chigaru and Lundu, though there was also severe malnutrition amongst people in the villages on Kuntaja's area, which was closer to Blantyre. In Chiradzulu District, a camp was set up to deal with people from Nchema's area, which lay to the east of Chiradzulu mountain, in an arid area (MNA, AFC 3/2/1).

The question of agricultural marginality in these areas has already been discussed in Chapter 2. The drought was clearly an important factor in causing the suffering here, and these areas were most vulnerable to drought. When the rains failed in 1922 these same areas had suffered most severely.[20] Contrary to the assumptions of the Malthusian theory of the famine, it was in these least densely populated parts of Blantyre District and in similar areas of Chiradzulu, that the famine was most acute, and not in the crowded areas near the townships. We saw how, in the course of the 1930s, more people had moved down from the highlands into these valley areas, encouraged by the government provision of boreholes. The Department of Agriculture attempted to define and determine the kinds of settlement and agricultural practices pursued by these newcomers, in an effort to secure their long-term food security. It could be argued, however, that in the short term these policies actually increased vulnerability to famine. In an area of poor soils and unreliable rainfall, peasant cultivators were attempting to farm extensively, making the best use of the resources available and minimising risks. In all likelihood, many households were still in the process of establishing a suitable agricultural system, having only recently moved into the area.

As we have seen, however, the failure of agricultural production goes only some way towards explaining the structure of the famine. Employment patterns are crucial, especially when seen in relation to government famine relief policy. In these more distant areas of the valley, there were fewer people engaged in 'formal' employment than there were in communities closer to the town. At the same time, there were more men absent as migrants, and this was another crucial factor (Bettison, 1958a). In normal times, people here raised cash and covered their food deficits in a variety of ways – by working for other Africans as *ganyu* labour, by engaging in craft industry, brewing beer and *kachasu*, sometimes growing cotton, and by migrating outside the country.

The *ganyu* labourers, did not reap the benefits which fell upon the more formally employed during the famine, and they were crucially dependent on the ability and willingness of their African employers to continue to employ and/or feed them. Much of this casual employment dried up as an immediate consequence of the drought, though some, as we have seen, continued to be provided by the richer African entrepreneurs. All in all, however, the casual *ganyu* labourers were a vulnerable group, and the first to complain of the breakdown of traditional community solidarity which might have cushioned them in such circumstances in the pre-colonial period.

The drought hit the cotton crop hard, so that there was no possibility of using cash from this source to cover food deficits. In 1949 only thirty-one tons of cotton were harvested in the whole of Blantyre District, and cotton-growing had never been a profitable enough exercise to have allowed the growers to accumulate substantial savings (Nyasaland Protectorate, Department of Agriculture, *Annual Report* 1949). Beer brewing and *kachasu* distillation were prohibited at the beginning of the drought, and so this source of income for women came to an end. Some non-agricultural cash-earning strategies held up for a while – but most eventually collapsed. As we have seen, some people continued to find employment in brick-making, and interviews also indicate how some families earned food by selling thatching grass to the more fortunate urban dwellers.

Somewhat ironically, it was these communities of people attempting to pursue a more purely agricultural livelihood which suffered most during the famine, and not the crowded peri-urban dwellers who in successive government reports in the 1940s were seen as the vulnerable ones. Of course, this outcome has as much to do with government famine policy favouring the urban dwellers as it has with any absolute level of famine vulnerability. But as the oral testimonies recount, even within the area most severely affected by famine there were vast variations in the level of suffering. There were people here who were in formal employment in the town or on the estates, and who therefore received free and subsidised food from employers. There were richer households with stores of food from previous years and *dambo* gardens which continued to yield; and there was the small group of traders and maize-mill owners whose activities I have already described. In most areas there was enough variation in circumstances, even during the famine, for there to be a ready market for famine relief food, ground into flour and sold in the market to those who could afford to buy it. There are many stories from the whole famine area of similar uses having been made of government supplies.

There was another dimension to the suffering, however, and other ways of defining the vulnerable groups. Both written and oral accounts emphasise the suffering of the young, the very old, and of women. To some extent this pattern is defined by biological factors. The very old, for example, would be expected to be more vulnerable to disease and death in any case, and the shortage of food added to their vulnerability. Young children who had been weaned were also biologically more vulnerable to lack of food, as were pregnant and lactating women whose food requirements were greater than normal.

In the Lirangwe feeding camp, which opened in January 1950, it was the children who showed the worst signs of malnutrition, and who suffered most from famine oedema (Nyasaland Protectorate Medical Department, *Annual Report* 1950, p. 5). Some oral testimonies confirm this, and add that old people also showed the same symptoms more quickly than did younger adults.[21]

Though there is much evidence for the physical vulnerability of these groups, suffering was not purely defined by biological need – there was often a social dimension to it as well. As in many famines, the old and disabled were often abandoned. Their lack of mobility meant that they were less able than others to forage for wild foods, and thus quickly became a burden on other members of the community. Such people, along with young children, were recognised by the government's famine policy to be vulnerable, and so they were recipients of free food issues from quite early on. Many old and disabled people, however, did not make it as far as the food distribution and feeding camps. Some were brought in on stretchers by their relatives, but many more were abandoned. Many oral testimonies contain accounts of how this happened, and also indicate the embarrassment and shame associated with it.

The case of young children also has a social dimension as they too were a dependent group, only marginally able to help themselves. Accounts exist of women feeding their children before themselves, but there are also many accounts of the abandonment of children. Women's accounts, outlined in Chapter 1, tell of the suffering of children and the psychological pain experienced by their helpless mothers. Some decided that it would be better to 'get rid' of their near-starving children than to watch their suffering, and the traditional midwives were charged with this role.[22] Over half the total of those admitted to feeding camps and hospital in 1949–50 were children aged 3 to 12 (Medical Department, *Annual Report* 1950, p. 5), and apparently abandoned children wandered the streets of Blantyre, begging and stealing food.

Colonial administrators were shocked by what they saw and report after report expressed their disappointment and disillusionment with the workings of African community and family life. Most officials felt that the events of the famine confirmed what they had long felt – that African societies in Southern

Malawi were dissolving under the pressures of modern economic influence, and had no 'social fibre' left. They had placed their hopes in the ability of the constituted Native Authorities and headmen to hold these communities together, and they had invested them with much administrative responsibility during the famine, but their performance was seen as disappointing. In his address to the Southern Province Provincial Council in April 1950, the Provincial Commissioner described this feeling:

At the beginning of January it suddenly became obvious to us that in certain areas there was considerable distress and that large numbers of the African population were actually in an advanced state of starvation . . . I was very distressed indeed and could not understand how it could be that 400 or 500 people could exist in one chief's area in that advanced stage of malnutrition without reports having been received by the District Commissioner . . . Mr Haskard, the District Commissioner, found a complete lack of sympathy amongst the villagers themselves concerning these poor people and he gave me one example of a village in Chief Chigaru's area. There was one family of eight women and children who were nearly dead from starvation and when he said to the village headman 'You should take immediate steps to get these people taken into Lirangwe so that we can get them into hospital' the answer he received from the village headman was 'That family is no good and if they died it is the best way we can get rid of them' . . . There were people in the villages very nearly dead and the village communities doing nothing to assist . . . this came as a great shock to me. I have been 26 years in this country and I never imagined for a moment that the African village community had ceased to look after its own people, and that points to the fact that your old customs of village community life are breaking down fast. (MNA, MP 12655, Address of the President, 17/4/50)

Clearly the important question here is how individuals in the communities of the famine area defined their responsibilities towards each other at times of crisis. This issue is brought into relief by an examination of the experience of women in the famine.

We have seen that certain biologically vulnerable groups – the old, the young and the pregnant – were more likely to suffer in the famine, but there is also evidence (outlined in Chapter 1) for the fact that women as a group experienced more hardship than men. In the following chapter I examine more closely the gender dimension of the famine structure, and attempt to explain this in relation to longer-term economic and social changes affecting women. At the heart of this study is the question of how, and into what units, societies break down under the pressure of a severe food shortage.

5

Gender and famine[1]

The distinctive feature of women's songs and stories about the 1949 famine is the emphasis they place on the role of marital relations in shaping the pattern of suffering. When asked about famine, women tell about family, marriage, divorce and children. In their pounding songs they sing about the role of husbands in the famine – either praising them for their exemplary behaviour or (much more frequently) berating them for their neglect. This chapter analyses the women's accounts of the 1949 famine and assesses the importance of gender in shaping the disaster. In so doing it attempts to locate the famine within a larger historical process of change in the economic role and social status of women.

As we have seen, many factors contributed to the creation of a food shortage in Blantyre District in 1949–50. But the explanation for the transformation of food shortage into famine, and the nature and severity of that famine, must lie in part in the institutionalised pattern of human relationships which we call the 'social structure'. Returning to a theme raised in the Introduction, it is important at one level to separate the analysis of problems of long-term food supply from that of the problem of famine. We need to consider who starves and why, and to relate this to established patterns of behaviour in normal times. But as the last chapter has shown, we must also consider the effect of state intervention and famine policy as a major factor in shaping the famine. In 1949 the colonial authorities' perceptions of and preconceptions about the social system they were dealing with, were themselves important in creating a pattern of suffering, and especially in determining the fate of women.

One of the attractions of analysing a famine to the student of African social and economic history, is the capacity of a crisis to illuminate and bring into sharp relief important areas of concern for which historical evidence is normally lacking. One of the most crucial of these areas is that covering family, kinship and marital relations. In particular, sexual and domestic politics are largely invisible in our sources, but an understanding of them and how they change over time is invaluable to the social historian. Whilst an anthropologist may, through extended observation, be able to describe intra-household relations at one moment in time, the substance of these relations rarely goes down in history except in a highly structured, idealised form. Relations between households are also often difficult to discern, except in cases of institutionalised dealings surrounding deaths, marriages or political conflict. What evidence we have for the late colonial period in Africa tends to be difficult to synthesise, as different observers and actors took different units of analysis as their starting points. Colonial government documentation (as with present-day surveys) often treats the household as an indivisible unit; colonial anthropologists generally ignored it for the lineage (but they considered this to be a social and political unit of little economic consequence), and oral testimony draws a blank on any issues we might call 'domestic'.

To anyone concerned with the study of food supply and famine, the near-blank in the sources on intra-household relations and food allocation is a great drawback. To understand famine we need to know about patterns of food consumption as much as about food production or procurement. It is perhaps not surprising that when asked to recall life forty years ago, an elderly woman is more likely to remember births, deaths and wars than she is to recall the seemingly timeless activities of cooking and eating. But these details are the stuff of social history, without which the relations between members of a community through such institutions as 'marriage' and 'kinship' cannot be understood.

Whilst people have very little recollection of who ate what in normal times, this is exactly what they do recall about a famine. The allocation of food within the community and within the family during a period of shortage, highlights the tensions and struggles which in normal times lie buried under the formal structure of social relations, and the famine is enough of an 'event' for such details to be consciously remembered. As was indicated in the description of the famine given in Chapter 1, men and women alive in the area today have differing recollections of the events of 1949–50. The nature of the evidence is, however, problematical. Some of the 'female' evidence comes through pounding songs which are said to have been composed during the 1949 famine. These songs are often very critical of men, or, more specifically, of husbands. The first problem with this evidence is the impossibility of dating it with any certainty. Some songs contain references to contemporaneous, or near contemporaneous events (the Second World War in particular), and to that extent they can be dated to the 1940s. But it is in the nature of the form itself that they will be modified and adapted over time in order to retain their relevance. In this respect it is interesting that the survival of such songs appears to be very patchy. In many villages in the general area affected by the 1949 famine, no-one recalled any such songs. In others they were widely known and sung with a confidence which implied repeated performance. In these villages older women explained that they were suffering current food shortages resulting from a series of poor harvests, but that younger people had little concept of 'real hunger', not having witnessed a famine of the proportions of 1949. The older women reminisced with the old songs and taught them to the younger women.

Despite adaptations and modifications, it is clear that most of these songs do refer to the events of 1949. No previous or subsequent famine reached the same proportions, or left such an imprint on local culture. Complicating the use of this evidence, however, is the fact that the famine also left its imprint on national political culture, and this has spawned a whole different repertoire of songs. In his speeches, President Banda often cites 1949 as 'the last great subsistence crisis' of Malawi. Ignoring much evidence to the contrary, political rhetoric has it that no-one in Malawi has gone short of food since Banda returned in 1958 to embark on saving the country from colonialism. The songs composed by members of the Women's League of the Malawi Congress Party, and performed widely at political meetings and broadcast over the radio, pander to this illusion. The tone of the 'official' songs about the famine is thus very different to that of the ordinary pounding songs, as this example illustrates:

Timagona nenjo	We slept without food
Musanabwele Ngwazi	Before your arrival. Ngwazi,
Forty-nine, forty-nine, forty-nine,	Forty-nine, forty-nine, forty-nine,
Anzathu anatisiya	Our relatives and friends left us.[2]

So famine is a 'live' issue, and in sifting the oral evidence one needs to be aware of this. Perhaps more difficult to allow for is the very form of the songs themselves. Pounding songs composed and sung in normal times are frequently critical of men and deeply concerned with family and marital relations. Sung by one or more women as they pound maize in the courtyards of hut complexes, they can be timed to provoke the maximum amount of embarrassment to the passing male villager, whose misdemeanours or inadequacies sound out across the village to the rhythm of the pestle. Just as the praise poem in Southern Africa has as a part of its form the convention that power may be openly criticised (Vail and White, 1983), so too the pounding song's form contains the possibility of expressing sexual antagonism in a socially acceptable way. It is therefore legitimate to ask how far songs about the 1949 famine are really centrally concerned with food shortage, and how far they are simply part of a continuous concern over marital relations. The stress on the behaviour of men, which emerges so clearly in the songs, could be interpreted as being in the nature of the genre rather than being a true reflection of events, and I will return to this question later.[3]

Despite all these problems, it seems to me that the songs and testimonies, if treated with caution, are indispensable to any analysis of the famine. Songs are at least the creation of the people who lived through the events, and as such must be valued since rarely in African social history 'has it been possible to demonstrate in any depth the part played by African perceptions in the unfolding of the events' (Vail and White, 1983, p. 887).

I start, then, by summarising the accounts of the famine told by men, and then turn to the women's testimonies and songs. The recollections of men are more difficult to obtain than those of women, partly because men are much more mobile than women, and not only during a famine. Many of the men who were living in Blantyre District at the time of the famine are no longer there, whilst others who live there now were absent when it occurred. As the description of the events of the famine in Chapter 1 outlined, a major feature of the famine was the migration of men.

In the pre-colonial history of much of Africa, famine has been held to be the cause of many wholesale migrations of communities. As we have seen, the Malawi region seems to have often been a refuge for such groups – some sections of the Yao, for instance, were said to have fled into the Malawi region in the eighteenth century as a response to famine in Mozambique. Wholesale migration of this kind was very rare in the colonial period, though the immigration of the Lomwe people into Malawi from the turn of the century comes close to it. Even the partial and temporary migration strategy carried with it substantial risks, as Michelle McAlpin has outlined for nineteenth-century India. She argues that up to the 1890s in India, migration was a strategy of last resort, carrying with it a number of serious risks, including the spread of disease (McAlpin, 1983). The evidence from India and elsewhere in Africa indicates that men were more likely than women to migrate in search of food at times of famine. In one study of Northern Cameroons it has been argued that this behaviour of male migration is so regular that it can be used as an indicator of the degree of shortage prevailing or impending. The authors argue that during a regular period of 'soudure' (hungry season) it is the women who take most responsibility for seeking available food resources, whilst during a severe shortage both men and women are involved in off-setting deficits. Within this, migration plays a large part and is primarily a 'male' response (Campbell and Trechter, 1982).

The success of such a strategy depends in part on the degree to which it is well-informed and directed. McAlpin contrasts the dangers of aimless wanderings of men from famine areas in India in the nineteenth century, with the clear advantages of well-informed labour migration in the twentieth century, when a few men from each village would be sent to 'scout' for work as soon as the failure of the early rains made a harvest failure inevitable (McAlpin, 1983). Oral accounts indicate that the migration of men during the 1949 famine fell somewhere between the 'aimless wandering' which led to exhaustion and the spread of disease, and the purposeful search for work which could benefit the whole community. The migration was clearly directed and reasonably well-informed, but it is also apparent that many men were in a very weak physical state when they embarked on their long journeys. As described in Chapter 1, many men migrated in search of work and food in the direction of their ancestral homes. Migration was patterned by a long history of marriage alliances, and whilst in general this migration strategy seems to have been a successful one for the men involved, it was nevertheless hazardous and many collapsed and died on the way.

Written accounts, and the oral testimonies of both women and of Yao village headmen, indicate that many of the more fortunate men did not return from their expeditions in search of food, but stayed away until the end of the famine. Village headmen were most often Yao men whose status allowed them to marry virilocally.[4] Their responsibilites kept them largely at home during the famine, and many in any case had larger than average land holdings and were more likely to possess stocks of food. Their administrative responsibilities during the famine included coping with the results of the mass migration of men from their villages:

> During 1949–50 people were totally preoccupied with getting food. People could not stay in one place. If they heard there was food somewhere they went to find it, no matter how far. They went to Ntcheu, Neno and Mwanza to work in the gardens of people who had plenty of food. They usually went in groups. Some men who had come from Ntcheu or Mwanza to marry in Lirangwe, went back to their original homes under the pretext of finding food – but they never came back! They left their wives and children starving.[5]

Apart from the stories of migration, male testimonies of the famine deal at length with the details of how food could be procured from employers. This, as we have seen, was an extremely important channel of food supply during the famine, and one which was almost entirely a male preserve.

Women's experiences of the famine, as reflected in the collective memory of their songs and stories, could be substantially different to those of men. They, along with the very old and very young, were more likely than men to end up relying upon government handouts. It is through the women's testimonies that we learn how the feeding camps were organised, and it was the women who most often took part in 'food for work' schemes. As we have seen, women stress how frequently they were abandoned by men, how harrowing it was to be left responsible for their suffering and dying children, how they became sterile, and how they were humiliated by the feeding system. The weakness of marriage ties is the main focus of their testimonies and songs. Whilst men claim that they died of 'anxiety' as a result of the burden of responsibility placed upon them, women retort that men died only because they maintained sexual relations with women in the areas to which they went to get food.[6]

These accounts and stories do not necessarily reflect the reality of the famine for all women. They rather constitute a collective female account of the famine which has other levels of meaning, and which reflects a number of continuing concerns. At the same time, however, they have a foundation in the reality of the famine experienced by certain groups of women.[7] Whilst we need not believe that *all* women suffered more than men, it appears that some groups of women were more vulnerable than the majority of men, and that this vulnerability had much to do with the structure of relationships in a changing matrilineal society. Whilst women in this society had the initial advantage of residing in their natal villages and being able to draw on the pooled resources of a large kin group, it was the men who had the external social and economic linkages – both with other ecological zones, and with the labour economy. These external linkages became more and more crucial as the famine increased in severity. The scarcer the food, the smaller became the units of consumption. Beyond a certain point the advantages of co-residence with kin ceased to be so apparent, and women were left increasingly dependent on their husbands (if they had any) or on themselves. It was at this point that their disadvantage *vis à vis* men became more obvious, and it is to this stage of the famine that so many of the songs and testimonies refer.

The structure of the famine, and in particular the pattern of gender differentiation within it, can only be understood when set in the context of longer-term economic and social change. In the rest of this chapter I examine two aspects of such change which became central during the famine: firstly, changes in the economic role of women which had occurred in this area over the preceding century; secondly, the functioning of the matrilineal system and the institution of marriage set within this.

The changing economic role of women

In Chapter 2 I outlined briefly the operation of the agrarian system of Southern Malawi in the early part of the nineteenth century. We saw that, amongst the Nyanja-speaking people of the Shire Highlands and the valley, there was no very clear sexual division of labour in agriculture. Agricultural production was relatively intensive, and men and women tended to work together on the same tasks. This had been especially so since the shifting forest-fallow system had been supplanted by a more intensive bush-fallow system. The latter required overall more labour, but less of the heavy land clearance which had been performed by men in the more extensive system which it replaced. Women helped clear the land, planted, hoed and cultivated along with the men, and took the major responsibility for harvesting and seed selection. The storage and processing of food crops were entirely the responsibility of women and seen as an extension of gender-defined domestic duties. Women's centrality to this agricultural system arose in two ways – firstly, through their heavy labour input, and secondly, through their rights to the land on which the crops were grown. Under the matrilineal system of inheritance which operated in Southern Malawi, rights to land passed through women, and it was generally through uxorilocal marriage that men gained rights to cultivation.[8] Village headmen and the male 'overseers' of sorority groups did, however, have independent access to land in their natal villages, and although land rights were women's rights, they were nevertheless administered by these men. It would also be mistaken to exaggerate the economic and political advantages which such rights conferred on women, especially in a situation of general land abundance such as prevailed in the nineteenth century. But it is nevertheless probable that their pivotal position in the land-holding system strengthened women's economic and political muscle.

Non-agricultural activities were more clearly defined along gender lines. Women were the salt-makers and pot-makers, while men fished, made iron goods, spun and wove cotton, and manufactured baskets. All of these items could be and were traded within the local and regional economy, but as the nineteenth century wore on trade in itself became more central to the economy and this brought a new shift in the sexual division of labour.[9]

The immigration of successive waves of Yao people into this area from Mozambique, and the progressive absorption of many Nyanja groups into Yao society, had important implications. Yao culture was a trading culture, the status symbols of which – imported cloth, guns, beads and an imported religion (Islam) – were almost totally appropriated by men. Agricultural production continued to be crucial to the functioning of the entire Yao economic system, as food was required as an intermediate trade good as well as for normal subsistence. But the value which society placed on agricultural activities was overtaken by that accorded to the more exotic involvement in the caravan trade, and this latter activity was the preserve of men. A Yao story collected by Alice Werner illustrates the male appropriation of exotic status symbols associated with long-distance trade, but also allows this to be ridiculed by the woman who stays behind:

> A man who had told his wife that he never ate bran-porridge went to the coast with a caravan, sold his ivory to advantage, and had a red fez given to him into the bargain. The party reached their home and were met with the usual rejoicings, and the man, wearing his new fez, sat down to wait while his wife prepared him a meal. This was, as usual, a long business; the woman first pounded the maize, then put the bran on a plate, and then took the grain down to the stream to wash it before the second pounding. The husband, growing more and more hungry as he waited, forgot his scruples or his fastidiousness, took the bran, poured it into his fez, poured some water on it, stirred it up and began to eat it. While he was doing so he saw his wife coming and put the fez half full of bran and water on his head to hide what he had been doing. His wife, however, was too quick for him and asked 'What is that on your head that you are hiding?'. He said, 'Medicine that I prepared for the journey' . . . Very soon the bran-porridge began to trickle down his

face. He said, 'Oh! my wife, hunger, hunger! Some hunger eats weeds of the field, some hunger eats what is bad. My wife, do not tell people that I have been seen with bran-porridge on my head, and I will pay you with goods.' So he paid her with goods. (Werner, 1906, p. 151–2)

The Yao men's vulnerability, this story seems to say, was created by his weakness in face of hunger and susceptibility to ridicule.

While men were away earning their red fezes, women took more responsibility for food production. But by the late nineteenth century the slave trade and the extension of firearms had made agricultural production impossible in many places. Landeg White has told in detail the story of Magomero in the Shire Highlands during this period (White, 1987). When the Universities' Mission in Central Africa (UMCA) missionaries arrived there, the local economy was based on raiding, and the survivors of the 1862–3 famine there were the successful raiding groups, not the food producers. Under these conditions, Nyanja agriculturalists either attempted to participate in this system on an equal basis by procuring firearms and taking slaves themselves, or they were forced into small pockets of refuge – Chisi Island on Lake Chilwa was one such place – becoming the 'mere fishermen' treated with derision in Yao oral testimony.

The implications of these changes for the role and status of women could be far-reaching. Women continued to be valued for their rights to land, their labour and (most importantly) their reproductive capacities. Political prestige in the late nineteenth century centred as much around the accumulation of people – followers, captives, wives – as it did around the possession of firearms (Vaughan, 1981). More women than men were taken as slaves, but fewer of them were sold over long distances. Most became the 'slave-wives' (or 'elephant wives') of their captors. Yao chiefs were able to build up large virilocal lineages based on the rights they claimed over the children of their unfree wives. Women became trade goods, exchangeable for cloth, ivory, beads or guns.[10]

The evidence for the decline of status of women is ambiguous, however. The matrilineal system survived intact in Southern Malawi and virilocal marriage never became the norm. Waves of immigrants made their homes in the area through conventional marriage alliances, even when others were doing the same through the force of arms. Even the most powerful Yao chiefs held a certain amount of respect for the 'owners of the land'. In the crowded Yao stockades disease and witchcraft were rife, and only Nyanja medicine was thought to be able to guard against it.[11] So long as they were not slaves, women maintained their crucial role in the social system and the matrilineal *mbumba* remained the fundamental unit of social organisation.

The early colonial period brought both change and continuity in the role and position of women. The gradual decline of slavery and slave marriage restored women to their pivotal position within the social system, while the increasing demands made by European settlers and the colonial administration on the labour of men, meant that women once again took on more responsibility for agricultural production. As was indicated in Chapter 2, the incidence and severity of demands made on male labour were variable, and on some estates of the British Central Africa and Blantyre and East Africa Companies were non-existent in the first part of the century. But the enforcement of hut tax, and the collusion of some European employers with local colonial officials, meant that overall there was some withdrawal of male labour from food production. The timing of the labour demands was crucial. Whilst many of the nineteenth-century 'male' activities could be timed for the dry season, wage-labour was demanded and coerced for the agricultural peak season. Where the demands on male labour were extreme (as on the Bruce estates in Chiradzulu) (White, 1987), and the rewards particularly low, this could significantly affect food production and place food security in jeopardy. There were a number of minor famines in the Shire Highlands during the early colonial period, but there is no evidence for any general 'crisis of subsistence' occurring. We must conclude that overall the intensification of female labour on food production, coupled with a different emphasis in the cropping pattern, were sufficient to save these communities from starvation.[12]

As the century wore on, so land in the Shire Highlands became scarcer and rights to land more valuable. To this extent the status of women may have been enhanced. Landeg White's study of villages on the Bruce estates of Magomero shows how the matrilineal system of inheritance and land-holding continued to dominate, even under the artificial circumstances of estate residence. The villages 'belonged' to the women, and rights to land (though ultimately removed from the hands of Africans altogether) passed through women. Whilst the men picked cotton for Bruce, the women ordered and organised the villages, grew the food crops, and reproduced the communities (White, 1987).

In the late 1940s the situation probably still prevailed in some parts of Blantyre District, but in others there had been further changes affecting the economic status of women. The major identifiable shift was in the relative values of food production against cash income from wages. A degree of land scarcity might enhance the status of women in this society by adding value to the rights in land accorded to them. But as land scarcity reached a more critical stage in some areas, so intensification of production without major technical change may also have reached its limits. For some groups food self-sufficiency became an unattainable goal, and whole communities became dependent on cash earned through wages to supplement their own food production. I have stressed in Chapter 2 that exchange had always been a feature of this agrarian system, and I have also stressed that increasing dependence on wages need not be seen as a precursor of famine. However, the relative decline in the value of own production did have implications for the economic status of women, and these implications were brought into sharp relief during the famine. Put simply, the resources over which women had most control – the land and the food products of that land – were becoming relatively less important to the overall economic strategies of households or larger family units. Whilst women took on more and more responsibility for food production, the returns to their labour in this were declining. This was not happening evenly, and in some parts of the Southern Province had not happened at all, but in the more crowded parts of Blantyre District it had been a clear tendency. It ws also a tendency in the newly colonised, marginal areas of the Middle Shire Valley, where agricultural production was in any case unreliable, and where the land rights of women in a situation of new settlement may have been less secure.

The increase in wage employment which I outlined in Chapter 4 was most pronounced in the late 1940s, and was almost totally the preserve of men. Male labour migration outside the country was also increasing, and remittances were playing an ever more important role in the local economy.[13] It is unfortunate that locally-specific figures are not available to demonstrate this, and the national aggregates obscure the wide variations in the levels of emigration and in the role of remittances. A national study made by the Colonial Office in 1949 estimated that each migrant labourer remitted approximately £9 per annum, to his family, allowing for some who did not remit at all (Great Britain, Public Record Office, CO 852/1035/2).

Women were very rarely employed in the 'formal' sector of the Southern Province economy, and then only on a very sporadic, seasonal basis. More frequently they engaged in *ganyu* labour for other Africans, but their most important source of cash income was through the sale of beer and *kachasu*, combined with trading small amounts of produce from their gardens.

Descriptions of how this economic system functioned locally are scanty for the 1940s, though the Department of Agriculture's village surveys do give some idea. I have already referred to the survey conducted in 1944 of Matope village in the area of Chief Kapeni, near the boundaries of Blantyre township (MNA, AGR 3/7). This was an area of high population density, and land was very scarce. Seventy per cent of the twenty households in the village cultivated less than 1.5 acres. Most of the men in the village divided their time between working in the town and working in their gardens, while the women worked in the gardens and brewed beer. Of the total man-days calculated to be available in the village 22 per cent were spent on the cultivation of food crops, and 78 per cent on other work (which included work for wages, brewing beer and domestic work). In eight out of twenty households, the woman was involved in brewing and selling either beer or *kachasu*, and this was particularly important where the woman was the head of household (this was the case in seven out of twenty households). Household number 3 was a woman living alone with three children, and brewing beer five or six times a year, and earning about £2 each time. In household number 6 the man died during the course of the survey, and the widow began brewing beer to support herself and her five children. Household number 9 consisted of a man, wife and three children, with only 0.19 of an acre. The man bought and sold vegetables, while the woman brewed and sold beer. Household number 11 consisted of a woman and two children, with one acre, earning cash through brewing beer about six times a year. Household 16 was a woman living alone, with 0.84 of an acre and brewing beer. Household 17 consisted of a woman with 0.37 of an acre, whose husband was away as a migrant in Southern Rhodesia. This woman also brewed beer, as did the woman in household 18 whose husband was away in the army.

Much more detailed information on the structure of household incomes was collected in a series of surveys conducted in the 1950s in the peri-urban villages of Blantyre-Limbe by the Rhodes-Livingstone Institute (Bettison, 1958, 1958b, 1958c, 1958d; Bettison and Rigby, 1961). Clearly we need to be wary of projecting these results backwards into the 1940s, as some of the findings may have represented post-famine adjustments, but from what we know of the 1940s from the Agriculture Department's research, it would seem justified to assume that some of these findings were relevant to the 1940s as well as to the 1950s. The surveys, despite a number of drawbacks, are particularly valuable for the attention they give to the question of gender and of how men and women generated and used cash.

In his study of seventeen villages in the Blantyre-Limbe area, David Bettison found a very high percentage of men involved in wage labour. This percentage varied depending on the distance of the village from the town. Within the 'peripheral' zone, lying within a four-mile radius of the town, seventy three per cent of the resident males were working in Blantyre-Limbe. In the extra-peripheral zone, within a four to eight-mile radius of the town, the percentage was 66 per cent, and in the 'rural zone', eight miles and more from the town, it was 53 per cent (Bettison, 1958a, p. 1). In another study of three villages in the extra-peripheral zone, 85 per cent of men had been in some wage employment outside their village in the course of the year (Bettison and Rigby, 1961, p. 6). Moving further away from the town there was a higher incidence of male absence (including migrants to Southern Rhodesia), so that whilst in the 'peripheral zone' 12 per cent of men were away from the village in which their wives lived, in the extra-peripheral zone 18 per cent were absent, and in the rural zone 35 per cent were absent (Bettison, 1958d, p. 61). It was also the case that the more rural the village, the more important was male self-employment in craft and service industries. The communities we have identified as having been most severely affected by the 1949 famine fell partly into Bettison's 'rural' zone, and partly within the 'extra-peripheral' zone.

Women were hardly involved in the wage economy at all, and this seems to have been little changed from what we know of the 1940s. Paid employment was available to some extent for women – as nursemaids in urban households, as temporary workers in tobacco factories, and assistants in African-owned brick-making enterprises. But in the 17 villages, 66 per cent of the women had *never* been in paid employment. Of those who had, 80 per cent had been employed only once, and this usually when they were very young (Bettison, 1958d, p. 77). Apart from producing food in their own gardens, the main occupations of the women surveyed were beer brewing and *kachasu* distillation, and petty trading in agricultural produce. The importance of beer or *kachasu* brewing as a source of income for women, was enormous, and the results confirm the picture sketched by the Department of Agriculture's surveys in the 1940s. The extent of brewing varied quite widely, however, from one village to another. In one village income from *kachasu* sales comprised 56 per cent of the total village cash income (compared to the 23 per cent accounted for by wages) (Bettison and Rigby, 1961, p. 6). Where women were household heads they relied almost entirely on *kachasu* distillation for the cash they needed (p. 24). Furthermore, the villages in which *kachasu* distillation took place had average household cash incomes of approximately twice the level of those in which there was no distilling. The researchers concluded that the overall effect of *kachasu* distillation was to increase the turnover of cash in the village and make available increased quantities of cash for expenditure on a number of other items (p. 151). Women in the *kachasu* distilling villages were often self-reliant in cash, and this was crucial in the case of male absenteeism. It was also important, however, when a second finding is taken into consideration, this being that within households men and women maintained largely separate income streams and budgets. Economic cooperation within the primary family was much more likely to occur between mothers and their daughters than along any other axis. Unmarried daughters were expected to be engaged in some cash-earning activity from a very early age, whilst unmarried sons lived largely free in their mothers' households (pp. 44–5).

Whilst the overall impression was one of female self-reliance, there were limitations to this, as Bettison and his colleagues pointed out. In the first place, *kachasu* distillation was not evenly distributed. There was evidence that the wage-levels of men might have had some significance for the economic activities of their wives, and to this extent the picture of different male and female income streams needs to be qualified. For example, women whose husbands fell into the lowest wage category were less involved in *kachasu* distillation than those in the category above, and this was presumably because they could not afford the capital outlay to embark on the production of *kachasu* (p. 95). Such women were more likely to resort to the much less profitable activity of petty trading, as were women in the 'rural' zone where there was a smaller market for manufactured alcohol. Bettison and Nyirenda's studies of the operation of urban and peri-urban markets in Blantyre showed women vendors to be confined to the least profitable trades and to be consistently more generous in their measures of goods than were men (Nyirenda, 1958, p. 15). Whilst male vendors obtained their supplies from a wide area, the women dealing in maize and maize flour were largely dependent on local supplies of maize – either from their own gardens or those of other peri-urban dwellers. Bettison found very low profit margins amongst maize flour vendors and concluded that the 'relatively even price of flour and its associations with female vendors, is probably no accident' (Bettison, 1959, p. 40).

The other limitation to female self-reliance in this economic system was created by the seasonal fluctuation in women's major income-generating activities. Bettison and his colleagues found that although male wage employment and self-employment were rarely permanent or constant, they were more stable than the 'marginal sources of income' controlled by women. The marked seasonal fluctuation in women's cash incomes was apparently 'linked to the decreasing availability of home-grown goods, and maize obtained from relatives in rural areas. This would affect the amount of beer and *kachasu* for sale and would cause a decrease in income from these sources' (Bettison and Rigby, 1961, p. 74).

Whilst women in normal times stood a good chance of being self-reliant, their dependence on agriculturally-related activities and their lack of connections with the formal wage economy, became crucial for some of them during the famine. Beer brewing and petty trading were the first activities to cease during the famine, along with most *ganyu* labour. This placed women in a situation of unprecedented dependence on men. Women did not, of course, experience the famine uniformly. Those whose husbands were in wage employment stood a better *chance* of gaining access to food than did those married to men who were not so employed. The fact that some of the women married to wage earners did not benefit from their husbands' positions is not to deny that as a group they were less likely to end up in the feeding camps. The gender dimension does not always override that of class and employment, but the fact that it sometimes does is nevertheless of interest.

In Chapter 4 I identified, by location and employment, those groups which appeared most vulnerable during the famine. These were groups living in the marginal agricultural land of the Middle Shire, and those in a wider area who were not employed in the 'formal' sector. Women in these groups were particularly vulnerable. As we have seen, women in the agriculturally marginal areas were more likely in any case to be heading households, than those living closer to town. When the famine struck they had no husband to depend on, unless they were lucky enough to be in receipt of remittances. If married, these women were classified by the colonial administrators as 'dependants' and assumed to be receiving help from their absent husbands. Oral testimony and written sources are explicit about the special vulnerability of these women, who, in the absence of their husbands depended very heavily on their matrilineal relatives. Mrs Solomon from Chief Machinjiri's area described the plight of her cousin Pochelia, during the 1949 famine, and this is a story repeated in many testimonies:

> My cousin, Pochelia, was one of those who received relief food. She had two children and her husband was in Salisbury and she never heard from him. At the beginning of the famine she got help from her relatives but later, when things got really tight, she no longer got help. One of the children died of hunger, and people urged the village headmen to take her to Lunzu for relief food, which he did.[14]

Many informants stressed that the government's policy of not giving married women free food was the source of much unnecessary suffering. In the case of this group, then, the pattern of their suffering was created by the interaction between long-term developments and short-term events and policies. Whilst in normal times such women were driven to self-sufficiency, in the famine they were structurally disadvantaged by their lack of entry to the formal wage economy and by government assumptions about the duties of absent husbands towards their wives.

The second particularly vulnerable group of women were those married to men who were not employed in the formal sector and who did not originate in the area. Such men, as we have seen, were more likely to migrate in search of food, and when these migrations took them in the direction of their original homes, they were open to the possibility of not returning. The fact that women rarely had such external contacts, and were in any case less mobile than the men because of their child-care responsibilities meant that this option was not usually open to them. Once again, some of these women received much support and help from other members of their families in the initial stages of the famine, and some had money saved from beer or *kachasu* manufacture which enabled them to remain independent for a time. Ultimately, however, many ended up as the recipients of relief food, along with the wives of migrants.

Women's songs and stories of the famine seem to draw heavily on the experiences of these especially vulnerable groups. As cultural constructions they are to some extent misleading as to the actual events of the famine and the real incidence of suffering experienced by women. They do, however, draw attention to the feeling of helplessness and vulnerability experienced by so many women during the famine, and the frustration they felt at being thrown into dependence on men.[15] They also reflect directly on the institution of marriage within a matrilineal society, and how this institution stood up to the famine, and it is to this issue that I now turn. For many women, the experience of the famine was structured not only by their objective position within a class structure and the economic entitlements or disadvantages associated with this, but also by their 'moral' entitlements and ties of affection within the social system.

Marriage and matrilineality

A famine crisis throws enormous strain on any social fabric, and highlights the tensions and divisions within it. Raymond Firth's account of his 'revisit to Tikopia' during a famine in 1952/3 vividly describes these strains and the dilemmas faced by individuals (Firth, 1959). On the one hand, a remarkable degree of social cohesion was maintained. Traditionally, in Tikopia, food was transferred from one economic unit to another or from one person to another, not by barter but by gift. This tradition was maintained even in the stringent conditions of famine (p. 75). There was no sale of food to the highest bidder, no profit-taking on small surpluses, and almost no capital transfers which would confer long-term advantages on those fortunate enough to possess spare food. At the same time, however, thefts of food were widespread and at the height of the famine almost the only people not to steal food were chiefs and members of their families. Where food was scarce but not desperately short, the pooling of supplies between households took place through the 'linking of ovens' (p. 84), in a similar way to that in which food was shared amongst matrilineal relatives at the start of the famine in Malawi. At the height of the famine in Tikopia, however, there was an atomisation of units of consumption down to individual households. Within households food was apparently shared equally. In a society which in normal times placed so much emphasis on hospitality, the crisis caused embarrassment and strain. Kinship ties had to be redefined. Those who might in normal times be treated as kin were now mere 'visitors' and food was not shared with them. The famine put a strain on social relations: 'People felt themselves to be in difficulty through not being able to fulfil the obligations demanded of them by custom, and some tended to compensate for this by aggressive behaviour' (p. 82). Overall, though, there was a maintenance of decorum. Firth concluded that 'while morals degenerated under the strain of famine, manners remained', and the ordinary modes of serving food were kept up (p. 83).

In Southern Malawi in 1949–50, as in Tikopia in 1952–3, there was both cooperation and conflict during the famine. But unlike in Tikopia, where it seems that only extended kin ties were placed under great strain, in Malawi the primary family unit was often pulled asunder. Interpreting this difference is not easy. It seems from Firth's account that the famine in Tikopia was less severe than that in Malawi. It could be argued that, had it become more severe, sharing there would likewise have been reduced to the minimum. However, evidence from elsewhere indicates that societies do break down in different ways in the face of famine, and that beyond a certain point there is no 'natural' pattern to this. The pattern which emerged in the 1949 famine in Malawi reflects on marriage within a matrilineal society, and on long-term change as well as short-term strain.

The colonial authorities always assumed that the household, consisting of man, wife and children, was the primary unit of production and consumption, and that food was shared equally within this unit.[16] The experience of the famine showed this to be a dangerous assumption, and drew attention to two rather divergent tendencies within the economic and social system. One was the continuing strength of the sorority group – the *mbumba*, and the other was the maintenance of separate economic spheres within the household.

In Southern Malawi in the late colonial period the basic social unit remained the matrilineal *mbumba* or sorority group. The *mbumba* was the effective descent group, consisting usually of a group of sisters and their children, 'overseen' by an elder brother or uncle. It rarely had a greater depth than four generations, and was liable to fission after reaching a certain size (Mitchell, 1971). In the cultural representation of this system the brother–sister tie was very strong, as was the avunculate exercised by the elder brother.[17] Ideally a village would consist of a number of *mbumba* groups, clustered around an original core group. In spatial terms this meant that most women lived in close proximity to their mothers, sisters, aunts and cousins, whilst maintaining separate dwelling units with their husbands and young children.

It was an adult woman's duty to provide basic foodstuffs for her family, and so when a girl reached adolescence she was expected to cultivate part of her mother's land. On marriage she was eligible for her own plot and this she would apply for from the village headman, or if the village was a large one, from the male head of a 'cluster' within it (Mitchell, 1956, p. 7). Sometimes she would inherit a plot of land from her mother or grandmother, though this transfer would still have to be approved by the headman. Along with her plot of land she would have her own grain bin or *nkhokwe* in which she stored the maize which was the product of her labour, and to which she alone had access. On marriage her husband would be expected to contribute labour to the production of this food, and thus gain the right to be fed from his wife's *nkhokwe* (Mitchell, 1956, p. 7).

We have very little information on how, in normal times, the *mbumba* group, or any wider cluster of matrilineally-related individuals, might have functioned as an economic unit. At one level the cultural emphasis was on the self-sufficiency of the unit consisting of a woman, her children and her husband, with the focus on the woman. The expectation was that each adult woman would support herself through the product of her labour on her plot of land, and that she would have sole control and access to her *nkhokwe*. We have seen, however, that in many parts of Southern Malawi by the late colonial period, food self-sufficiency through direct production was no longer possible, with many households buying quantities of food with cash earned from (predominantly male) wage labour, or through brewing and trade. In such cases, the ideal 'hearthhold' centred around the woman and her grain-bin, may not have reflected a changing reality.[18] However, Bettison and his colleagues found this ideal still functioning strongly in the peri-urban villages of Blantyre-Limbe in the 1950s.

Both because of the strength of this ideal, and because of the strong methodological bias in the surveys towards the households as the primary economic unit, one can do little more than speculate on the possible economic functions of the wider matrilineal group. Bettison and Rigby's work on patterns of income and expenditure concluded that households tended to be independent economic units, and that whilst 'a certain amount of gift exchange, labour exchange on arduous tasks, and similar intra-community advantages were observed, these were rarely well developed' (Bettison and Rigby, 1961, p. viii). We have seen, however, that whilst they emphasised the household as an economic unit, they also concluded that it was characterised by 'a tendency for the person obtaining cash to keep it for his or her *individual* uses' (p. 63). They also concluded that the main lines of economic cooperation within these communities were gender-specific ones, such as that between a mother and her daughter (and thus spanning more than one primary household in most cases) (p. 45).

The ambiguities in the results were partly a function of the methodological difficulties encountered in the surveys. Exchanges and gifts of food between households were found to be difficult to monitor, though they clearly could be very significant to any one individual's livelihood. Even more difficult to assess with any accuracy was the transfer of goods within the household. Bettison had hoped to monitor these transfers as they would 'throw into relief the theoretically interesting relationship of a wage-earning, or at least independently earning husband, living uxorilocally in a matrilineal village whose economic base was by no means self-supporting'. Irregularities in field returns apparently invalidated the results of this attempted study, and no conclusions could be drawn (p. 43).

Transfers between and within households thus remain almost invisible in the data, but there are a few things we can say with some certainty. Firstly, there were some productive activities carried out by women which often involved the active cooperation of female members of the matrilineal group. Harvesting was one of these. Women would frequently combine to harvest each other's gardens in turn, even though the produce would then be stored in individual, separate granaries. Beer brewing and *kachasu* distillation were also often carried out by two or more women in cooperation, and given the evidence for the importance of this industry in the 'female' economy of the area, such cooperation is surely significant (Bettison and Rigby, 1961, p. 45). Perhaps more important, however, and completely overlooked by researchers and commentators, was the fact that the *consumption* of food was often not an entirely household-based activity. Although it was assumed that a woman would provide the staple food independently for her household and cook it on her own hearth, meals were rarely consumed by households as a unit, but in gender-defined groups drawing on several households. Men from separate households would sit together in the village and their wives would bring food to them from their separate kitchens. The women and children from these households would also sit together and eat together. Whilst the food was cooked on separate fires, it was consumed communally, and there thus arose the possibility of exchange and sharing at the point of eating.[19] This form of sharing was perhaps more significant than the exchange of unprocessed foods between households. If for some reason (illness, labour shortage, old age) a woman was not able to provide all her own staple food needs, the deficit could at least be partially made good by her female relatives with whom she ate. Sharing at this stage also had the advantage of obscuring a woman's lack of self-sufficiency and enabling her to maintain respect.

The importance of the *mbumba* group as a unit of consumption has parallels elsewhere in the matrilineal belt of Central Africa, as well as continuing to be important in Southern Malawi today. Betty Preston Thomson's nutritional studies conducted in Northern Rhodesia between 1947 and 1950 uncovered a similar phenomenon (Thomson, 1954). Commenting on the difficulties of measuring individual food intake with any accuracy, Thomson gives some examples of the sharing of food. Although women in these Lala villages tended to eat separately in their huts with their children, and not communally as in Malawi, there was nevertheless a great deal of sharing and interchange of food. As Thomson pointed out, even when a bowl of food was sent to one person specifically, this did not mean that that person ate all the food in the bowl. One old woman, for instance, received food from her married daughters, but shared it with her grandchildren. Three married sisters in the same village all cooked separately, but 'were always in and out of each other's huts after cooking, helping themselves to each other's foods' (p. 48). Chet Lancaster's study of the Goba in Zimbabwe, conducted in the 1960s, noted that whilst dependent children and husbands always ate from the mother's nuclear family hearth and granary, seating arrangements within compounds were broken up along age and sex lines (Lancaster, 1981, p. 225). In these matrilocal compounds co-resident married daughters formed one group with their own daughters, their sisters and mother, and sometimes their mother's mother. The grain from one woman's granary was commonly shared within the extended family compound:

> This casual 'family' sharing is difficult to quantify, but when closely allied households fail to produce enough grain in any one year, the nuclear household with sufficient grain (or

other resources convertible into grain) may temporarily expand to share its supply and, in effect, form a temporary eating unit. (Lancaster, 1981, p. 225)

During the early stages of the famine, and presumably throughout the famine in some cases, this expansion of the consumption unit was extremely important in cushioning the less fortunate women and their families from the worst effects of food shortage. Oral accounts emphasise that food was shared between mothers and their adult daughters, amongst sisters, and other female relatives, in a pattern similar to the 'linking of ovens' noted by Firth in Tikopia. This was especially important for those women whose husbands were absent and not remitting money, or whose husbands had migrated at the start of the famine and not returned. Had the household really been the only functioning economic unit in normal times, then presumably this form of sharing would have been more difficult to achieve during a crisis, and the level of suffering of the weaker would have been greater.

As time went on, however, it seems that the units of consumption became smaller and smaller. Oral accounts stress that by January 1950 the custom of *ubombo* had broken down altogether. Not only was there widespread theft, but also the abandonment of the old and the young. Those who had at the beginning of the famine often shown great generosity, now turned away all but their immediate families, and within some of these families sharing broke down. People ate alone, in the dark and secretly. It was at this stage of the famine that the most vulnerable groups of women – the wives of migrants, the divorcees and the abandoned – began to suffer. Sharing between women of the same extended family was relatively easy when the food came from the grain-bins which were the women's property.[20] But as the famine wore on, so increasingly the available food within the *mbumba* unit was coming from 'male' sources – via employers, or as a result of the men's journeys to other areas. Such men, if they were married uxorilocally in their wives' villages, may not have seen the feeding of their sisters-in-law and families as a priority, and while in theory all these women would be under the protection of an elder brother, in practice he was unlikely to be able to support all of them. Marriage ties became crucial at this stage. For a woman to be married was to have direct access and first claim on 'male' sources of food. But in many cases marriage ties proved fragile.

Amongst the matrilineal peoples of Southern Malawi marriage had never been accompanied by any protracted ceremonial or exchange of goods. When Clyde Mitchell studied marriage amongst the Yao of present-day Machinga District in the 1940s, he found a high divorce rate.[21] Colonial observers frequently attributed the instability of marriage to the disruptive effects of 'modern times', but there is some evidence that marriage had never been so strong a bond as certain matrilineal ties. In the culture of this area a husband was depicted as a 'visiting cock', and his degree of incorporation into his in-laws' village was not great. There was no custom, as there was amongst the matrilineal peoples of the Central Province, of the bridegroom performing services for his parents-in-law which would entitle him to remove his bride to his own village after a certain period.[22] Uxorilocal marriage was thus the norm, though within this system village headmen and guardians of sorority groups had the right to remain in their mothers' villages and bring their wives to live with them.

A number of factors were at work in the colonial period which were affecting the operation of this institution. In particular, the rights and duties of a husband were being redefined in response to colonial policies (especially taxation policies) and to economic changes including the accumulation of inheritable wealth by some groups. Though hardly representative of society as a whole, the opinions of members of the African Protectorate and Provincial Councils in the 1940s are worth noting. These Councils were composed of male representatives of both the 'traditional' and the 'modern' African elite, including chiefs (Traditional Authorities) and non-chiefly coopted members. The chiefly members had a clear vested interest in the continuance of the matrilineal system, but even they sometimes expressed disquiet on the question of inheritance, for instance.

In the Southern Province African Council the subjects of marriage and inheritance arose frequently. In 1947 Chief Chikowi from Zomba District produced a list of twenty brick-built houses which had fallen into ruins in his area as the result of the death of one party to a marriage, and the prevailing rules of inheritance.[23] A husband and wife might build a 'good house' together and live in it together, but if the wife died then her relatives would turn the husband out of the house, which would then be left to fall into disrepair. In the same session Chief Somba made a plea for the interests of the children of a marriage to be taken into account, adding that they should be able to 'look forward to receiving the property by inheritance', which by matrilineal rules was impossible. He also complained that when a woman died her relatives usually took the children away, 'and the husband was left to do his own housework'. Mr Bandawe, a non-chiefly member from Blantyre, thought that times had changed and that customs should change accordingly:

> By the old custom the husband was nothing better than a cock expected to produce children but given no right over them. Whereas the children's uncle used to look after the children, now the husband did, and the time had come for them to say definitely that their old custom had died, and that henceforth a man should be the absolute owner of his property and children. (MNA, ADM 1/22)

This was wishful thinking on the part of Mr Bandawe and all the men he represented, for the matrilineal system proved remarkably resilient. The Rhodes-Livingstone studies of the 1950s indicated that uxorilocal marriage and matrilineal inheritance were still by far and away the norm, even in the peri-urban areas where one might have expected change to come about first.[24] There was undoubted opposition to the system on the part of men like Mr Bandawe, and on the part of the colonial government which saw the whole system as unprogressive. There was much discussion of matrilineality within the Department of Agriculture, as it was believed that for the conservation legislation to work, men would have to become more involved and have a greater stake and security in land than was common. In 1949 Clyde Mitchell was engaged to write a report on the social structure of T A Malemia's area in Zomba, where the Domasi Community Development scheme was being initiated. He concluded that matrilocal marriage was not in itself inimical to economic and political change, but that the high divorce rate of the area was.

> When long range plans for improvement are considered it must be remembered that a man will not expend great energy and expense on a project in his wife's village when his expectancy of continuing to live in that village is low . . . (MNA, MP 19376, Report on Social Structure, 1950)

The scheme encountered many problems which were seen to be created by the matrilineal system and made a unique but rather short-lived attempt at social engineering. Patronymics were required for tax registration, and the settlement of deceased estates on non-traditional lines was supported. Legislation was drawn up at the Native Authority level which would control land settlement, forbid fragmentation, encourage the nomination of heirs and 'provide protection for the man who wants to develop a holding for his own family' (MNA, MP 19376). Predictably the scheme encountered opposition from the traditional leaders, though it attempted to coopt them, as well as wider opposition from those (including many women) who resented the enforcement of conservation rules seen intrinsic to 'social progress'.

Elsewhere in Southern Malawi there was no such concerted effort to undermine matrilineality on the part of the authorities, though many tendencies in legislation were working in this direction.[25] District court divorce cases show, however, that women sometimes used the colonial legal system to resist attempts by men to subvert the matrilineal system. European magistrates did not always support women in these cases, though they were characteristically ambivalent in the face of appeals to 'custom'. Whilst the matrilineal system was seen as an obstacle to progress, any system was better than none, and many officials feared the creation of a 'social vacuum' in which no rules operated.

The earliest court cases were heard in a period when slave and semi-servile marriage was still common, and in such cases a woman had usually been captured or bought and taken to live at her 'owner's' home. There were many gradations of slave marriage and the positions of such women could differ quite markedly one from another. Often brothers and uncles of these women would attempt to use the European court to reclaim them as their own, and the cases demonstrate clearly how male status in a matrilineal society was closely bound up with the accumulation of dependent women. Sometimes cases were brought by the women themselves, who wished to return to their natal homes. In a case of 1909 for instance, a woman sued for separation saying that when she was a small girl she had been 'stolen' and had been placed in her captor's hut: 'I have lived with him ever since and have four children by him, but now I have found my brother and want to live with him' (MNA, BA 1/2/1 Case 138). Sometimes, however, the women concerned elected to stay with their 'husbands', despite the irregularity of their marriages. Women appear to have resisted attempts to regard them as mere chattels, arguing for choice in where and with whom they should live. The impression remains in these cases, however, that they were frequently regarded as commodities to be haggled over between men of different groups.[26]

With the decline of slave marriage, the cases coming before the Blantyre District Court frequently revolved around the issue of uxorilocal marriage in a matrilineal society. Men sued for the 'restoration of conjugal rights' when their wives refused to join them in residence at their place of work. In one typical case heard in 1909 the husband complained that his wife had gone to her mother's home at Michiru (on the outskirts of Blantyre) and demanded that he follow her there and build a house for her. It was shown in court that the woman's mother and family had previously lived at Kapeni's, where the husband had built a house, as was demanded of him by custom. The family had then left to settle at Michiru. The magistrate judged in this instance that 'a man cannot be expected to be constantly moving about to suit his mother-in-law's whims' (MNA, BA 1/2/1, Case 233). In another typical case the husband pleaded that his wife should leave her family's village and live with him at Ndirande near his work. His wife said in court that she did not want to leave her husband, but neither did she want to abandon her garden and her own family. In this case a compromise solution was worked out, involving the woman spending some time with her husband, and some at home, and stipulating that she should not have to move prior to having harvested the crops in her garden (MNA, BA 1/2/1, Case 196).

Whilst men generally sued for the restoration of conjugal rights, and fought against the demands of their wives to reside with their maternal families, so women increasingly used the courts to sue for divorce. In the course of the early colonial period it seems that women began to redefine the duties of their husbands to include not only the traditional one of building a hut for them in their maternal villages, but also paying the tax on this hut. In so doing they were making use of the tendencies within colonial legislation to force a man to be responsible for his wife and own children. It was perhaps a rather ambiguous move for women to take, as many were simultaneously resisting the demands of their husbands for them to live virilocally. A woman who could prove that her husband had not been paying her tax was usually granted a divorce in the district court (though if she sued for divorce on grounds of ill-treatment she was unlikely to be granted it) and be free to remarry:

> My husband has deserted me for four or five years. I now want to remarry. He married me when I was a small girl and before I grew up he went away to work and has not come back. For the last four years I have lived alone with my mother and paid our tax. Now I am tired of paying tax and I want to marry Saiti, an *askari*. (MNA, BS 1/1/1, Case 86)

A woman could also effect a divorce by *refusing* her husband's offer of tax payment, as one distraught man recounted to the court in 1907:

> N.K. gave me his daughter long ago and we lived quietly. At length the woman refused to sleep with me and I knocked down my house because my wife would not pay a tax with my money. She bought a tax with 6/- of her own. (MNA, BS 1/1/1, Case 64)

A woman could use the same refusal to avoid living in a polygamous marriage, for although polygamy was uncommon in Southern Malawi, Ngoni men who were marrying into this area often attempted to maintain two wives, including one in their Central Province homes.

> I married N. five years ago and another wife three years ago, and now N.'s father say he does not want me to have another wife, and N. refuses the money which I sent her to pay her tax. (MNA, BS 1/1/1, Case 103)

One of the major difficulties faced by the courts in dealing with any of these cases was how to establish whether a marriage had existed in the first place. No goods changed hands at marriage in this system, but in theory each marriage partner had to have appointed witnesses or *ankhoswe* who could be called upon to arbitrate in any marital dispute. Increasingly, however, it seemed that 'marriages' were conducted without *ankhoswe*, and this presented problems when one or other party demanded compensation. By the 1940s such marriages without formality were apparently the norm in Blantyre District and some 'elders' saw this as subversive of their authority. In the Southern Province African Council, Chief Katuli outlined the system of *ankhoswe* and went on to say that 'many of the present marriages take place on the agreement between the man and woman without first obtaining the consent of the woman's parents so that *chinkhoswe* should be fixed'. This kind of marriage did not 'offer due respect to the responsible persons of the family (*mwini mbumba*)' (MNA, ADM 1/22 16/9/46). Chief Somba said that when cases of marriage without *ankhoswe* came before him, 'the parties were asked how long they had been together and whether they still loved each other'. If they no longer wanted each other he called for whatever property they had in their hut and divided it equally 'telling them that they had no right to compensation because there were no *ankhoswe* and their marriage was not regular with the Native Authorities, or in church, and in fact was no marriage at all'.

A new problem had apparently arisen by the 1940s as a result of the laxity of marriage alliances, combined with changing economic circumstances. Children of 'irregular unions' were now defined by the members of the Provincial council as 'illegitimate'. Mr Kumbikano explained the problem presented by these children:

> In the old days illegitimate children caused no trouble as there was plenty of food. Times were now different and more difficult and the mother alone could not look after the child. The burden of a come-by-chance child was left with the mother, and women were still dependent upon male support. (MNA, ADM 1/22, 16/9/46)

Chief Somba explained that the object of the *ankhoswe* system had been to prevent this sort of thing from happening 'but the girl would not listen and went wrong and very rarely would the men own up, thus it was very difficult for the chiefs or parents to bring a case'. Mr Bandawe, as always in favour of radical solutions, believed that they should deal with the problem 'by changing their customs'.

Even more perplexing were the problems posed by 'inter-tribal' marriages. In Blantyre District, as we have seen, marriage links between the matrilineal Yao and patrilineal, *lobola*-giving Ngoni, had been common since the beginning of the century, when many Ngoni men came south to work on the European estates of the Shire Highlands. They frequently married into Yao communities there, and conforming to matrilineal rules, they took up residence there. By so doing they were gaining a more secure foothold in the wage economy of the south, as well as access to food from their wives' gardens. In the 1950s Bettison found Ngoni immigration into Blantyre District still continuing along lines established in this early period. One example was Mlanga village in Chief Kapeni's area. Many of the inhabitants of this village in the 1950s came from Kachindamoto's area of Dedza District, though the original 'core' of the village was Yao:

> This association is said to have arisen from a trade in meat established in the village with the permission of the central lineage some three or four decades ago. The chief sent a number of his followers from Dedza to reside in the village and manage his business. Some of the men have remained despite the closing of the business many years ago. The contact between the chiefs' followers in Dedza and in Mlanga village provides immigrants with a place to settle at the present time. (Bettison, 1958d, p. 25)

In another example an Ngoni 'accretion' in a Yao village had been established by a man who had come to work in Blantyre in 1926. Once he found work other men had followed to take up residence there (p. 16). In Bettison's peri-urban studies, 33.9 per cent of the population classified themselves as Ngoni (compared to 35.9 per cent who were Yao) (Bettison, 1958c, p. 18), but there were very few Ngoni central lineages in the villages surveyed. Ngoni residence was most commonly in the form of 'accretions' to Yao villages or through inter-tribal marriage. Bettison concluded that despite the tribal mix, the 'typical Yao matrilineal structure' dominated in the peri-urban villages (Bettison, 1958d, p. 43).

The pattern of the early colonial period of Ngoni men conforming to uxorilocal rules appears to have persisted. In Bettison's survey uxorilocal marriages represented 73 per cent of the total sample, and this figure included a significant proportion of marriages in which one (or both) parties were Ngoni (Bettison, 1958c, p. 32). The court records do indicate, however, that specific problems arose in marriages between Yao women and Ngoni men. When older, an Ngoni man might sometimes wish to return to live in his natal home, and this caused problems if his wife refused to accompany him. If an Ngoni man died whilst in the south, his relatives frequently arrived to exert their patrilineal rights over his wife and children. If *lobola* had been paid, and thus the marriage conformed to Ngoni rules in one respect, then the court usually upheld the right of the father's relatives to the 'ownership' of the children. In many cases, however, *lobola* was not paid for wives from southern matrilineal areas, and so the issue was more confused. Cases of child custody and uxorilocal versus virilocal residence were common in the Blantyre courts in the period for which records survive. Such issues continued to perplex the Blantyre chiefs in the 1940s. In 1946 the Southern Province African Council debated these issues and resolved that when a man from a patrilineal area married a woman from a matrilineal area, and when no *lobola* had been paid, then matrilineal custom should be followed (MNA, ADM 1/22 Provincial Council Meetings, Agenda and Proceedings: Southern Province, 1945–7).

Bettison's study in the 1950s found that Yao women were most likely to be married to Yao men, but that the pattern of Yao–Ngoni marriage was still strong. He also found a large number of 'unattached' women (32 per cent of the total), most of whom he described as 'grass widows' whose husbands were absent (Bettison, 1958c, p. 24). The majority of these grass widows were Yao women under the age of 39, and as Ngoni men were found to have a greater tendency than others to migrate outside the country (p. 81), it seems likely that many of these 'grass widows' were Yao women married to Ngoni men. These were the very women whose plight during the famine is highlighted in oral accounts.

The evidence on long-term change in marriage and the matrilineal system is patchy, but I have tried to fit what is available together, as without this longer perspective the events of a short-term crisis cannot be adequately understood. There is no conclusive evidence to show that the late 1940s was a particular period of crisis for the social system, despite the propensity of colonial administrators and traditional leaders to see it as such. It is very difficult to say, for instance, whether divorce had become very much more frequent by the late colonial period, or whether marriage without sureties had really been unknown in the past. After all, the immediate pre-colonial past to which this period has to be contrasted was one in which women were frequently bought and sold as slave wives – hardly a picture of conventional marriage by any standards. The traditional leaders who sat on the Provincial and Protectorate Councils had their own reasons for portraying the past differently, and for claiming that their previous control was being undermined. Similarly, court cases, whilst useful for showing the strains in a system, are biased towards the problematical, and this does need to be constantly borne in mind.

The experience of women during the famine, then, cannot be seen as the result of a new and extreme crisis in the social system which exposed them to starvation in a way which would have been impossible before. There are some strands we can draw together, however, which support the view that *some* groups of women were emerging as vulnerable in this period, to a degree which was more pronounced than in the previous fifty years. Central to this was the interaction between economic variables and the social system. The latter was, as we have seen, subject to strain and struggle over a long period, and not just in the 1940s. Furthermore, some of the changes I have documented could be very localised in their effects, and should not be seen as constituting a uniform and unilinear development in the position of women. The work of Mandala (1983) on the Lower Shire and White (1987) on the estates of the Shire Highlands, when taken together, make this point very clear. Both see a deterioration in the economic position and status of women occurring in the 1930s and 1940s, but for entirely different reasons. In the case of the Lower Shire, Mandala argues that the decline of cotton cash-cropping and its replacement in the economic system by labour migration and cattle keeping, undermined the economic independence of women. White, on the other hand, sees the *rise* of the tenant tobacco industry on the Bruce estates (occurring at about the same period) as being prejudicial to the interests of women. Tobacco was a totally 'male' crop, over which the women had little or no control. Clearly the mere existence of a cash-cropping economy, therefore, does not define the economic role and status of women, and needs to be seen as acting together with a number of other variables, the most crucial being the availability of land and the degree of control over it exercised by women. The history of the Bruce estates shows this dramatically, for when the government decided to appropriate this land at the end of the 1940s and reallocate it to African tenants, the decline in status of the women was quickly reversed as they suddenly found themselves in control of a very valuable asset. Just a few miles away, on Native Trust Land, the situation was entirely different, with land shortage continuing to become more critical.

What I have documented in this chapter then, are elements of change in the economic and social system of parts of Blantyre District, which were affecting women in their relationships with men. Some of these changes are generalisable to a much wider area, but it needs to be constantly borne in mind that they interact with local circumstances to different effect.

To summarise the evidence of this chapter, it would seem that despite many pressures, the matrilineal system still provided the basic framework for social and political action in Southern Malawi in the late 1940s. The linkages between women and their brothers were particularly pivotal to the functioning of this system. Much less prominent in the culture, but more significant from an economic point of view, were the gender-specific linkages between women, their sisters and mothers, and other female matrilineal relatives. For whilst an elder brother had clear social obligations towards his sisters and their children, his economic obligations were less clear cut. He might be expected to help a sister if she was in need, but rarely would this help take the form of direct gifts of food, as the food upon which he himself drew was held by his wife in her grain-bin (Mitchell, personal communication, 1985). Female relatives, on the other hand, constantly exchanged food, despite (or in some cases, because of) the strong prevailing ideal that an adult woman would be able to provision herself and her children with the product of her land. Closely related women commonly ate together, and this facilitated discreet exchange of food which cushioned those temporarily unable to provide for themselves, as well as the very old or sick.

The institution of marriage within this social system was structurally unstable and was in the process of being redefined, partly in response to some of the new economic circumstances of the colonial period and the tendencies of colonial legislation. Women were actively involved in redefining the institution. They defended their rights to uxorilocal marriage and to close cooperation with matrikin. At the same time they attempted, in line with colonial thinking, to enforce a greater degree of financial responsibility on their husbands. There was a tension between these two approaches which emerges clearly in the marriage cases coming before the Blantyre District Court. Undoubtedly these tendencies were prevalent in the whole of the Southern Province matrilineal areas, but in Blantyre District there was the added dimension provided by the presence of a large number of Ngoni men from the Central Province who conformed to the matrilineal system at one level, but who under some circumstances were liable to fight for the rights over children and residence which were theirs within a patrilineal framework.

Like any other social system, that of Southern Malawi was an arena of struggle and compromise, of conformity and non-conformity, and probably always had been. Similarly there had always been economic change influencing the operation of this system. Probably the most extreme example of this could be found in the historically brief period of the height of the slave trade. By the late 1940s there were other economic factors at work which were of significance for social relationships. One was the gradual, creeping land shortage which had become severe in places and which necessitated some communities, or families within these, becoming more dependent on cash sources of income than ever before. This was of particular significance to women as a group, because it meant that the resources over which they had control were becoming less central to the reproduction of society. This is not to say that *all* women experienced a decline in economic status within their households or wider units. Land was very unevenly distributed within villages, and so it is only for some women that this generalisation would hold true. However, this was an important development affecting increasing numbers of women, and especially significant when taken in conjunction with the second major economic change, which was the accelerating growth of wage labour (both local and migrant). At the level of the 'formal sector' this was virtually a male preserve, though women were involved in the growing sector of casual intra-African employment. As we saw in Chapter 4, economic differentiation within African communities of Southern Malawi gathered pace in the 1940s. Women were of course members of all the emerging class groups, and even in the most disadvantaged of these groups they developed economic strategies to ensure themselves a level of self-sufficiency and independence from their husbands. The evidence for the importance of beer brewing and *kachasu* distillation within the local economy is testimony to this. For those women whose husbands were absent as migrants such strategies were particularly important. The major limitation to this self-sufficiency, however, was that women's cash-earning activities were subject to a seasonal fluctuation much more pronounced than that of the major 'male' strategies. This meant that for part of the year some women experienced a decline in income, and at such times they would rely more heavily on their husbands, or on transfers of cash from their brothers, combined perhaps with food from more fortunate female relatives.

What happened in the 1949 famine was an extreme exaggeration of this pattern of the seasonal dependence of some groups of women on their menfolk. When the rains failed and the crops failed, some women lost their direct entitlement to food from their own gardens, stored in their own grain-bins. But they also lost much of their indirect entitlement as their usual cash-raising strategies – beer brewing, *kachasu* distillation, petty trading and *ganyu* labour – either dried up through lack of demand or were prohibited by the authorities. Male cash-earning strategies became more crucial. Those men who were in formal wage employment were particularly privileged in their access to scarce food supplies, and some of this food reached their wives, children, sisters. But the extent to which women shared in this access depended on a number of moral and emotional factors unforeseen by the colonial authorities who constructed the famine policy. Some men took their duties as husbands, brothers, fathers and uncles, very seriously, but ultimately there had to be a narrowing of obligations. A woman with either a husband or a brother in wage employment stood a better chance of access to food than one without such links, but the access was not guaranteed. In a society in which the rights and duties of husbands and brothers were the subject of constant negotiation, some women found themselves without male support of any kind.

The most vulnerable of all the women, however, were those without male support but for whom the colonial authorities took no direct responsibility during the famine. Married women whose husbands had abandoned them, and wives of long-term migrants who did not remit money, constituted this group. Only after pressure from village headmen and chiefs did the authorities concede that these women might be eligible for free food. To this extent, the suffering of women in the famine was constructed as much around government famine relief policy as it was around marriage and kinship structures.

In their songs and stories, women in the Blantyre area have appropriated the experiences of this most vulnerable group in the famine as 'women's experience', and give the impression that all women suffered equally. From individual life-histories it is clear that this is not true, and that the class position of any given woman was an important factor in determining how and if she personally suffered. It is also clear, however, that gender could act as an independent variable, though the degree to which this was true, and the emphasis to give to it in any analysis, is not easy to determine. In Southern Malawi, where women in normal times had quite considerable control over foodstuffs, had independent sources of cash income, and lived within social forms which facilitated food-sharing, we might expect the sufferings of women in the famine to have been less than they would under similar circumstances in other societies. When famine occurred in patrilineal areas of Zimbabwe in the 1890s, for instance, women were frequently evicted from their husbands' villages, and left destitute (personal communication, Terence Ranger, 1985). In the Indian sub-continent, where in normal times female children and women are often nutritionally disadvantaged *vis à vis* males, one might also expect the suffering of women during a famine to be more acute than it was in Southern Malawi. Whilst there is much literature on the nutritional deprivation of women and girls in normal times, there is very little literature on women's experience of famine. If gender does act as an independent variable, then in the construction of famine relief policies it needs to be taken into account.

6

After the famine: a conclusion

Viewing the famine as a Malthusian crisis, the Department of Agriculture saw its occurrence as a confirmation of its views on African agriculture, the need for conservation measures, and greater government intervention. The main lines of the Department's policy were not altered by the experience of the famine, but pursued with greater vigour and urgency as a result. In 1950 an increasing number of subordinate European Field Staff were employed 'in an attempt to inculcate into African peasants certain basic elementary principles and practices in the shortest possible time' (Nyasaland Protectorate, Department of Agriculture, *Annual Report* 1950, p. 5). There was to be greater intervention by the Department, and greater concentration of efforts on those Africans seen as 'progressive elements' who could act as examples to the masses. In the short term, however, there was one important change in policy, and this was the raising of the producer price for maize – a measure which, as we have seen, had been long resisted by the Department.

In 1950 maize was bought by the Maize Control Board at 1d. per lb, which was double the price paid prior to the famine. Buying by the Board was permitted in all areas where a surplus seemed likely. It was a good harvest, despite the difficulties some people experienced in getting seed, and despite the fact that so many people were weakened by hunger at the time when their labour was most needed on the crop. After the inflated prices of the famine, it was feared that producers would not sell, even at this comparatively high official price. But the fear proved unfounded, and large surpluses were produced. A total of 10,400 tons were bought, of which 70 per cent came from three districts: Lilongwe and Dedza in the Central Province and Mulanje District in the South (Nyasaland Protectorate, Department of Agriculture, *Annual Report* 1950, p. 6).

In 1951 the official price remained the same, and a record surplus of 28,500 tons was bought by the Maize Control Board (MCB), who guaranteed to purchase all surplus maize offered for sale at the official price (Nyasaland Protectorate, Department of Agriculture, *Annual Report* 1951, p. 5). In the same year a record tobacco crop was also produced, which implied that maize was not necessarily being grown at the expense of other crops. Already, however, the spectre of the famine was receding somewhat in the memories of officials of the Department of Agriculture, who viewed with alarm the increase in maize mono-cropping. By 1952 the maize surplus purchased had risen to over 40,000 tons, and the Annual Report of the Department again expressed concern that the increase in the area under maize was 'prejudicing the introduction of balanced crop rotation and adding to the danger of erosion' (Department of Agriculture, *Annual Report* 1952, p. 3). By 1953, a policy decision had been taken which, it was hoped, would discourage this tendency. Areas seen as marginal to maize production were not provided with official markets. These areas were defined in a number of ways. Surplus maize production was to be discouraged in areas where it was seen as desirable to stimulate the production of particular cash crops – cotton in the Lower Shire being a prime example. In other cases, high population density and/or unsuitable soil or topography were given as reasons. Areas where labour was required to work on European plantations (such as the tea estates in Mulanje) were also deemed unsuitable for surplus maize production. Finally, those areas which were close to urban markets were to have their maize trades 'freed', and official markets were not to be provided here. Blantyre District was the main example of this category.[1] In Blantyre, Mulanje and Chiradzulu, where restrictions were placed on maize buying, an official market for sorghum was established, and some surplus produced. Sorghum had proved itself a valuable crop during the famine, and along with the root crops, began to receive more attention from the Department (Nyasaland Protectorate, Department of Agriculture, *Annual Report* 1954, Part I, p. 4).

The Department's policy of limiting maize purchases to certain areas met with opposition from the Governor, and other non-agricultural officials, for whom the memory of the famine – its cost to the administration, the threat of political insurrection it held, the administrative difficulties it posed – was vivid. In 1953 the Governor attacked the Department's maize policy, arguing that this should be directed towards producing the maximum possible surplus of maize, and that the country could not regard itself as safe until it could keep 50,000 tons of maize in store. He argued further that the Department's policy was negative and dangerous, and that maize ought to be regarded as the most important economic crop as 'there can be no doubt that food in this part of Africa is going to become the greatest single problem in the next generation' (MNA Secretariat MP 21331: H.E.'s minute on maize production policy 9/3/53).

The practical problems of storage, however, combined with a slump in the price of maize on the world market, together strengthened the Department of Agriculture's arguments. In 1955 there was overproduction of maize both in neighbouring countries and elsewhere, and the world price fell to below the price at which Malawian maize could be sold (Nyasaland Protectorate, Department of Agriculture, *Annual Report* 1955, Part I, p. 2). In 1956 a large stock was sold at a loss on the world market (Department of Agriculture, *Annual Report* 1956, p. 2), and in 1957 the price paid to the producer was dropped to $\frac{2}{3}$d per lb, resulting in a fall in the surplus purchased (Department of Agriculture, *Annual Report* 1957, p. 6). This went hand in hand with a greater degree of activity on the part of African traders whose activities were now regarded as essential and benign, and who moved surpluses from one area of the country to another. Much of this surplus was being bought by them at the old official price of 1d. per lb (p. 4). By 1959 the Department was openly declaring a change in maize marketing policy. As soon as the African Produce and Marketing Board (a successor to the Maize Control Board) had purchased its basic requirements, the market was 'freed', and licensed buyers could choose either to purchase directly from the Board or from the growing number of African traders (Nyasaland Protectorate, Department of Agriculture, *Annual Report* 1959, p. 4).

Although the Department gradually withdrew from direct intervention in marketing in the course of the 1950s, it did not withdraw from other areas of agricultural policy which it regarded as crucial. The famine had, according to the Department's thinking, merely emphasised the need for a more aggressive policy on conservation, and this was pursued in the 1950s with some important political results. Departmental thinking also became more wedded to the elitist model of development argued by some in the 1940s. Whilst the 'masses' were to be forced to adhere to elementary conservation rules, the future of agricultural production was seen to lie in the development of a 'yeoman' class, and extension advice was directed increasingly towards such individuals. This policy was partly dictated by the limited resources available to the Department. In its 1957 Annual Report it declared a change of emphasis (which in fact, had been evident for some years) in its extension programme:

> Whereas in the past effort has tended to be thinly dispersed over the mass of the population to effect simple general improvements in cultural and conservation matters, present policy is increasingly to concentrate on comparatively limited objectives with the more responsive individuals and communities where tangible results can be expected. (p. 12)

Though limited resources were part of the explanation for this emphasis, there was also a conception underlying it of the type of 'development' possible and desirable. I have already noted this trend of official thinking in the 1940s, and it was given greater prominence with the appointment of R. W. Kettlewell as Director of Agriculture. In his 'Outline of Agrarian Problems and Policy in Nyasaland', written in 1955, Kettlewell argued that population increase was the major problem being faced in Malawi, and that radical solutions were needed

(Nyasaland Protectorate, *Outline of Agrarian Problems*, 1955). These included the active encouragement of family limitation ('if economics are left to teach that lesson it will be learned too late', p. 6), as well as the encouragement of family emigration within the Federation of the Rhodesias and Nyasaland:

> With a federal outlook on Rhodesian and Nyasaland problems it will be possible further to assist the needs of a static labour force in Rhodesian industry by means of more family emigration from Nyasaland. (p. 6)

Kettlewell's agricultural policy was to a large degree determined by his concern over population. He argued (as he had done in the 1940s) that the objective must be 'to create a class of professional farmers with sufficient land to derive a reasonable standard of living, and to remove the subsistence cultivator from the land into other employment' (p. 3). Policy would then take two lines. Firstly, farming would have to be intensified, and this necessitated a 'correct' land tenure system which would encourage the individual 'yeoman' farmer. Secondly, other occupations would have to be encouraged, and adequate wages paid to those who were not selected as 'farmers'. He wanted, in particular, to bring an end to the 'straddling' strategy of so many low-paid workers who 'maintain one foot on the land, usually in the shape of an unaided and unenlightened wife, in order to provide some security and supplement in a low-wage economy' (p. 6).

The 'Master Farmers' scheme was one of the programmes arising out of this policy. Individuals were sought out who were regarded as 'promising' farmers. They enrolled in the scheme, and in return for abiding by its stringent rules, were rewarded with free fertilizer, bonuses, and Master Farmer medals. The problem, however, was to find enough such individuals who were able and prepared to accept the conditions of the scheme. In 1951, for instance, the Provincial Agricultural Officer for the Southern Province had reported on the disappointing results of his search for potential Master Farmers. It had not been possible to recommend any single award in the Province that year, and the number of 'collaborators' was very small (MNA, AGR 3/2 1951 Provincial AO to DA Zomba 19/12/51). In both Blantyre and Zomba districts there were none. According to him, the majority of prospective candidates fell down on the condition of resting land and rotating crops. These were just two of a long list of conditions all seen as crucial to the model of agriculture being aimed at. Potential Master Farmers had to agree to:

(1) Practise all soil conservation measures advocated by the Department of Agriculture and the Natural Resources Board.
(2) Observe completely all agricultural rules and regulations applicable to the locality.
(3) Practise crop rotation and the use of a fallow period.

(4) Maintain a high standard of husbandry, including seed selection.
(5) Cultivate a variety of crops.
(6) Apply farmyard manure or a compost to at least part of a garden.
(7) Show good management and housing of livestock, and where possible, the preservation and use of manure, and preferably the employment of cattle for draft purposes.
(8) Show possession and good management of a few fruit trees, and the preservation of domestic timber trees as well.
(9) Cultivate a few vegetables for household consumption.
(10) Possess adequate storage facilities for crops.

(MNA, AGR 3/2 Director of Agriculture to Provincial Agricultural Officers, 11/11/50)

The pursuance of this policy was made doubly difficult by the fact that the most obvious candidates – the 'progressive', individuals with sufficient resources – were often also the politically active and hostile. Throughout the 1930s and 1940s attempts had been made to foster the attitudes of the potential Master Farmer amongst Native Authorities and Village Headmen, as members of the 'traditional' elite to whom increasing administrative powers were being given.

Courses for traditional leaders were held at the Jeanes Training Centre at Domasi, which was later to become the nucleus of the Domasi Community Development Scheme.[2] Here chiefs and their wives were instructed on how to build improved housing, on agricultural techniques and conservation, on health and sanitation. They were encouraged to send their heirs to school so that 'if and when these become chiefs, they may have had as good an education as the best of their people' (MNA, NS 1/8/3 Report on Second Course of Native Authorities May 1935). But the problem of disrespect for chiefs on the part of the younger educated people was already a subject of discussion in the 1930s. Instructors at the Jeanes Centre in 1935 suggested that this problem might be helped by the invention of new signs of respect ranging from 'the Hitler salute to a curtsey or the removal of headgear' to replace the kneeling posture which younger people often objected to (MNA, NS 1/8/3).

In general the policy of enhancing the status of traditional leaders was not a success, and in any case education did not always work in favour of government policy. The mass literacy campaign which formed part of the Domasi Community Development Scheme in the 1950s, for instance, had some unexpected results as the anti-Federation campaign of the nationalists gathered pace. One of the questions on the rural science paper of the Kwaca literacy school in Domasi in 1953 was 'What good purposes do bunds serve?', and the unanimous written answer of the candidates was 'Bunds are bad' (MNA, NS 3/3/1).

Greater intervention on the part of the Department only stimulated heightened opposition. The 'progressive' educated elite of the Southern

Province largely supported the Nyasaland African Congress campaign against political federation with the Rhodesias, and they were not impressed by the Department's Master Farmer Scheme. In 1949 they had submitted a memo to the Secretary of State making clear their view of how agricultural development should proceed:

> Nyasaland being a purely agriculture [*sic*] country depending on produce by the efforts of the masses, Congress wish that Africans must now be assisted to own mechanical agricultural implements if they are to play a greater part in the production of both foodstuffs and other economic crops. The day of a hoe and a handle is far gone and it will be of great help if they could be helped to procure small power tractors for the production of foodstuffs and their tobacco and cotton. They will have to pay for them but on easy terms. Also extensive agricultural training will be undertaken if the Africans are to take greater part in the production of food and cash crops. The country's resources are such that they cannot support a great number of Europeans as field supervisors. Therefore the establishment of an Agricultural Training Centre is quickly and urgently required . . . (MNA, AGR 3/2 extract from memo of NAC to Secretary of State, n.d.)

The Director of Agriculture dismissed these appeals with the reply that there were obvious dangers in 'enabling an untrained and unenlightened community to expose vast tracts of land to the evils of soil erosion by the use of mechanical appliances', and that in any case mechanisation could not succeed until 'traditional' attitudes towards land tenure had been modified (MNA, AGR 3/2, Director of Agriculture, 15/4/49).

In so far as the famine brought about an increased intervention on the part of the Department of Agriculture in cultivation practices of ordinary people, so it can be said that it contributed towards the development of an effective nationalist movement in Malawi. Agricultural, and especially conservation, policies became the focuses of popular agitation and opposition throughout Malawi, and united strategically the educated elite with the mass of the rural population (White, 1987; Beinart, 1984).

In the famine areas of Blantyre District itself, the increased energy with which the Department of Agriculture pursued its conservation programme was seen as a direct consequence of the famine, and by some as a 'punishment' for it. Mr Peter of TA Kapeni's area remembered that in 1950 the government officials ordered them to make *migula*, or large bunds, to prevent soil erosion. Those who did not oblige were tried at Msenje Court and fined £3, and if they could not afford to pay they were arrested and imprisoned.[3] The impression of the government punishing them for the famine was strengthened by the levying of a 'famine tax' of 2s. 6d. per adult man in the areas in which relief food had been distributed (Interviews and MNA, AFC 3/2/1 and AFC 3/1/1).

Most informants recall that after the famine more people planted cassava as an insurance crop, and that the fast-maturing variety known as *chitekere* became more common.[4] If the Department of Agriculture was anxious to discourage the strategy of 'straddling' between wage labour and agriculture, the effect of the famine was, if anything, to encourage this. Mr Champimpha of TA Chigaru recalls how, in 1950, when he was working as a clerk at Malamulo mission in Thyolo district, he sent his wife back to her home in Lirangwe to open a maize garden, and from then on he went there at week-ends to help her: 'We did this so as to secure a maize store for ourselves.'[5]

In the course of the 1950s Blantyre District produced an increased officially marketed surplus of sorghum, and of seed cotton – the latter in response to better prices – while the Trust Land African tobacco industry faded. The demand for pulses on the part of Indian traders fostered a new cash-crop industry in the area, and by 1956 3,795 short tons of pulses were bought by the Produce Board in markets in Blantyre District (Nyasaland Protectorate, Department of Agriculture, *Annual Report* 1956). But the main lesson of the famine must have been that there were considerable advantages to be gained by links into the wage economy, and for women, by establishing a secure, independent cash income, so that the main pre-famine lines of economic change in the area were probably continued afterwards.

The majority of women continued to engage in beer and *kachasu* manufacture and small-scale trading, and they were employed on the estates in slowly increasing numbers. Amongst the small educated elite of Blantyre District there was some male reaction against this female independence, and a new conception grew of the role of the 'respectable' woman in the home. This conception was encouraged by the increasing activities of the Social Welfare Officers in Blantyre District, evidenced in the setting up of Women's Institutes. In Kuntaja's area in 1951 the members of the WI were engaged in making children's dresses for presentation to the Mitsidi orphanage (MNA, MP 20933, Report of Social Welfare Officer, 1951). By 1947 some representatives to the Southern Province African Council had already argued that women should not be allowed to work for wages on the estates, and the meeting recommended to the government that no married African woman should be employed on paid work unless her husband had agreed and that employers of labour should be required to give adequate reasons why they required to employ African female labour before they were permitted to employ such labour (MNA, ADM 1/22, Record of 7th Session, 5–7 May 1947).

It is doubtful if such decisions made much impact on more than a minority of women, though the pattern of formal wage employment being a largely male preserve continues in Malawi up to the present day.

Today Malawi enjoys an unusual reputation in Africa for being self-sufficient in (and sometimes an exporter of) foodstuffs. President Banda is constantly reminding his people of this, and of the sufferings of the 1949 famine caused, it is claimed, by the policies of the colonial government. In fact, the lines of agricultural policy adopted by Banda's independent government were very little different from those of the colonialists. For much of the post-independence period the peasant sector has been taxed for the benefit of a growing large-farm sector, through the operations of the official marketing board, Admarc (Kydd, 1985). Wages remain extremely low by the standards of the region, and labour emigration has ceased to be available as an alternative employment strategy. In what one might be tempted to see as a re-run of the story of 1949, maize producer prices were depressed in the 1970s, and at the end of that decade a serious famine occurred, which was especially severe in both the Lower and Middle Shire Valley. Subsequently, the maize price was increased, and since then a regular surplus has been produced. For the most part, the people of Malawi do not starve, though they are very poor by all measurements. With an annual population growth rate of 3.1 per cent, the problems of land pressure and exhaustion in the south of the country are serious, though whether they can be seen as constituting a Malthusian crisis in the 1980s is just as open to question as it was for the 1940s.

The famine of 1949 was not a drama on the scale of that faced in the 1980s by the people of the Sahel and the Horn of Africa. It was a famine structured by the social and economic developments of the preceding one hundred years, and cannot be understood in terms of a simple 'subsistence crisis'. In Chapter 2, as in the Introduction, I have questioned the validity and usefulness of the 'subsistence agriculture' framework in analysing the famine. Subsistence, in Southern Malawi, had long been predicated on some degree of exchange.[6] In the course of the colonial period this tendency went much farther, and specialisation increased to the point at which there were many communities no longer attempting or expecting to grow more than a small proportion of their subsistence needs. Although colonial observers saw this development as a natural precursor of famine, I have argued that this perspective was incorrect, and resulted in a misleading interpretation of the causes of the disaster. Because such a large number of people in Southern Malawi were dependent on the market for a large part of their subsistence needs, the analysis of food supply has had to move from a local to a national (and international) level, to look at factors such as pricing policy, political manipulation of markets, government intervention, and so on. Moving between one level of analysis and another, between local factors and the wider influences, allows us to build up a more accurate picture of the trends in food supply in colonial Malawi, and their causation. This is not the whole story, however. At some point it becomes essential to distinguish this analysis of the longer-term trends in food supply from the analysis of the famine itself, for whilst the former supplies an important component of the explanation for the famine's occurrence it does not tell us who starved and why. To understand these questions we need to look more closely at the nature of economic differentiation in the area in which the famine occurred, and see how this meshed with social relations and, most crucially, with government famine policy.

There is no doubt that the colonial government's intervention in providing famine relief saved many people from starvation. Its ability to move foodstuffs, not only within the country, but half-way across the world, meant that large-scale starvation was avoided. Its reluctance and tardiness in intervening, however, and its definition of the social structure with which it dealt, meant that unnecessary suffering occurred amongst some groups, and these groups were to a large extent determined by the policy itself. There seems little point in asking the question whether fewer or more people would have starved in a pre-colonial context, as such a famine would not have occurred in a comparable form.

Some groups would have been more vulnerable in the pre-colonial past, some less so, but there were areas of overlap as well. Those whose vulnerability to starvation was defined to a great extent by biology – the very old, and the young, for instance – were probably less liable to starve in 1949 than they had been in the past, since the colonial government defined them as a group worthy of direct attention in the feeding programme. Wage labourers in the formal sector of the economy also had their subsistence largely ensured by government policy and intervention. Others were less fortunate, however. The marginal agricultural producers of the Middle Shire Valley were probably more vulnerable to food insecurity as a consequence of the intervention of the colonial Department of Agriculture. Those who had a link into the formal wage economy were safer, but those who did not were left to depend on older forms of social security involving kinship links. The evidence of the famine shows that many of these forms survived. Patron–client relations and kinship ties certainly did save a great many people from starvation, though they were perhaps less assured than they had been in the past. In the 1862–3 famine it was those people without 'protectors' who suffered, as the society was structured around servile relationships. In 1949 the colonial government had in part taken over the role of patron. We have seen that, when it seemed politically apt (as with the wage labourers) this patron would act to protect its clients, but in other cases (women, for instance) it devolved the responsibility onto a social system the workings of which it did not fully comprehend and which was being constantly influenced by its own policies.

The history of the 1949 famine draws attention to the need for analysis at a number of different levels. Aggregate figures may tell us something about long-term trends in food production, but these trends in themselves do not determine the occurrence or non-occurrence of a famine. We need constantly to move backwards and forwards from the large issues of policy, world markets and intervention, to the local circumstances of the famine area to gain a total picture. Policy and prices are mediated the whole time through regional and local economic and social structures. Conversely, the identification of an apparent 'Malthusian crisis' in a localised area is an inadequate determinant of famine if the population of that area is closely linked to wider economic and political structures through which it reproduces itself. Malthusian theories in this case are singularly unhelpful, working as they do within a vacuum. The argument that government intervention in marketing and pricing inhibited surplus food production in some areas of colonial Malawi seems to provide part of the explanation for long-term food supply trends, but does not in itself explain the occurrence of famine. When pressed, the government relinquished much of its shaky control over food markets in any case. Less government intervention may have helped to secure a freer supply of foodstuffs into the areas in which there was a shortage, but would not have guaranteed access to food on the part of the most vulnerable groups. For the latter, it was more rather than less intervention which was needed. Withdrawal from market relations (as advocated by some for the present-day Sahelian region) would not seem to have been a viable alternative.

It will be clear by now that there are no definitive lessons to be drawn from this one historical example – merely a confirmation of the complexity which characterises all modern famines. It is conventional for historians to attempt to justify their focus on the past when there are so many pressing problems awaiting attention in the present. One feels this most acutely in a study of famine – a problem very much present in the lives of so many Africans today. In the Introduction I outlined some of the literature which takes a comparative, historical perspective on famine. Surveys which draw on wide-ranging examples to describe an apparently common phenomenon are of limited use, I think, unless (like Amartya Sen's) the analysis is firmly located within a political economy framework. Pasting together the common, recurrent ingredients of a famine drama provides the basis for a novel of human drama and suspense – as in Graham Masterton's recent bestseller *Famine*, set in America. But it is not adequate for a useful analysis. As Mike Watts has pointed out (Watts, 1983), a useful historical analysis is one which moves beyond the description of common existential conditions to examine the different developmental attributes of famines:

> A typology of famines would, then, not only address obvious differences in the technological conditions of production, communications systems, and the structure of the agrarian economy, but would also identify the strategic importance of the market, the changing terms of trade, commoditization, and exchange entitlements. In this way, the etiology of famine is neither a neo-Malthusian inevitability nor the mechanical outcome of a decline in food availability, but may emerge from discrepancies between price and purchasing power. (p. 462)

The example of 1949 has shown that it is futile to search for a single cause of a famine crisis. It has also shown that it is necessary to separate, to some degree, the analysis of long-term trends in food availability from the analysis of the crisis itself. The current famine crisis in Africa brings out this need for analytical separation very clearly. One writer on the current famine in Africa has been moved by the profusion of garbled, unhelpful accounts, to identify '14 Fallacies about Famine' (Currey, 1981). Number one is Currey's list of fallacies is the one that states that famines are acute and large-scale food shortages, and moves from this definition to an assumption that forecasting should concentrate on identifying prospective shortfalls in production. In Currey's view, forecasting should 'be geared to prevent the tragedy of famine, not to the forewarning of a request for emergency food aid', and points out that the two are *not* synonymous. Maintaining some analytical separation between levels of explanation, and being clearer as to whether we are discussing a famine crisis, a long-term food availability problem, or a food *production* problem, would contribute enormously to the generation of solutions.

The conflation of issues and ensuing confusion, is not completely accidental, of course, but springs ultimately from the dominant Western ideological biases. Keith Griffin made this point succinctly when, along with other experts, he was called to give evidence to the House of Commons Foreign Affairs Committee on famine in Africa. The dominant Western ideology of free enterprise, free trade and free movement of capital influences our perception of famine and its causation (just as it did for the observers of colonial Malawi). The emphasis on fast growth, rather than on the distribution of the fruits of that growth, contributes to the confusion between the analysis of long-term food supply problems and that of famine. The corollary of this emphasis on growth rather than distribution, as Griffin points out, is a hostility to government interventions to improve the distribution of income, or the distribution of food. This despite the historical evidence that famine has never been solved without large-scale government intervention, and despite the fact that there is evidence that a timely introduction of food rationing in Ethiopia would have prevented the worst of the crisis of the mid 1980s.

This brings us to another issue on which there has been much confusion in analysis of the current crisis, and that is the issue of responsibility. As I pointed out in the Introduction, at the back of much of the Western media coverage of the present famine in Africa is a neo-Malthusian model, of varying sophistication. Often at the forefront, however, has been criticism of African governments – both for their agricultural policies which seem to have discriminated against the small-scale food producer, and for their mishandling of the crisis once it occurred. This issue was clearly to the forefront of the minds of many members of the House of Commons Committee, as well it might be. As Griffin stated in his evidence to that Committee, 'In a world composed of sovereign nation-states the government of each country must assume the larger part of the responsibility for ensuring that everyone under its administrative authority has enough to eat. This responsibility is an inescapable consequence of the way the world is presently organised.' But, as he goes on to say, this does not imply that hunger is exclusively a national phenomenon, or that it can be dealt with entirely at that level. Supra-national forces at work, for which the West holds much responsibility and which affect the longer-term availability of food, include the pattern of international trade, the stockpiles of grain in the West, the investment in Africa by Trans-National Corporations, and so on. Griffin adds to this another, less commonly cited list: the Western ideological bias in favour of free trade; ideas about the efficacy of the transfer of technology; preconceptions of the nation-state which avoid a class analysis – these are all contributory factors at one level of explanation. African countries may be, in theory, sovereign states, but the level of intervention in their development policies on the part of Western agencies has steadily increased since the post-war period and cannot be ignored in explanations of famine causation.

The recognition that our ideological views colour our perceptions of famine is one step in the right direction. At the same time, the example of the 1949 famine demonstrates that one should not focus exclusively on these large-scale international economic and political determinants of famine. Incorporating such factors in one's total analysis does not imply that one should deny the very specific local knowledge and experience of the communities concerned. It is my view that these different perspectives can, and must, be considered simultaneously.

In a recent special issue of the *Review of African Political Economy* on war and famine, the editors find most useful to their analysis a focus on the larger issues, not specific to a famine situation. These include the role of imperialism in 'disarticulating African social formations in the process of converting people to wage labour, export commodity production and economic domination by TNCs [Trans-National Corporations]'; the rise of national bourgeoisies which divert surpluses from the peasantry to their own pockets; the role of the state in subordinating the rural producer, and of development strategies which give priority to linkages with the international market rather than to internal self-sufficiency. Yet they also recognise that there is at the same time a need to focus on rural producers themselves, to understand and respect their adaptive ability and production potential.

The methodology used in this study of the 1949 famine has highlighted the need for this focus, for it is only by talking to survivors of the famine, and by hearing their own accounts of the processes at work, that I have been able to reconstruct the event. Yet I have also been at pains to emphasise that 'taking the peasants' point of view' does not mean that one should abstract rural communities from the total environment in which they operate. Taking the peasants' point of view does not mean that one should hold an idealised vision of subsistence communities and their moral order, and doing so only serves to confuse the real issues and real problems facing rural communities in the Third World today.

Notes

Introduction

1 Amongst the most frequently cited works on the physiology of starvation is that edited by Keys in 1950 (Keys *et al.*, 1950).
2 For this history see Vail, 1983; McCracken, 1983 and 1986: White, 1987 and Mandala, 1983.
3 This question has been tackled most ably for the Lower Shire Valley of Malawi by Elias Mandala (Mandala, 1983).
4 For an examination of this see the bibliographical study of famine by Janet Seeley (Seeley, 1986).
5 See, for instance, the debate on the history of the Kenyan peasantry (Njonjo, 1981; Ng'anga, 1981; Cowen, 1981a and 1981b) and full discussion of these issues in Iliffe, 1983 and Kitching, 1980.
6 For example, the influential work of Meillassoux (1981) and Rey (1973). For a review of this literature and its contribution to African historiography, see the special issue of the *Canadian Journal of African Studies*, 19, (1), 1985, entitled *Modes of Production: The Challenge of Africa.*
7 Sen has recently been criticised for underestimating the importance of Food Availability Decline (Bowrick, 1985), but in general his approach still appears to be found useful by many working on the problems of famine.

The 1949 famine

1 Present-day Malawi (formerly Nyasaland) was made a British Protectorate in 1891, and became part of the Central African Federation (along with Southern and Northern Rhodesia) in 1953. It achieved independent status in 1964. Throughout the book I refer to the territory as Malawi, and also use current spelling for place names.
2 For the economy of the Shire Highlands in the colonial period see Vaughan, 1981; White, 1987. For the tobacco industry see McCracken, 1983 and 1986.
3 *Kachasu* is a strong distilled liquor, manufactured from maize and sugar.
4 In 1942 Blantyre District had been incorporated into a larger unit named Blantyre Administrative Unit and comprising the districts of Blantyre, Neno, Chiradzulu and Chikwawa, with a total population of 270,690. The Traditional Authorities, or chiefs, had administrative and judicial responsibilities accorded them by the District Administration (Native) Ordinance of 1933.
5 For the history of the tea industry see Robin Palmer (1985).
6 Malawi National Archives. All files are referred to by the abbreviation MNA, followed by departmental notation and number. See bibliography (p.170).
7 Interviews with J. Manyazi; Village Headman Nyani; Christine Somba. (There is a full list of interviews on pp. 167–9.)
8 Songs sung by Bekana Saimon and others at Masulani Village, Traditional Authority (TA) Chigalu.
9 Interviews with Wilfred Kampazaza; Village Headman Somba; Ida Jemusi; Rabson Frank.

10 Interviews with Herbert Peter; James Chisala; Mai Nambewe Joni; Village Headman Gulani.
11 Interviews with Jameson Chisala; Mai Nambewe Joni; Lapken Moses Kanyenga.
12 Interview with Victor Misonje.
13 Interview with J. Manyazi.
14 There is a large literature on responses to drought and famine, demonstrating the importance of migration, exchange of goods, and, crucially, the sale of labour (O'Leary, 1980; McAlpin, 1983; Cutler, 1984; Sen, 1980; Smith, 1983; Laya, 1975; Wood, 1976; Caldwell, 1977; Campbell and Trechter, 1982).
15 Sung by Mrs F. Michael, Kandio Village, TA Kapeni.
16 Sung by Mr Mubulala, Chikande Village, TA Kuntaja.
17 The following are the most frequently mentioned famine foods:
nthudza and *mapoza* – wild fruits
mapeta and *chilazi* – varieties of yam which had to be cooked and washed several times before they were safe to eat.
gugu – a kind of grass, likened to sorghum
matomolo – fruit which looks like a mango
dzikolekole – roots, a bit like potatoes
matondo – a wild fruit
mphandula – a wild bean
kalongonda – a wild bean
Also frequently mentioned are bamboo roots, banana roots and water-lily roots (all of which were processed into flour), and green mangoes (cooked into a liquid).
18 The symptom of which they complained is known as 'famine oedema' and was almost certainly not caused by the eating of these foods (Keys *et al.*, 1950, vol. 2: *The Edema Problem*).
19 Interview with Bekana Saimon.
20 Interview with Donald Mpira.
21 Interview with Dawa Somba.
22 Interview with Malita Gulani.
23 Interview with Rabson Frank.
24 Accounts of the famines of the 1970s and 1980s in Ethiopia and the Sahel also include examples of the desertion by men of their wives and children (Shepherd, 1975, p. 19; Holt and Seaman, 1976, pp. 4–7; Wood, 1976, p. 72; Sen, 1980, p. 102). There are other accounts, however, of men making the journey to the relief centres and returning to their families with food (Laya, 1975; Smith, 1983).
25 Sung by Mrs F. Kamowa, Mbera Village, TA Kapeni. See also pp. 123–4, and interviews with Mrs S. Ganet and Agnes Siwetela (whose husband left her during the famine and never returned).
26 The *mbumba* is a matrilineal sorority group. The issues of matrilineality and marriage are discussed at length in Chapter 5.
27 For a discussion of the role of amenorrhea in lowering the birth-rate during famine see Ladurie, 1979, pp. 255–73.
28 Sung by Mrs F. Michael, Kandio Village, TA Kapeni.
29 Interview with Elizabeth Gomani. In the early stages of starvation human lactation usually appears to be little affected, but because of the relationship between lactation and psychological conditions, maternal anxiety can sometimes bring about the termination of lactation. Furthermore, once *severe* chronic malnutrition sets in, lactation declines and ceases (Jeliffe and Jeliffe, 1971, p. 56).
30 Sung by a group of women in Kandio Village, TA Kapeni.
31 For example:

Ndingopita Limbe	I must go to Limbe
Ndikwakwere bus	And board a bus,
Makwacha ndine ndemwe	My body will pay the fare.
Makonyora, aye makonyora.	In Lilongwe, my body will do,
Lilongwe makonyora	In Limbe, it will do,
Limbe makonyora	In Blantyre it will do,
Blantyre makonyora	And in Salisbury it will do.
Salisbury makonyora.	

Song collected in Kandio Village, TA Kapeni, Blantyre District.

32 Sung by Bekana Saimon, Masulani Village, TA Chigalu.
33 Interviews with Donald Mpira, Michael Phiyo, Flackson Madyera.
34 Distribution centres were opened in Blantyre District, Chiradzulu District, the Domasi area of Zomba District, Fort Johnston (now Mangochi) District, and in Mulanje District (all in the Southern Province). In the Central Province centres were opened in the lakeshore areas of both Dowa and Dedza Districts, and in the low-lying areas of Ntcheu District (MNA, AFC 7/2/1: Memo on Famine Relief, 1950).
35 Interviews with Dawa Somba, J. Manyazi and Mrs N. Mandauka.
36 Interview with Dawa Somba.
37 Interview with Dorothy Kabichi.
38 Interview with Village Headman Somba.
39 Interview with Mrs N. Kaulembe.
40 Interviews with Mrs M. Chimpeni and others.
41 Interviews with Dorothy Kabichi, Dorofe Jemusi, Christine Somba, Village Headman Gulani, and Mrs N. Mandauka.
42 Nyasaland Protectorate, Medical Department, *Annual Report for 1950*, p. 5. In a despatch to the Secretary of State for the Colonies, the Chief Secretary estimated that, overall, 100–200 people had died directly or indirectly through lack of food (MNA, MP 12347: Chief Secretary to All Administrative Staff: Circular Letter 14/3/50). This was almost certainly a gross under-estimation, judging by the oral testimonies collected.
43 Interviews with Lapken Moses Kanyenga, Mary Likala, Wilfred Kampazaza.
44 Interview with Herbert Peter.
45 Interviews with Agnes Siwetala and others.
46 Interview with Rabson Frank.

2 Famine as a Malthusian crisis

1 See for instance, the remarks of the first Commissioner for British Central Africa, Harry Johnston: Johnston, 1897, pp. 424–5.
2 See Chapter 5 for the important implications of this, and also Vaughan and Hirschmann, 1983. For comparative material see Thomson, 1954, Lancaster, 1981. and A. Richards 1939.
3 For the history of the Maravi Empire see Alpers, 1968; Phiri, 1977: Schofeleers, 1972; Langworthy, 1975.
4 *Life and Work*, March 1903, reported the account by an elderly Yao man, of the drought of the 1860s: 'Drought is rarely felt in the hill country but often in the River and Lake. Long ago, the year the Yaos came into the district, there was a severe drought. Then people had gardens, hoed, but the heat destroyed them, and the people had to retreat to the river to find water and wet soil on which to plant.'
5 For a demographer's account of these likely effects see Cordell *et al.*, 1983.
6 Discussions within the Department of Agriculture are recorded in MNA, MP 3/2 Native Agriculture: General, 1945–7.
7 For a critical discussion of the notion of 'carrying capacity' see Ellen, 1982, pp. 41–6.

3 Famine as a failure of the market

1 Although Laurens van der Post in his introduction to *Venture to the Interior* implies that there were some in Whitehall who thought that the mountainous areas of Malawi might help feed the world (an implausible suggestion to those who know them): 'The matter was urgent. Production of food in the world, and particularly in the Empire and Britain, was beginning to fall in a sort of geometric retrogression, to keep up with increases in population. Moreover, as our troubles with the Argentine so clearly showed, anything that could help to make Britain independent of alien sources of food should be done, and done as quickly as possible. There was a chance that these areas might help.'
2 In 1939 the number of adult males in the Protectorate fit to leave their villages for work was

estimated at 329,000. Of this number, an estimated 87,292 made a livelihood at home in the areas of economic production and distribution; 62,513 were employed for wages by 'non-natives' within the Protectorate. By 1949 there were an estimated 83,054 persons employed in industries within the Protectorate owned by non-natives plus another 26,138 in government employment. (Labour Department, *Annual Report* 1939, and 1949).

3 There are innumerable expressions of this concern in the internal correspondence of the Department of Agriculture, and in the Department's Annual Reports. See Chapter 2.

4 Some of this maize sold in Mulanje may have been smuggled over the border from Mozambique.

5 See Chapter 4 for a more detailed discussion.

4 Food entitlement and employment

1 Phyllis Deane was appointed to undertake an economic survey of Nyasaland for the Colonial Office, with a view to proposing a fiscal reform. She investigated closely the popular view that Africans were hoarding money, and concluded:

I think one can over-estimate the increases in material well-being of the African. Most of his income is subsistence income and I have found no reason to assume a real increase in that, in spite of a higher price level . . . Just how much idle money does in fact lie buried in the floors of African huts is very difficult to judge. Much of it may well be absorbed by the increased velocity of inter-African trade. Africans are charging and receiving from other Africans very inflated prices for fish, meat and similar 'luxury' foodstuffs. This money, which would normally be attracted to the European or Indian stores in return for manufactured items which are now unobtainable, and would then pass through the banking system, is nevertheless circulating briskly in the villages. (MNA, LB 5/4/1 Fiscal Survey: Phyllis Deane to H. R. Butters (Chairman) 12/12/46)

2 See discussions in the Fiscal Survey Committee: 'A statement made on the comparative cost of commodities in native markets at Blantyre, Limbe and Zomba, in respect of 1939, July 1945, May 1946 and November 1946, observed that there was no price control in these markets and that black marketing was rampant, African exploiting African' (Minutes of the 2nd meeting of the Committee of Fiscal Survey, 13/11/46, in MNA, LB 5/4/1).

3 For the Master Farmer Scheme see the Annual Reports of the Department of Agriculture, which chart its progress in the late 1940s and 1950s. Also the discussions within the Department contained in MNA MP 3/2: Native Agriculture:

The Domasi Community Development Scheme near Zomba included a small land settlement programme. In 1951 the only 'settlers' (also Master Farmer candidates) were five men, all of whom had non-agricultural sources of income or capital. One was a former carpenter who still practised his trade off-season; the second was a former instructor at the Jeanes Training Centre at Domasi; the third was a retired hospital assistant; the fourth a retired detective sub-inspector of the Nyasaland Police, and the fifth a cinema operator. (MNA, NS 3/3/1 Domasi Community Development Scheme: Final Report of Officer-in-Charge to Chief Secretary, 9/9/55)

4 Interview with Jameson Chisale.
5 Interviews with Mr Katsabola and Adam Diliza.
6 Interview with Mr Kumpanda.
7 Interview with Adam Diliza.
8 Interview with Mai Damalesi Mondawa.
9 Interview with John Njoka.
10 Interview with Mr Mtelongo.
11 Interview with Layiti Rabson.
12 Interview with Thomson Champimpha.
13 Interview with John Sakamoyo.
14 Interview with John Sakamoyo.
15 Interview with Beyadi Misomali.

16 Interview with Mai Nambewe Joni.
17 Interviews with Herbert Peter, Lapken Moses Kanyenga, Berton Nthengo and Mr Mashalabuti.
18 A list of non-officials who assisted in the distribution of relief foodstuffs is contained in MNA, MP 12344: Famine Precautions 1949: Staff Arrangements. The list included both missionaries and estate owners, as well as the anthropologist, J. Clyde Mitchell (personal communication, 1985).
19 Interviews with J. Manyazi, Village Headman Gulani, Frackson Dausi and Samuel Fabiano.
20 The 1922 famine was not as severe as that of 1949 but was nevertheless the most serious since the turn of the century. The areas affected were the Middle Shire Valley of Blantyre and Neno Districts (as in 1949), parts of Zomba District, Liwonde in the Upper Shire Valley, and parts of Chiradzulu and Chikwawa Districts. This was the first famine in which the government took direct responsibility for distributing relief food. In Blantyre District the 1922 famine is known as 'Njala wa Chirimba' after the place from which food was distributed.
21 Interviews with Dorothy Kabichi, Mrs Nkupumula, Dorofe Jemusi and many others.
22 Interview with Michael Phiyo.

5 Gender and famine

1 An earlier version of the argument presented here appeared in my article 'Famine and Family Relations: 1949 in Nyasaland', *Past and Present*, 108 (1985), 177–205.
2 Song sung by members of the League of Malawi Women, 1984.
3 Landeg White makes extensive use of pounding songs in his history of Magomero village on the Bruce estates of the Shire Highlands (White, 1987). He argues that although pounding songs are often used as a vehicle for criticising husbands this is not an exclusive concern, and their content depends much on the particular circumstances. On the Bruce estates in the 1930s it seems that the chief preoccupation voiced in the songs was the rivalry between women, which was in part brought about by a shortage of husbands on the estates (pp. 253–6).
4 Clyde Mitchell's work provides a detailed description of the functioning of the Yao social and political system in the 1940s, and lays much emphasis on the role of the Yao village headman. Most of Mitchell's work was carried out in the Yao 'heartland' of Mangochi and Machinga, and some is not easily generalisable to the more crowded districts of Blantyre and Chiradzulu. (Mitchell, 1956; Mitchell, 1949; Mitchell, Gluckman and Barnes, 1949).
5 Interview with Village Headman Somba.
6 Interview with Mrs F. Kamowa.
7 I am indebted to Richard Werbner of Manchester University for demonstrating to me the importance of this point.
8 See Mitchell, 1956 for a description of land rights amongst the Yao, and also White, 1987 for the operation of these customs on the Bruce Estates.
9 Elias Mandala places much emphasis on this in his study of the Lower Shire Valley, arguing that by the late nineteenth century in the southern part of the valley a 'distinctly gender-based economy was developing' through the expansion of non-agricultural, male-dominated activities such as trading, and iron and cloth manufacture (Mandala, 1983, p. 161).
10 For comparable evidence see Wright, 1970.
11 There is much evidence for this in the Yao accounts of the nineteenth century in *Amachinga Yao Traditions*, vols. I and II, and in the diary of the White Fathers' Mission at Mpondas on Lake Malawi (Linden, 1974 and 1975).
12 Tenants on estates suffered a number of disadvantages, including the compulsory withdrawal of male labour from food production on some estates, but in general the women on estates had more land at their disposal for producing food than did their counterparts on Trust Land. Landeg White's study of Magomero clearly demonstrates the importance of this (White, 1986).
13 Mandala has demonstrated the growth of labour migration from the Lower Shire Valley at around the same period, and also sees this as having undermined the economic status of women (Mandala, 1983, p. 259).
14 Interview with Salome Alfred Solomon.

15 Similar frustrations are apparent in the songs and testimonies of women on the Bruce estates during the period when the male-dominated tobacco industry was the main source of tenant livelihood (White, 1986, Part II, Chapter 2).
16 This was the assumption underlying the calculations on food availability contained in the Department of Agriculture's records and Village Surveys (MNA, AGR 3/7).
17 In her survey of family structure amongst the 'Central Bantu' Audrey Richards concluded that: 'The matrilineal system of Nyasaland differs from those of Northern Rhodesia in the greater strength of the brother–sister group, the more pronounced avunculate exercised by the elder brother in a society in which primogeniture is emphasised, and the growth of villages around a sororal extended family core rather than around a father–daughter grand family' (A. Richards, 1950, p. 236).
18 For a discussion of this disjuncture in present-day Southern Malawi see Vaughan and Hirschmann, 1983.
19 A detailed description of eating conventions is contained in Platt's Report of a Nutrition Survey in Nyasaland, carried out in Nkhota-Kota District and in Ndirande area of Blantyre (MNA, Q 267 Nutrition Survey, 1940).
20 This point was emphasised to me by Clyde Mitchell (personal communication, February 1985).
21 Mitchell found that eight out of every ten men and women over the age of forty had experienced divorce at some time in their lives (Mitchell, 1971, p. 186).
22 Mitchell did find, however, a practice amongst the Yao whereby the son-in-law was expected to work in his mother-in-law's garden. This did not earn him the right to remove his bride. (Mitchell, 1950, p. 8.)
23 MNA, ADM 1/22 Provincial councils: Meetings, Agenda and Proceedings, Southern Province 1945–8. Record of 7th Session, 5–7 May 1947. See also the evidence in White's (1986) study of Magomero, and especially the song quoted on p. 322 beginning 'I am crying for my iron sheets'.
24 Bettison found that uxorilocal marriage represented 73 per cent of his sample in the seventeen peri-urban villages studied (Bettison, 1958d, p. 32).
25 See especially the cases in MNA, BA 1/2/8. Blantyre District Court, Native Civil Cases, 1925–9. For Ngoni customs at this period see Margaret Read, 1956. See also Chanock (1985) for a full and fascinating account of the positioning of Africans within the colonial legal system, and the functioning of the marriage and 'morality' legislation.
26 Some cases involved the exchange of wives between men, for example case 235 in MNA, BA 1/5/3.

6 After the famine: a conclusion

1 MNA, MP 21331 Maize Production Policy 1952–3. Director of Agriculture's précis for the Executive Council on policy laid down in 1951. 8/7/52:

Maize Control Board Purchases in recent years from areas in which maize production as a cash crop might be discontinued.

	Production (short tons)			Reasons for discontinuing
	1950	1951	1052	
Port Herald	324	27	100	South of Chiromo (B, C); north of Chiromo Aa, D
Chikwawa	81	—	1,000	West of Shire Aa
Cholo	415	1,068	600	Whole district B,C,E
Mlanje	416	1,435	2,700	S. Mlanje – B,E
Blantyre	—	769	700	Within 20 miles of township – B, C,D,E Chiradzulu – B,C,D,E Lisungwe – Aa
Zomba	274	1,732	2,900	S. Zomba – B,C,D,E. Kawinga Ab,B Chingale Aa
Fort Johnston	—	2,482	2,800	Lakeshore – B,A. Namwera's, Nyambi and W. hills – Ab,B.
Ncheu	208	281	250	Whole district – Aa, Ab, B
Lilongwe	100	360	400	Fort Manning area – Ab, N.E. Lilongwe Ab, B, C.
Kota-Kota	—	250	100	Whole district Ab,B
Kasungu	—	380	100	Whole district B

Key to Table. Reasons for unsuitability:

A – areas in which desirable to stimulate other economic crops: (a) cotton, (b) groundnuts.

B – areas unsuitable due to soil conditions or topography

C – areas in which population density too great

D – areas with alternative local markets such as townships, or where annual shortages can be anticipated

E – areas where labour required to work on estates.

2 The history of the Jeanes Training Centre is outlined in Vaughan, 1983 and documented in: MNA, NS 1/8/5. MNA NS 1/8/3, MNA NS 1/8/4, MNA NSG 1/4/1, MNA, M2/15/2, MNA, MP 66/34/11, MNA, S1/111/34, MNA, NSL 1/5/2, MNA, S1/308/27, as well as in the files on the Domasi Community Development Scheme already cited.

3 Interview with Herbert Peter.

4 Interviews with Sonice Mbendeka, Lapken Moses Kanyenga, Justin Chipinga, Wilfred Kampazaza and others.

5 Interview with Thomson Chompimpha.

6 Elias Mandala emphasises this point with respect to the Lower Shire Valley (Mandala, 1983).

List of oral interviews

These were mostly conducted between March and June 1983. Unless otherwise indicated, they were carried out in Blantyre District. Many informants were interviewed on more than one occasion. TA = Traditional Authority.

1 With Herbert Peter, John Kwadya Village, TA Kapeni
2 With Ida Jemusi, Mtendera Village, TA Kapeni
3 With Dorothy Kabichi, Mpira Village, TA Kapeni
4 With Mai Nkupumula, Champira Village, Lunzu
5 With J. Chasauni, Kamlenga Village, TA Machinjiri
6 With Issa Mpira, Mpira Village, Lunzu
7 With Donald Mpira, Mpira Village, Lunzu
8 With Michael Phiyo, Chitima Village, TA Kapeni
9 With Mr P. Katsabola, Lunzu Trading Centre
10 With Dorofe Jemusi, Machinjiri Village, TA Machinjiri
11 With Mrs J. Chomboko, Mpira Village, Lunzu
12 With John Sakamoyo, Champira Village, Lunzu
13 With Manase Chikondi, Mpira Village, Lunzu
14 With W. Kumpanda, Lunzu Trading Centre
15 With John Njoka, Machinjiri Village, TA Machinjiri
16 With Adam Diliza, Machinjiri Village, TA Machinjiri
17 With Nabanda Gomu, Machinjiri Village, TA Machinjiri
18 With Jameson Chisale, Kamlenga Village, TA Machinjiri
19 With Nambewe Joni, Chitima Village, TA Kapeni
20 With Kasamu Monole, Chitima Village, TA Kapeni
21 With Mr K. Katemba, Lunzu market
22 With Mr Mayani Ngolo, Chitima Village, TA Kapeni
23 With Mr Dawa Somba, Somba Village, TA Lundu
24 With Christine Somba, Somba Village, TA Lundu
25 With Thomson Champimpha, Gulani Village, TA Chigalu
26 With Malita Gulani, Gungulu Village, TA Chigalu
27 With Mr J. Manyazi, Gulani Village, TA Chigalu
28 With Mrs N. Mandauka, Somba Village, TA Lundu
29 With Village Headman Somba, Somba Village, TA Lundu
30 With Mrs N. Kaulembe, Somba Village, TA Lundu
31 With Alesi Dankeni, Somba Village, TA Lundu
32 With Mrs M. Chimpeni, Somba Village, TA Lundu
33 With Village Headman Gulani, Gulani Village, TA Chigalu
34 With Mr Bwanali, Somba Village, TA Lundu
35 With Mr L. H. J. Somba, Malanga Village, TA Kapeni
36 With Mr Beyadi Misomali, Malanga Village, TA Kapeni
37 With Anderson Ford, Malanga Village, TA Kapeni

38 With Adawa Dimusa, Malanga Village, TA Kapeni
39 With Frackson Dausi, Malanga Village, TA Kapeni
40 With Layiti Rabson, Malanga Village, TA Kapeni
41 With Victor Misonje, Malanga Village, TA Kapeni
42 With James Dimusa, Malanga Village, TA Kapeni
43 With Elizabeth Gomani, Malanga Village, TA Kapeni
44 With Julius Gomani, Malanga Village, TA Kapeni
45 With Tumalire Gositi, Malanga Village, TA Kapeni
46 With Gilbert Chikuse, Malanga Village, TA Kapeni
47 With Malita Chiluwe, Malanga Village, TA Kapeni
48 With Rabson Frank, Gulani Village, TA Chigalu
49 With Fred Misi, Malanga Village, TA Kapeni
50 With Flackson Madyera, Somba Village, TA Lundu
51 With Frank Ngwaya, Gulani Village, TA Chigalu
52 With Damalesi Mondiwa, Gulani Village, TA Chigalu
53 With Ellena Lozani, Maziyaya Village, TA Machinjiri
54 With Virginia Yotani, Kaluzu Village, TA Machinjiri
55 With Wilfred Kampazaza, Mananani Village, TA Machinjiri
56 With Julius Makoleni, Ntukula Village, TA Machinjiri
57 With Salome Alfred Solomon, Mthini Village, TA Machinjiri
58 With Wesley Mataka, Manaseni Village, TA Machinjiri
59 With Mary Likala, Chigojo Village, TA Machinjiri
60 With Amos Fred Manondo, Yosefe Village, TA Machinjiri
61 With Justin Chipinga, Maziyaya Village, TA Machinjiri
62 With Rodney Luanja, Luanja Village, TA Machinjiri
63 With Victor Masamba, Tadako Village, TA Machinjiri
64 With Halton Chadoko, Changata Village, TA Machinjiri
65 With Selina Jailosi, Padoko Village, TA Machinjiri
66 With Lapken Moses Kanyenga, Padoko Village, TA Machinjiri
67 With Sonice Mbendeka, Kawajika Village, TA Machinjiri
68 With Berton Nthengo, Maziyaya Village, TA Machinjiri
69 With Agnes Siwetela, Nkwajika Village, TA Machinjiri
70 With Walter Chota, Nkwajika Village, TA Machinjiri
71 With Justino Pote, Kandio Village, TA Kapeni
72 With Mr Albert, Mbera Village, TA Kapeni
73 With David Kachoka, Kandio Village, TA Kapeni
74 With Mr Salima, Masulani Village, TA Kapeni
75 With Andrew Limbika, Mbera Village, TA Kapeni
76 With Samuel Fabiano, Mbera Village, TA Kapeni
77 Anon., Chikanda Village, TA Kumtaja
78 With Mr Mashalubuti, Mbera Village, TA Kapeni
79 With Michael Pote, Kandio Village, TA Kapeni
80 With Mr J. Namonde, Kandio Village, TA Kapeni
81 With Mr Liwonde, Kandio Village, TA Kapeni
82 With Mr Roben Juma, Masulani Village, TA Chigalu
83 With Mr Bekana Saimon, Masulani Village, TA Chigalu
84 With Mr Ballon Kachere, Masulani Village, TA Chigalu
85 With Mrs Albert, Mbera Village, TA Chigalu
86 With Mr Lenison Phiri, Mbera Village, TA Chigalu
87 With Mrs S. Ganet, Kandio Village, TA Kapeni
88 With Austen Magwangula, Kandio Village, TA Kapeni
89 With Mrs F. Kamowa, Mbera Village, Ta Kapeni
90 With Mr Gama, Chigongwaya Village, TA Kuntaja
91 With Mrs F. Michael, Kandio Village, TA Kapeni
92 With Mrs Makuluni, Chinkande Village, TA Kuntaja

93 With Mr P. Mubulala, Chinkande Village, TA Kuntaja
94 With Mr S. K. Phiri, Bwanasompho Village, TA Kuntaja
95 With Village Headman Nyani, Nyani Village, TA Malemia, Zomba District
96 With Mary Limani, Binali Village, TA Mwambo, Zomba District
97 With Evelyn James, McMaurice Village, TA Mwambo
98 With Mrs Solombera, Somba Village, TA Mwambo, Zomba District
99 With Lucy Chiseko, Tulesia Village, TA Mwambo, Zomba District
100 With Adalia Kazembe, Makawa Village, TA Mwambo, Zomba District
101 With Lucy Sam, Mlandani Village, TA Mpama, Chiradzulu District
102 With Grace Namadingo, Nyani Village, TA Malemia, Zomba District
103 With Kamwendo Mperewere, Suluku Village, TA Kuntumanje, Zomba District
104 With Village Headman Njala, Njala Village, TA Zomba District
105 With W. H. Mtelongo, Tulesia Village, TA Mwambo, Zomba District

Bibliography

Archival sources

Great Britain

Public Record Office: CO 852/1035/2. Memo on the Economy of Nyasaland, 1948–9

Malawi

Malawi National Archives (MNA)

(i) Secretariat Files (prefixes MP and S)

MP 4/72 Department of Agriculture: Report on the 1949 drought
MP 12352 Famine Precautions 1949: Food Stocks in Villages
MP 12348 Famine Precautions 1949: Beer Brewing and Consumption
MP 12655 Southern Province Provincial Council Meetings, 1949–51
MP 12385 Famine Precautions 1949: His Excellency's demi-official correspondence with the Colonial Office and Other Governments
MP 12355 Vol. II: Import of Foodstuffs through Other Governments
MP 12324 Famine Precautions 1949
MP 12359 Famine Precautions 1949: Fish Supplies.
MP 12353 Famine Precautions 1949: African Emigration
MP 12375 Famine Precautions 1949: His Excellency's Tour of the Southern Province
MP 12932 Famine Precautions 1949: Miscellaneous Correspondence with Unofficial Bodies
MP 18690 1949 Famine: Report on the out-turn of the 1948/9 and 1949/50 Harvests
MP 12347 Famine Precautions 1949: Progress Reports and Communiqués
MP 14399 Nutrition, 1944–52
MP 4/68 Department of Agriculture: Crops and Foodstuffs: Maize Production, 1947–9
MP 34/2 Maize Control Ordinance and Rules
MP 34/10 Maize Control Ordinance and Rules, 1949
MP 35/26 Foodstuffs Committee, 1946–8
MP 3/2 Native Agriculture: General, 1945–7
MP 12258 History of the British Central Africa Company, 1948
MP 12405 History of the Blantyre and East Africa Company, 1949
MP 1100 Agricultural Policy: Food Production, 1943–6

MP 10797 Question of the Elimination of Competitive Buying of Foodstuffs in Foreign Territories, 1944
MP 10802 World Food Shortage, 1946–7
MP 34/1 Marketing of Native Produce Ordinance, 1945
MP 19376 Domasi Community Development Scheme, Annual Report, 1950
MP 12344 Famine Precautions: Staff Arrangements
MP 12036 Domasi Community Development Area, 1949–54
MP 66/34/11 Jeanes Training Centre, 1942
MP 21331 Maize Production Policy, 1952–3
MP 20933 Social Welfare Officer, Southern Province, Annual Reports 1952–9
SI/111/34 Jeanes Centre Scheme for Chiefs' Instruction in Agriculture in Connection with Jeanes Training Centre, 1934
SI/308/27 Establishment of a School for Training of Native Supervisory Teachers, 1927

(ii) Provincial Administration: Southern Province (prefix NS)
NS 3/1/19 Annual Reports, Zomba District, 1947–9
NS 3/1/18 Annual Report for the Lower River, 1949
NS 3/3/3 Nutrition in the Colonial Empire, 1940–2
NS 3/1/13 Annual Report for the Southern Province, 1948
NS 1/3/9 Mulanje Native Foodstuffs Growers Association, 1943–5
NS 3/3/1 Domasi Community Development Scheme, 1949–54
NS 1/8/3 Jeanes Training Centre: Courses for Chiefs, 1936–7
NS 1/8/4 Jeanes Training Centre: Courses for Chiefs, 1937–9
NS 1/8/5 Jeanes Training Centre: Courses for Chiefs, 1940–6

(iii) District Administration: Blantyre District (prefix NSB)
NSB 7/4/1 Blantyre District Ulendo Reports, 1946–9
NSB 7/1/2 Annual Reports, Blantyre District, 1929–31
NSB 7/1/3 Annual Report for Blantyre and Neno Districts, 1933
NSB 7/1/4 Annual Reports for Blantyre and Central Shire Districts, 1937 and 1938
NSB 7/1/5 Annual Report for Blantyre and Central Shire Districts, 1939
NSB 7/1/6 Annual Report for Blantyre and Central Shire Districts, 1940
NSB 7/1/1 Blantyre District, Annual Reports, 1922–8
NSB 3/2/1 Blantyre: Agricultural Policy, 1943–9
NSB 3/12/1 Cost of Living, 1947–9

(iv) District Administration: Domasi District (prefix NSG)
NSG 1/4/1 Jeanes Training Centre, 1939–52

(v) District Administration: Liwande District (prefix NSL)
NSL 1/5/2 Jeanes Training Centre, 1941

(vi) African Foodstuffs Commission (prefix AFC)
AFC 7/2/1 Memo on Famine Relief
AFC 3/2/1 Camps for Advanced Cases of Malnutrition
AFC 3/1/1 Feeding of the Aged and Infirmed who are Destitute
AFC 2/1 Distribution in Townships

(vii) Department of Agriculture (prefix AGR)

AGR 3/2/156 Native Agriculture, General, May 1931–January 1939
AGR 3/7 Village Surveys, 1944
AGR 4/10 Food Shortage, 1941–5
AGR 3/2 Native Agriculture, General, 1951

(viii) Medical Department (prefix M)

M2/5/6 Cerebro-Spinal Meningitis, 1924–37
M2/15/2 Jeanes Training Centre, 1934–9
M2/17/16 Nutrition, 1941–3

(ix) Administration (prefix ADM)

ADM 1/22 Provincial Council: Meetings, Agenda and Proceedings, Southern Province, 1945–8

(x) Labour Department (prefix LB)

LB 14/3/3 Notes on the 1945 Census
LB 4/2/1 Conditions on Estates, 1941–51
LB 5/4/1 Fiscal Survey, 1946

(xi) Police Department (prefix POL)

POL 5/2/2 Police Monthly Reports, Blantyre, 1949

(xii) Court Records, Blantyre District (prefix BA)

BA 1/2/1 Blantyre District Court Records, 1909–12
BA 1/2/8 Blantyre District Court, Native Civil Cases, 1925–9
BA 1/5/3 Blantyre District Criminal Cases (Native) 1909–12

(xiii) Court Records, Ncheu and Upper Shire Districts (prefix BS)

BS 1/1/1 Ncheu and Upper Shire, Native Civil Cases, 1906–10

(xiv) Miscellaneous

Q 267: Report of a Nutrition Survey in Nyasaland by B. S. Platt, 1940
Blantyre District Notebooks

Government publications

British Central Africa Gazette, vol. 3 (13), July 1896, Zomba

Great Britain, Foreign Affairs Committee, 1985, *Famine in Africa*, House of Commons Paper 56, London: Second Report from the Foreign Affairs Committee Session, 1984–5. HMSO

Malawi Government, 1975, Blantyre Planning Team, *Report No. 14: Land Use and Physical Aspects of City Environment*, Ministry of Works and Supplies, Blantyre

Nyasaland Protectorate, 1921, *Report of a Commission to Enquire into and Report upon Certain Matters connected with the Occupation of Land in Nyasaland Protectorate* (Land Report, 1921) Zomba

Nyasaland Protectorate, 1932, *Report of the Census of 1931*, Zomba
Nyasaland Protectorate, 1946, *Report of the Census of 1945*, Zomba
Nyasaland Protectorate, Labour Department, *Annual Reports, 1939–50*, Zomba
Nyasaland Protectorate, Department of Agriculture, *Annual Reports, 1949–50*, Zomba
Nyasaland Protectorate, Maize Control Board, *Reports of the Trading Sessions 1947–8, 1948–9 and 1949–50*, Zomba
Nyasaland Protectorate, 1951, *Report of the Medical Department for 1950*, Zomba
Nyasaland Protectorate, 1955, *An Outline of Agrarian Problems and Policy in Nyasaland*, by R. W. Kettlewell, Zomba

Books and articles

Acland, J. D. 1971, *East African Crops*. London.

Allan, W. 1949, *Studies in African Land-Use in Northern Rhodesia*. Rhodes-Livingstone Papers, 15. London.

Alpers, E. A. 1968, 'The Mutapa and Malawi Political Systems to the Coming of the Ngoni Invasions', in *Aspects of Central African History*, edited by T. O. Ranger. London.

Alpers, E. A. 1975, *Ivory and Slaves in East–Central Africa: changing patterns of international trade to the later nineteenth century*. London.

Amanze, J. 1980, 'The Bimbi Cult and Its Impact among the Chewa, Yao and Lomwe of the Upper Shire Valley', University of Malawi, Department of Sociology, Student research paper.

Ambirajan, S. 1979, 'Malthusian Population Theory and Indian Famine Policy in the Nineteenth Century', *Population Studies*, 30 (1), 5–14.

Anderson, D. 1984, 'Depression, Dust-Bowl, Demography and Drought: the Colonial State and Soil Conservation in East Africa during the 1930s', *African Affairs*, 83 (332), 321–45.

Arrighi, G. 1970, 'Labour Supplies in Historical Perspective: A Study of the Proletarianisation of the African Peasantry in Rhodesia', *Journal of Development Studies*, 6 (3), 197–234.

Arrighi, G. and Saul, J. 1973, *Essays on the Political Economy of Africa*. New York.

Aykroyd, W. R. 1974, *The Conquest of Famine*. London.

Aziz, S. 1975, *Hunger, Politics and Markets: the Real Issues in the Food Crisis*. New York.

Bates, R. 1981, *Markets and States in Tropical Africa*. Berkeley and Los Angeles.

Beinart, W. 1984, 'Soil Erosion, Conservationism and Ideas about Development: a Southern African Exploration, 1900–1960', *Journal of Southern African Studies*, 11 (1), 52–84.

Bernstein, H. 1985, 'Agrarian Crisis in Africa and Neo-Classical Populism', Paper presented to the Seminar on Peasants, Institute of Commonwealth Studies, University of London.

Berry, S. S. 1984, 'The Food Crisis and Agrarian Change in Africa: a review essay', *African Studies Review*, 27 (2), 59–112.

Bettison, D. G. 1958a, 'Migrancy and Social Structure in Peri-Urban Communities in Nyasaland', in *Present Interrelations In Central African Rural and Urban Life*, Rhodes-Livingstone Institute, 11th Conference Proceedings, Lusaka.

Bettison, D. G. 1958b, 'Cash Wages and Occupational Structure, Blantyre-Limbe, Nyasaland', *Rhodes-Livingstone Communication*, 9, Lusaka.

Bettison, D. G. 1958c, 'The Demographic Structure of 17 Villages, Blantyre-Limbe, Nyasaland', *Rhodes-Livingstone Communication*, 11, Lusaka.

Bettison, D. G. 1958d, 'The Social and Economic Structure of Seventeen Villages, Blantyre-Limbe, Nyasaland', *Rhodes-Livingstone Communication*, 12, Lusaka.

Bettison, D. G. 1959, 'Price Changes in African Markets, Blantyre-Limbe, Nyasaland', in *Further Economic and Social Studies, Blantyre-Limbe, Nyasaland*, edited by A. Nyirenda, H. D. Ngwane and D. G. Bettison. Lusaka.

Bettison, D. G. and Rigby, P. J. A., 1961, 'Patterns of Income and Expenditure, Blantyre-Limbe, Nyasaland', *Rhodes-Livingstone Communication*, 20, Lusaka.

Bhatia, B. M., 1967, *Famine in India*. London.

Bowrick, P. 1985, 'How Professor Sen's Theory can Cause Famines', Paper presented to the Agricultural Economics Society Conference, Edinburgh, 1985.

Bryceson, D. F., 1980, 'Changes in Peasant Food Production and Food Supply in Relation to the Historical Development of Commodity Production in Pre-Colonial and Colonial Tanganyika', *Journal of Peasant Studies*, 7, 281–321.

Bryceson, D. F. 1982, 'Peasant Commodity Production in Post-Colonial Tanzania', *African Affairs*, 81 (325), 547–69.

Buchanan, J. 1885, *The Shire Highlands*. London.

Cahill, K. M. (ed.) 1982, *Famine*. New York.

Caldwell, J. C. 1977, 'Demographic Aspects of Drought: an Examination of the African Drought of 1970–74', in *Drought in Africa*, edited by D. Dalby *et al*. London.

Campbell, D. J. and Trechter, D. D. 1982, 'Strategies for Coping with Food Consumption Shortage in the Mandara Mountains Region of Northern Cameroon', *Social Science and Medicine*, 16, 2117–27.

Canadian Journal of African Studies. 1985, 'Modes of Production: the Challenge of Africa', Special Issue. 19, (1).

Chanock, M. 1985, *Law, Custom and Social Order: The Colonial Experience in Malawi and Zambia*. Cambridge.

Christensen, C. 1978, 'World Hunger: a Structural Approach', in *The Global Political Economy of Food*, edited by R. F. Hopkins and D. J. Puchala. Wisconsin.

Cordell, D., Gregory, J. and Piché, V. 1983, 'The Social Reproduction of Health and Disease in Africa: a Demographic Perspective', Paper presented to the African Studies Association meeting, Boston.

Coulson, A. 1977, 'Agricultural Policies in Mainland Tanzania', *Review of African Political Economy*, 10; 551–67.

Cowen, M. 1981a, 'The Agrarian Problem', *Review of African Political Economy*, 20, 57–63.

Cowen, M. 1981b, 'Commodity Production in Kenya's Central Province', in *Rural Development in Tropical Africa*, edited by J. Heyer, P. Roberts and G. Williams. London. 121–42.

Cowen, M. 1982, 'The British State and Agrarian Accumulation in Kenya', in *Industry and Accumulation in Africa*, edited by M. Fransman. London. 142–70.

Cowen, M. 1983. 'The Commercialisation of Food Production in Kenya after 1945' in *Imperialism, Colonialism and Hunger*, edited by R. Rotberg. Lexington.

Crow, B. 1984, 'Famine and Plenty', manuscript prepared for the Open University, Milton Keynes.

Currey, B. 1981, '14 Fallacies about Famine', *Ceres*, 14 (2), 20–5.

Cutler, P. 1984, 'Famine Forecasting: Prices and Peasant Behaviour in North-Eastern Ethiopia', *Disasters*, 8 (1), 48–56.

Drummond, H. 1888, *Tropical Africa*. London.

Ellen, R. 1982, *Environment, Subsistence and System: The Ecology of Small-Scale Social Formations*. Cambridge.

Firth, R. 1959, *Social Change in Tikopia: a Re-Study of a Polynesian Community after a Generation*. London.

Food and Agriculture Organisation (F.A.O). 1946, *World Food Survey*. Washington: F.A.O.

Food and Agriculture Organisation (F.A.O). 1949, *Report on World Commodity Problems*, Fifth Session Conference. Washington: F.A.O.

Guardian, The, 1985, 'Africa on Verge of Unprecedented Crisis'. 16/2/85. London and Manchester.

Guyer, J. I. 1983, 'Women's Work and Production Systems: a Review of Two Reports on the Agricultural Crisis', *Review of African Political Economy*, 27/28, 186–92.

Hetherwick, A. 1887, 'Notes on a Journey from Domasi Mission Station, Mt Zomba, to Lake Namaramba, August 1887', *Royal Geographical Society Proceedings*, 10, 26.

Holt, J. 1976, 'The Scope of the Drought' in *Rehab: Drought and Famine in Ethiopia*, edited by A. M. Hussein. London.

Hopkins, R. F. and Puchala, D. J. (eds.). 1978, *The Global Political Economy of Food*. Wisconsin.

Hussein, A. M. (ed.). 1976, *Rehab: Drought and Famine in Ethiopia*, African Environment, Special Report 2, London: International Africa Institute.

Iliffe, J. 1983, *The Emergence of African Capitalism*. London.

Iliffe, J. 1985, 'The Poor in the Modern History of Malawi', in *Malawi: An Alternative Pattern of Development*, Centre of African Studies, University of Edinburgh, Seminar Proceedings 25, 243–93.

Jeliffe, D. B. and Jeliffe, P. 1971, 'The Effects of Starvation on the Function of the Family and of Society', in *Famine: a Symposium dealing with Nutrition and Relief Operations in Times of Disaster*, edited by G. Blix *et al.* Stockholm: Swedish Nutrition Foundation.

Johnston, H. H. 1897, *British Central Africa*. London.

Keys, A. *et al.* (eds). 1950, *The Biology of Human Starvation* (2 vols.). Minneapolis.

Kitching, G. 1980, *Class and Economic Change in Kenya: The Making of an African Petite-Bourgeoisie, 1905–70*, New Haven.

Kjekshus, H. 1977, *Ecology Control and Economic Development in East African History*, London.

Klein, I. 1984, 'When the Rains Failed', *Indian Social and Economic Review*, 21 (2).

Kydd, J. 1985, 'Malawi in the 1970s: Development Policies and Economic Change' in *Malawi: An Alternative Pattern of Development*, Centre of African Studies, University of Edinburgh, Seminar Proceedings 25, 293–381.

Ladurie, E. Le Roy, 1979, 'Amenorrhea in Time of Famine, the Seventeenth to Twentieth Centuries', in *The Territory of the Historian*, by E. Le Roy Ladurie, (trans. Ben and Sian Reynolds). Hassocks.

Lancaster, C. S., 1981, *The Goba of the Zambesi: Sex Roles, Economics and Change*. Norman, Oklahoma.

Langworthy, H. 1975, 'Central Malawi in the Nineteenth Century', in *From Nyasaland to Malawi*, edited by R. MacDonald. Nairobi.

Laws, R. 1879, 'Journey along Part of the West Side of Lake Nyasa, 1878', *Royal Geographical Society Proceedings*, 1, 305–32.

Laya, D. 1975, 'Interviews with Farmers and Livestock Owners in the Sahel', *African Environment*, 1, 49–93.

Life and Work in British Central Africa, March 1903. Blantyre.

Linden, I. (ed.), 1974 and 1975, 'Mponda Mission Diary, 1889–1891: Daily Life in a Machinga Village', *International Journal of African Historical Studies*, 7 (2, 3 and 4) and 8 (1).

Livingstone, D. and Livingstone, C. 1865, *Narrative of an Expedition to the Zambezi and Its Tributaries and the Discovery of Lakes Chirwa and Nyasa, 1858–64*. London.

Lofchie, M. 1975, 'Political and Economic Origins of African Hunger', *Journal of Modern African Studies*, 13 (4), 551–67.

McAlpin, M. 1983, *Subject to Famine*. London.

McCracken, K. J. 1983, 'Planters, Peasants and the Colonial State; the Impact of the Native Tobacco Board on the Central Province in Malawi', *Journal of Southern African Studies*, 9 (2), 172–92.

McCracken, K.J. 'British Central Africa, 1905–40', in *Cambridge History of Africa* (vol.7). Cambridge.

Mallory, W. H. 1928, *China: Land of Famine*. New York: American Geographical Society Special Publication, No. 6.

Mandala, E. C. 1982, 'Peasant Agriculture, Gender and Intergenerational Relations: the Lower Shire Valley of Malawi', *African Studies Review*, 25 (2/3), 27–44.

Mandala, E. C. 1983, 'Capitalism, Economy and Society: The Lower Tchiri (Shire) Valley of Malawi, 1860–1890', PhD, University of Minnesota.

Masterton, G. 1981, *Famine*. London.

Meillassoux, C. 1981, *Maidens, Meal and Money*. Cambridge.

Mitchell, J. C. 1949, 'The Political Organisation of the Yao of Southern Nyasaland' *African Studies*, 7 (3), 141–59.

Mitchell, J. C. 1956, 'Preliminary Notes on Land Tenure and Agriculture among the Machinga Yao', *Human Problems in British Central Africa*, 10, 1–13.

Mitchell, J. C. 1971, *The Yao Village* (first published 1956). Manchester.

Mitchell, J. C., Gluckman, M. and Barnes, J. A. 1949, 'The Village Headman in British Central Africa', *Africa*, 19 (2), 82–106.

Ng'anga, D. M. 1981, 'What is Happening to the Kenyan Peasantry?', *Review of African Political Economy*, 20, 7–16.

Njonjo, A. V. 1981, 'The Kenyan Peasantry: A Reassessment', *Review of African Political Economy*, 20, 27–40.

Norman, L. S. 1934, *Nyasaland Without Prejudice*. London.

Nyirenda, A. A. 1958, 'Markets and Price-Fixing in Blantyre-Limbe', *Rhodes-Livingstone Communication*, 17, Lusaka.

O'Leary, M. 1980, 'Responses to Drought in Kitui District, Kenya', *Disasters*, 4 (3), 315–27.

Palmer, R. 1985, 'The Nyasaland Tea Industry in the Era of International Tea Restrictions, 1933–50', *Journal of African History*, 26, 215139.

Phiri, K. M. 1977, 'The Chewa of Malawi in the Nineteenth Century: an Assessment of the Decline of the Maravi Political System', Paper presented at the International Conference on Southern African History, Roma, Lesotho.

Poleman, T. T. 1977, 'World Food: Myth and Reality', *World Development*, 5 (5–7), 383–94.

Post, J. D. 1977, *The Last Great Subsistence Crisis of the Western World*, Baltimore.

Rangeley, W. H. 1953, 'Mbona – the Rainmaker', *Nyasaland Journal*, 6, January 1953.

Raynault, C. 1977, 'Lessons of a Crisis', in *Drought in Africa (2)*, edited by D. Dalby *et al.* London. 17–29.

Read, M. 1956, *The Ngoni of Nyasaland*. Manchester.

Review of African Political Economy, 1985, 'War and Famine', Special Issue. 33.

Rey, P. 1973, *Les Alliances de Classes*. Paris.

Richards, A. 1939. *Land, Labour and Diet in Northern Rhodesia*. Oxford.

Richards, A. 1950. 'Some types of Family Structure amongst the Central Bantu' in A. R. Radcliffe-Brown and Daryll Forde (eds.), *African Systems of Kinship and Marriage*. Oxford.

Richards, P. 1983. 'Ecological Change and the Politics of African Land Use', *African Studies Review*, 26 (2), 1–72.

Rimmer, D. 1983, 'The Economic Impact of Colonialism on Domestic Food Supplies in British Tropical Africa', in *Imperialism, Colonialism and Hunger*, edited by R. Rotberg. Lexington.

Schofeleers, J. M. 1972, 'The History and Political Role of the Mbona Cult among the Mang'anja', in *The Historical Study of African Religion*, edited by T. O. Ranger and I. Kimambo. London.

Scott, E. (ed.). 1984, *Life Before the Drought*, Boston.

Seeley, J. 1986, 'Famine in Africa: A Bibliographical Survey', *African Research and Documentation*, 39.

Sen, A. K. 1981, *Poverty and Famines: an Essay in Entitlement and Deprivation*, Oxford.

Sen, A. K. 1983, 'The Battle to Get Food', *New Society*, 3/10/1983, 405–38.

Shenton, B. and Watts, M. 1979, 'Capitalism and Hunger in Northern Nigeria', *Review of African Political Economy*, 15/16, 53–62.

Shepherd, J. 1975, *The Politics of Starvation*, New York.

Smith, G. E. 1983, *Counting Quintals: A Monitoring Report on Famine in Tigray*. London.

Sorokin, P. 1975, *Hunger as a Factor in Human Affairs*. Gainsville.

Stevens, C. 1980, *Food Aid and the Developing World: Four African Case Studies*. New Delhi.

Thomi, H. 1978, 'Food Imports and Neo-Colonialism', in *The Political Economy of Food*, edited by Vilho Hale. Farnborough.

Thomson, A. 1983, 'Egypt: Food Security and Food Aid', *Food Policy*, 8 (3).

Thomson, B. P. 1954, *Two Studies in African Nutrition: An Urban and a Rural Community in Northern Rhodesia*, Rhodes-Livingstone Paper 24, Lusaka.

University of Malawi, *Amachinga Yao Traditions* (3 vols), Department of History, Chancellor College.

Vail, L. 1981, 'The Making of the Dead North: a Study of Ngoni rule in Northern Malawi, *c.* 1885–1907', in *Before and After Shaka: Papers in Nguni History*, edited by J. Peires. Grahamstown.

Vail, L. 1983, 'The Political Economy of East-Central Africa', in *The History of Central Africa*, vol. 2, edited by D. Birmingham and P. Martin. London and New York.

Vail, L. and White, L. 1983, 'Forms of Resistance: Songs and Perceptions of Power in Colonial Mozambique', *American Historical Review*, 88 (4), 883–920.

Vaughan, M. 1981, 'Social and Economic Change in Southern Malawi: a Study of Rural Communities in the Shire Highlands and Upper Shire Valley, up to 1915', PhD thesis, University of London.

Vaughan, M. 1982, 'Food Production and Family Labour in Southern Malawi: the Shire Highlands and Upper Shire Valley in the Early Colonial Period', *Journal of African History*, 23, 351–64.

Vaughan, M. 1983a, 'Which Family?: Problems in the Reconstruction of the History of the Family in Africa', *Journal of African History*, 24, 275–83.

Vaughan, M. 1983b, 'Better, Happier and Healthier Citizens: The Domasi Community Development Project, 1949–54', Staff Seminar Paper, Department of History, Chancellor College, University of Malawi.

Vaughan, M. 1984, 'Men, Women and Food Supply in the History of Southern Malawi', Paper presented to the Workshop on Conceptualising the Household, Harvard University, November 1984.

Vaughan, M. 1985, 'The Politics of Food Supply: Colonial Malawi in the 1940s', in *Malawi: An Alternative Pattern of Development*, Centre of African Studies, University of Edinburgh, Seminar Proceedings 25.

Vaughan, M. and Hirschmann, D. 1983, 'Food Production and Income Generation in a Matrilineal Society: Rural Women in Zomba, Malawi', *Journal of Southern African Studies*, 10 (1), 86–99.

Watts, M. 1983, *Silent Violence: Food, Famine and Peasantry in Northern Nigeria*. Berkeley and Los Angeles.

Webster, J. B. 1977, 'From Yao Hill to Mount Mulanje', Seminar Paper, Department of History, Chancellor College, University of Malawi.

Werner, A. 1906, *The Natives of British Central Africa*. London.

White, L. 1987 (forthcoming), *Magomero*, Cambridge.

Wood, A. P. 1976, 'Farmers' Responses to Drought in Ethiopia', in *Rehab; Drought and Famine in Ethiopia*, edited by A. M. Hussein. London.

Woodham-Smith, C. 1962, *The Great Hunger*. London.

Wright, M. 1970, 'Women in Peril: a commentary on the life-stories of captives in nineteenth century East-Central Africa', *African Studies Review*, 20, 800–19.

Index

ঙ

ACA9429 afro